# THE IMPORTANCE OF TEACHING SOCIAL ISSUES

John Dewey's *My Pedagogical Creed* outlined his beliefs about teaching and learning. In this volume, prominent contemporary teacher educators follow in Dewey's footsteps, articulating their own pedagogical creeds as they relate to educating about social issues. Through personal stories, each contributor reveals the major concerns, tenets, and interests behind their own teaching and research, including the experiences underlying their motivation to explore social issues via the school curriculum. Rich with biographical detail, *The Importance of Teaching Social Issues* combines diverse voices from curriculum theory, social studies education, science education, and critical theory, providing a unique volume relevant for today's teachers and education scholars.

**Samuel Totten** is Professor Emeritus of Curriculum and Instruction at the University of Arkansas, Fayetteville.

# THE IMPORTANCE OF TEACHING SOCIAL ISSUES

## Our Pedagogical Creeds

*Edited by Samuel Totten*

Routledge
Taylor & Francis Group

NEW YORK AND LONDON

First published 2015
by Routledge
711 Third Avenue, New York, NY 10017

and by Routledge
2 Park Square, Milton Park, Abingdon, Oxon, OX14 4RN

*Routledge is an imprint of the Taylor & Francis Group, an informa business*

*Library of Congress Cataloging-in-Publication Data*
Totten, Samuel.
    The importance of teaching social issues : our pedagogical creeds / by Samuel Totten.
    pages cm
    Includes bibliographical references and index.
    1. Social justice—Study and teaching. 2. Social problems—Study and teaching.
    3. Critical pedagogy. I. Title.
    LC192.2.T68 2015
    370.11'5—dc23
    2014007510

ISBN: 978–1–138–78852–7 (hbk)
ISBN: 978–1–138–78853–4 (pbk)
ISBN: 978–1–315–76551–8 (ebk)

Typeset in Bembo
by Swales & Willis, Exeter, Devon

# CONTENTS

# PREFACE

## Education in a Time of Crisis

*H. Svi Shapiro*

UNIVERSITY OF NORTH CAROLINA AT GREENSBORO

### Education and the Crisis of Democracy

There is surely little doubt that we face a deep crisis of meaningful citizenship in this country. And in this regard education has abdicated its responsibilities. Indeed, schooling contributes in important ways to the evisceration of civic culture and the erosion of identities that are capable of seriously enacting democratic citizenship. Meaningful citizenship—what Stuart Ewan (1998) refers to as a "democracy of expression" is more and more replaced by what he calls a "democracy of consumption." For many people—young people, especially—choice, power, and freedom are increasingly reduced to one's capacity to buy. The marketplace defines "democratic" action more than the polling booth or public engagement and advocacy. The credit card defines one's eligibility as a citizen. That most critical aspect of democracy—the capacity to exert power over one's circumstances— is reduced to the ability to shop from the ever-expanding, dizzying array of available products. Advertisers have appropriated the language of democratic life so that change, innovation, renewal, and the energy of public life are concentrated and distilled into the excitement of fashion, automobile ownership, the latest upgrade in the technology of communication, or the promise of optimal experiences offered through travel, drink, or sex. What is clear is how far this focus is from Ewan's democracy of expression. If democracy is about a shared search for a better society, consuming is all about what *I have acquired or experienced*. If democracy is about improving our common wellbeing, consumption relentlessly offers the prospect of "getting an edge" and being one-up on our neighbor in looks, acquisitions, opportunities, and style. A possessive and competitive individualism is at its motivational core (Bauman, 2007). In sharp contrast to this is a democracy of expression, a concern that constitutes the capacity to name and articulate the circumstances that enable or limit a full and satisfying human existence, not just for oneself but for all of us who are members of our shared polity.

Yet it is a rarity when schooling offers students the opportunity to develop that capacity for expression that enhances democratic life and citizenship. School for most students is primarily about the process of domestication and conformity as they learn the grammar and syntax of test-taking skills and become adept at the search for the single correct answer on the test sheet. Creative thought, critical questioning, the articulation of ideas and insights about students' lives and concerns have little place in the classrooms of most young people (Purpel, 2004). The suffocating regime of standardized testing squeezes out any possibility of educating young people to develop genuine curiosity about their world, a passion to pursue and understand life's purpose, and the will to challenge accepted truths and conventions. Most of all, schools now develop accountants of test scores and grade point averages, and adept manipulators of college résumés through the accumulation of curricular and extra-curricular experiences. Little here can contribute to a mind that is alert and awake to the challenges we face as a human community, and which is imbued with the desire to question deeply and boldly those social, moral, and epistemological assumptions and categories that shape our dangerously divisive, wasteful, and materialistic world. What Hannah Arendt (1977) called so aptly the "banality of evil" starts in school with the message about doing what one is told to do without question or reflection. When success in school comes to mean rote memorization, the search for the single right answer, and intellectual conformity or timidity, then we have created the conditions in which human beings learn that it is right to abdicate their capacity for moral autonomy and "wide-awake" thoughtfulness and decision-making (Greene, 2000). The shrinking ability to see knowledge as having any transformative power other than as the crass instrument of individual advantage is also the consequence of the world of spin that engulfs political and corporate life in the United States. People are taught, first and foremost, to see themselves as consumers who choose sides regarding matters of temporary and shifting taste or convenience. Intellectual conviction and ethical commitment are replaced by cant, spin, and short-term interests. In the face of the extraordinary and intensifying power of elites—corporate, political, and military—to structure the language and set the limits of public debate in this country, any significant and new educational vision must be one that includes the prospect of a critically reflective, boldly questioning, and imaginatively creative citizenry.

## *Education and the Struggle for Community*

The crisis of democratic citizenship is also the crisis of community. The withering of what Cornel West (2004) refers to as *parrhesia*—the capacity for bold and courageous thinking—is also the erosion of social cohesion and communal interdependence. And in each case schools are an important (though certainly not the sole) factor in this decline. School is, after all, that place in which children first learn the "culture of separated desks." It is the place where they are first formally introduced to a world-view in which life's rewards—material and symbolic—are seen as the product of an endless struggle with one's neighbors. The mentality of the bell-curve instructs them that scarcity of affirmation, recognition, and reward is part of the very DNA of human existence (Kohn, 2004). It is a social imperative, they learn, to acquire those skills, manners, dispositions, and knowledge that give them an advantage over the next individual. Whatever is said about friendship, sharing, and caring in our schools and classrooms, the real effect of the curriculum is to teach the centrality of competition and individualism in our social relations. In this world, children learn that not everyone can be someone; some of us are inevitably destined for failure and invisibility. To be "somebody" rests on the capacity to classify another as being "nobody." It is a lesson relentlessly emphasized through schools' constant attention to the markers of success and failure, validation and rejection. It is a message that deeply penetrates students' understanding of human existence. The world is a predatory place. The fear of failure hangs over all of us, and with it a distrust and suspicion towards those who appear to have acquired something more than we have. It is a world in which envy, dissatisfaction, and an incessant drive towards invidious comparison permeate our lives. From the gold stars of kindergarten to the status hierarchy of college selection, schooling is an insistent socialization into the world of hierarchy, status, and human separation. We are, through this process, driven apart not brought together; led to see ourselves as working against another, rather than with one another; and primed for an aggressive egoism rather than an open-hearted generosity (Eisler, 2006).

In this landscape of painful human fragmentation and separation, the hunger for connection, genuine friendship, closeness, and camaraderie find expression—but often in ways that still bear the marks of a hostile and fearful environment. The construction of community here is rooted in a zero-sum world of enemies; connection among us is predicated by our hostility towards, and fear of, those who appear to threaten our way of life. It is easy to see how young people are socialized into this kind of world-view. The poison of a community constructed through invidious comparison with others who are viewed as inferior, immoral, or bent on our destruction has very deep roots in our culture (Maalouf, 2000).

The enormous challenge in the 21st century is to allow and facilitate the genuine recognition and flourishing of all those communities that have hitherto been made invisible by the exercise of hegemonic cultures and, at the same time, to ensure that fierce allegiance within these communities does not preclude a sense of wider human connection and interdependence. *It is, I believe, the task of education to both facilitate the former while also encouraging the latter.* This means that education has a double role around the issue of community. Schools need to provide the space in which particularistic identities can be nurtured. They need also to build and encourage communities of a much wider span in which a universal human ethic and consciousness flourishes. It is surely necessary to assert as never before the connectedness of the human species (and of course the interdependence on Earth of all life). We face as a human community threats to our very existence as a species from pollution, climate change, water shortages, nuclear armaments, the spread of disease across national borders, and violence that makes no distinction between combatants and innocent civilians. Education will have to be a part of a process that asserts and supports identities that are a complex weave of the particular and the universal, the local and the global, the partial and the whole (Shapiro, 2006). We know enough now about the meaning of identity to understand the importance of rootedness and place to human wellbeing. But we also are increasingly aware of the malignant and dangerous consequences to others when such identity refuses to acknowledge the bonds that connect all of our species as social, ethical, and spiritual beings. Citizenship education today must be one that is concerned with our plural identities *and* the social cohesion stemming from our common concerns and needs as human beings.

## Schooling and Global Justice

Of course, it is impossible to address the pressing question of community in our lives if we do not acknowledge its inseparability from issues of social justice. Community is, after all, that mode of being in which each of us is visible and recognized within the circle of human presence. Each of us takes our place within this circle as a presence of inestimable value, equally empowered and responsible for what is collectively undertaken, and fully supported and secure in the care of one's neighbors. The evidence points to a deep hunger for community among human beings, yet the practices and reality of our daily lives constantly contradicts its possibility (Lerner, 2008). We are, in school and elsewhere, constantly subjected to a process that creates a world of winners and losers—a hierarchy of worth and recognition in which, as John Holt (1983) once noted, a few learn to get what they like, and many learn to like what they get. School is, in the words of educational historian Joel Spring (2011), first and foremost a "sorting machine" that socializes the young into a world of inequality. The primary and most insidious lesson of education is the legitimacy of unequal treatment and differential human value. School is nothing if it is not a vehicle for the transmission of hierarchical distinctions of respect, worth, ability, and economic expectations. It is the seeding ground for a society in which we accept astonishing inequalities in the circumstances of our lives—access to health care, decent housing, availability of food, opportunities for rest and recreation, security of employment, dignity and respect—both in the community and on the job (Klein, 2008).

Talk of a national community is mocked by the extraordinary differences in children's lives consequent upon differences of race, wealth, and gender. All the talk of "no child left behind" is pure obfuscation in a society where social and economic inequalities bear down heavily on children's lives, hopelessly blighting the possibilities for success or achievement among so many. And talk of a shared national interest is, much of the time, a cover for glaring and increasing inequalities in the lives of citizens (Judt, 2010).

To educate towards the now pressing vision of human community cannot be separated from the need to move human consciousness away from the impulse to sort, select, and rank, and to find and to legitimate winners and losers. In our schools this will be no easy task, since education is almost unimaginable today when it not about such a process. Yet, we need to be reminded that, despite the power and influence of such ideas, other ethical, political, and spiritual visions persist. These visions speak to the continuing possibility of a world in which all are affirmed in their worth, respect, and autonomy; in which all deserve to live with decency and security; and in which meaning is found through the sharing of our earthly resources. Such a vision must surely infuse what Raymond Williams (2001) once referred to as the long revolution that we are called upon to make both in our schools and throughout our social institutions.

## Towards a Pedagogy of Peace

All of this rests on the belief in a universal human ethic. It is an ethic rooted in the concept of the infinite value and preciousness of each and every human life. Its first imperative is to refuse violence against others. We cannot separate a vision of education centered on the quest for democracy, community, and social justice from the need for an education that negates the violence that pervades our culture (Shapiro, 2010). In this regard, a major responsibility of education today should be to cultivate a culture of peace. In the end, this goal cannot be separated from the need to cultivate the bonds of universal human community and a culture of democracy. The first challenge of educating for peace is overcoming the dualistic and Manichean thinking that shapes so much of human consciousness in our world (Hedges, 2002). At every turn we learn to understand our world as one constructed from rigid and binary categories: black vs. white, male vs. female, gay vs. straight, disabled vs. able, native vs. alien, Europe vs. Africa, our country vs. another, and so on. We learn to view all things through a prism that separates and opposes one side from another. And to this separation we add the qualities that give "our side" its supposed superiority. This is a way of constructing a reality that ensures not just a world of immoveable divisions but one in which we come to see our attributes, allegiances, and preferences as the stuff that makes us better than, more deserving than, more enlightened than, and, in extreme cases, even more genetically superior than, all others. This polarized us/them world is the recipe for inevitable and certain prejudice and hatred. Fear and anger corrode all relationships. Resentment of mistreatment and the ache of dehumanization fill the lives of those distinguished by their supposed failings and pathologies, and fear of the encroachment of the other shapes the psychology and politics of those who hold themselves as superior. If we don't act with force to restrain and contain the other, it is held, then we may succumb to their influence. In this view, security comes through the domination and suppression of others.

Educating for peace works within what appears to be a paradoxical world-view. It asserts, on the one hand, the ancient spiritual wisdom that all human life is of inestimable value. In this view all people have unconditional or infinite worth. It asserts that all our distinctions and separations obfuscate the fundamental oneness of existence and the endless recycling and regeneration of our common origins within the elemental stardust of the universe. From this perspective, education means to emphasize the precious value and meaning of all life. It shifts our focus from the qualities that separate us, and polarize us, to those that connect us and speak to our similarities. Security, in this view, depends not on our capacity to dominate or exclude, but on our willingness to show generosity and open-heartedness towards others (Sacks, 2006). Our wellbeing, as Michael Lerner (2008) suggests, depends on the wellbeing of everyone on our planet.

While educating for peace requires that we see the essential humanity of all people, it also requires that we fully recognize the way in which our lives have been conditioned and shaped through the particularity of our language, history, gender, culture, and class. What has the experience of living meant for this person and those who share that particular experience? It has been said that one's enemy is someone whose story you have not heard. Peace education certainly demands the possibility of dialogue in which one's life can be shared with others. It means cultivating a hermeneutical approach to "truth" in which the emphasis is less on whose view is right than on simply hearing what it means to grow up understanding one's world through a particular set of circumstances. It is a process that emphasizes sympathetic listening rather than the impulse to quick judgment. It means to struggle with one's own immediate assumptions and prejudices in order to truly hear the challenges and obstacles in the life of the other. Such dialogue breaks down or deconstructs the simplistic and damaging binary view of identities. In its place emerges a more complex and fluid understanding of one's neighbor (Levinas, 2006)—someone who is different in some respects from oneself yet so similar in others; a person whose being is not solely defined through a single characteristic of religion, race, nationality, disability, etc.; and a person who is not fully formed and complete, but someone whose life is evolving and changing.

Of course the sharing and naming of experience can only be a part of what it means to educate for peace. There must also be exploration of the culture of violence—the social conditions that predispose us towards the harming of others on the macro scale we now witness. We have to look at what Zygmunt Bauman (1998) has termed *adiaphorization*—the tendency, so pronounced in our world, to become desensitized to the pain and humiliation of others. We have to look here at the way violence becomes entertainment, the way wars are depicted through the mass media as video games, and the overall consequence of the barrage of violent images and themes on our sensibilities as human beings. We have to consider how poverty and unemployment sap human beings of hope for a better future and open the door to a nihilistic rage. Or the way domination—cultural, economic, and political—humiliates and dehumanizes people and can become a catalyst for suicidal revenge. And we must recognize the way that so much of the violence in the world is overwhelmingly perpetrated by men. Here we have to consider the way masculinity is constructed around the axis of power and dominance (Shiva, 2006). Vulnerability, dependence, and the desire for nurturance are regarded as signs of human weakness (read femininity) that evoke hostility and disgust and are an incitement to violent suppression, whether in oneself or in others.

A fuller and more radical expression of democracy, social justice, a culture of peace that teaches us to practice non-violent means of resolving human conflicts, and relationships between people that celebrate and affirm the bonds of community and interdependence among us are some of the great challenges before us in this century. Their failure to be seriously addressed confronts us with threats to the very possibility of a desirable human future. All of these challenges will require efforts and interventions in a multiplicity of ways, both within our individual lives and across the landscapes of our public institutions. There can be no doubt of the extraordinary importance of education to making these changes. Education is, after all, that sphere where reason, reflection, imagination, and the capacity to act with thoughtfulness and creativity is stirred and nurtured. Yet it is clear that this is far from where the present discourse of education has taken us. Schools have become instruments of conformity and passivity. They are enthralled with the language of management and controlled outcomes, and measured by their usefulness to the state as the means to supply trained workers and warriors.

In this time of great danger (and also extraordinary possibility), educators are called towards a prophetic role. We must insist that, in the conditions that now confront us, the present educational agenda only reinforces and even compounds our problems. To educate today must instead be an act that helps transform human consciousness and conscience. *The vision that animates our work as educators must be rooted in the ancient quest for Tikkun Olam—the effort to repair and heal our world as a place of generous and loving community, in which there is a just sharing of rewards and obligations, where human differences are mediated by respect and recognition; a world of ecological sanity and responsibility, where there is the widest diffusion of opportunities for human beings to participate in shaping the world they live in.* No matter how far-fetched or unrealistic such a vision may appear to be in relation to the present concerns of schooling, this is no time for timidity. The immense dangers and the extraordinary suffering within which we are now engulfed demand from us bold, daring, and imaginative thinking. Anything less is an irresponsible negation of our obligations to coming generations.

*The Importance of Teaching Social Issues: Our Pedagogical Creeds* returns us to that most powerful and succinct vision of educational purpose, John Dewey's "My Pedagogic Creed," a statement written at the end of the 19th century, but one that still resonates in the context of 21st-century American education. Perhaps its resonance is especially strong today given the cultural, political, and economic influences that currently bear down on public schooling. Dewey's call that the child's interests, inclinations, and powers be central to pedagogy, that school should nurture the social and moral dispositions of an individually responsible, democratic, and socially just society, that the life of a school should be built around an active participative community, and that education should never induce a passive conformity among students or a rote style of learning, continue to speak forcefully to those of us concerned with education today. Most powerfully, Dewey articulates the belief that education must be connected to social change and respond to the social challenges that confront civilization.

More than one hundred years later, the contributions to *The Importance of Teaching Social Issues: Our Pedagogical Creeds* collectively and powerfully update Dewey's original vision. In ways that echo our most famous philosopher of education, the chapters in this book speak, too, of the need for education to respond to the moral, political, social, and technological issues and challenges that currently beset our world. Among the many insights the reader will find here is an insistence that schools develop among students a critical understanding of their world, the importance of social justice and human rights in a globalized society, the need to understand how power and prejudice can distort our lives, the way that knowledge is socially constructed, the importance of care and sustainability, and the need for education to attend to not only the cognitive but the social and political realms of life.

Drawing, in revealing and often moving ways, on the authors' own educational experiences and reflections, this book, in sum, is a badly-needed attempt to forge a renewed vision of education. It reflects the creative insights, broad intelligence, and the sometimes courageous willingness to think "outside the current box" of educational thinking which has more and more defined schooling in the most narrow and limited of ways. My fervent hope is that it will contribute to a reawakening of the critical and creative spirit in our thinking about the purposes and practices of education, and provide a hopeful rejoinder to those who have lost faith in the ground of education as a source of possibility and renewal.

## References

Arendt, H. (1977). *Eichmann in Jerusalem*. New York, NY: Penguin.

Baumann, Z. (1998). *Modernity and the Holocaust*. Ithaca, NY: Cornell University Press.

Bauman, Z. (2007). *Liquid Modernity*. Cambridge, England: Polity Press.

Ewan, S. (1988). *All Consuming Images*. New York, NY: Basic.

Eisler, R. (2006). *The Real Wealth of Nations*. San Francisco, CA: Berret-Koehler.

Greene, M. (2000). *Releasing the Imagination*. New York, NY: Jossey-Bass.

Hedges, C. (2002). *War Is a Force That Gives Us Meaning*. New York, NY: Public Affairs.

Holt, J. (1983). *How Children Learn*. Cambridge, MA: Da Capo Press.

Judt, T. (2010). *Ill Fares the Land*. New York, NY: Penguin.

Klein, N. (2008). *The Shock Doctrine: The Rise of Disaster Capitalism*. New York, NY: Picador.

Kohn, A. (2004). *What Does it Mean to Be Well Educated?* Boston, MA: Beacon.

Lerner, M. (2006). *The Left Hand of God.* San Francisco, CA: Harper.

Levinas, E. (2006). *Humanism and the Other.* Urbana, IL: University of Illinois.

Maalouf, A. (2006). *In the Name of Identity.* New York, NY: Penguin.

Purpel, D. (2004). *Reflections on the Moral and Spiritual Crisis of Education.* New York, NY: Peter Lang.

Sacks, J. (2006). *The Politics of Hope.* London, England: Vintage.

Shapiro, H.S. (2006). *Losing Heart: The Moral and Spiritual Miseducation of America's Children.* Mahwah, NJ: Lawrence Erlbaum.

Shapiro, H.S. (2010). *Educating Youth for a World beyond Violence.* New York, NY: Palgrave.

Shiva, V. (2006). *Earth Democracy, Justice and Peace.* Cambridge, MA: South End Press.

Spring, J. (2011). *The Politics of American Education.* New York, NY: Routledge.

West, C. (2004). *Democracy Matters.* New York, NY: Penguin.

Williams, R. (2001). *The Long Revolution.* Orchard Park, NY: Broadview Press.

# INTRODUCTION

*Samuel Totten*

One constant in any society is the impingement of social issues. While not all social issues are controversial, they generally revolve around conflicting viewpoints as a result of various factors, including people's political beliefs, religious beliefs, and views concerning race, class, and gender, etc. That said, it is also true that numerous social issues have not only been extremely controversial but have riven society. Even a short list of the latter in relation to the United States and its citizens is noteworthy: slavery, the "Red Scare," the battle for civil rights, the Vietnam War, the nuclear arms race, Second Amendment rights versus gun control, and the National Security Agency's wholesale collection and analysis of the phone and email data of U.S. citizens for so-called intelligence purposes.

Ridding society of social issues is impossible. And, since that is the case, it behooves citizens of a society to prepare its young, the proverbial future leaders of the nation, to learn how to address such issues in as an intelligent, thorough, and rational manner as possible. When a social issue is particularly controversial—for example, a woman's right to choose ("pro-choice") versus foes of abortion ("pro-life")—that is easier said than done. Then, again, that underscores the critical need to prepare future voters and decision-makers how to deal with such issues, civilly, constructively, and efficaciously.

U.S. educators throughout the 20th century, and now in the 21st, have wrestled with the best way of preparing young people to thoughtfully approach the study of social issues. The history of such efforts is rich and brings to mind some of the most renowned educators of the past century who have engaged in such work: George Counts, Harold Rugg, Lawrence E. Metcalf, Maurice P. Hunt, Donald Oliver, James Shaver, Fred Newmann, Byron Massialas, Shirley Engle, and Anna Ochoa, among many others (including a vast number of contributors to this book, *The Importance of Teaching Social Issues: Our Pedagogical Creeds*).

The fact that social issues can, and often do, rip asunder the fabric of society has induced educators with vastly different backgrounds, philosophies, and goals to develop a host of models and approaches for helping teachers to educate the young about social issues (as well as how to analyze them in an intelligent manner). Even a short list of some of the more notable approaches is impressive, not to mention quite eclectic: Harold Rugg's textbook program; Hunt and Metcalf's Reflective Thinking and Social Understanding Model; Donald Oliver, James Shaver, and Fred Newmann's Public Issues Model; Massialas and Cox' Reflective Inquiry Model; and the Engle/Ochoa Decision-Making Model for Citizenship Education. And that is not to mention a host of other approaches, including Science Technology Society (STS), multicultural education, critical pedagogy, and teaching for social justice.

To this day, educators continue to wrestle with developing and implementing the most efficacious approaches to preparing young people to become adept at dealing with social issues. This is as it should be. Fresh minds, new research, and a rethinking of past approaches and models are more likely to lead to more engaging and powerful means to nurture students' interest in, and ability to thoughtfully engage in thoroughly examining, social issues.

## John Dewey's Pedagogical Creed

In 1897, John Dewey published "My Pedagogic Creed" in the *School Journal*. It was succinct (three pages, single-spaced typed) and comprised of five sections, or what he referred to as "articles": Article One, What Education Is; Article Two, What the School Is; Article Three, The Subject Matter of Education; Article Four, The Nature of Method; and Article Five, The School and Social Progress.

It is an interesting document in that it provides one with a clear sense of Dewey's major concerns, interests, tenets, and approaches to teaching and learning. It seems, to me, that anyone who teaches in our nation's schools (K through university) should, almost automatically, really, craft his/her own list of beliefs/tenets—not for the sake of publication, but as a way of clarifying one's own thinking and to provide one with the means to continually reflect upon, examine, and, when needed, revise, his/her beliefs/tenets. That, in turn, is likely to prod one to become more reflective about one's beliefs, aims, and practices. If nothing else, it should assist one to stay current, and thus avoid stagnation: to help one, as it were, not to fall into the trap of teaching in a mindless and/or perfunctory manner or teach an "inert curriculum" (Whitehead, 1967, pp. 1–2).

Each and every line of Dewey's creed begins with "I believe . . ." At the center of Dewey's creed is the child—and, ultimately, the education and growth of each child on his/her journey to becoming a responsible and productive member of society. The society that Dewey is implicitly speaking about is that of a democracy.

In addressing the latter, Dewey states the following:

I believe that the only true education comes through the stimulation of the child's powers by the demands of the social situations in which he finds himself. Through these demands he is stimulated to act as a member of a unity, to emerge from this original narrowness of action and feeling and to conceive of himself from the standpoint of the welfare of the group to which he belongs.

*p. 1*

Though Dewey does not specifically mention social issues here, what he says is certainly germane to the critical need to prepare students to address social issues within the society in which he/she resides.

In fact, *nowhere* in his pedagogical creed does Dewey address the critical need for teachers and schools to incorporate the study of social issues into their curricular programs; however, throughout his creed Dewey does touch on what is at the heart of many educators' pedagogical beliefs and efforts to prepare the young to care about, analyze, reflect on, and address social issues, be they of a local, regional, national, and/or international nature. For example, in his pedagogic creed, Dewey states the following:

- "I believe that all education proceeds by the participation of the individual in the social consciousness of the race";
- "I believe once more that history is of educative value in so far as it presents phases of social life and growth. It must be controlled by reference to social life. When taken simply as history it is thrown into the distant past and becomes dead and inert. Taken as the record of man's social life and progress it becomes full of meaning. I believe, however, that it cannot be so taken excepting as the child is also introduced directly into social life";
- "I believe that the only way to make the child conscious of his social heritage is to enable him to perform those fundamental types of activity which makes civilization what it is";
- "I believe that education is the fundamental method of social progress and reform";
- "I believe that education is a regulation of the process of coming to share in the social consciousness; and that the adjustment of individual activity on the basis of this social consciousness is the only sure method of social reconstruction."

## The Pedagogical Creeds of Noted Teacher Educators vis-à-vis the Critical Need to Incorporate the Study of Social Issues into Schools' Curricular Programs

This book is comprised of the pedagogical creeds/statements of 23 noted teacher educators who have dedicated a large part of their professional careers to thinking and writing about, advocating for, and implementing the teaching of social issues into the school curriculum. Two of the major goals of the teacher educators whose pedagogical creeds appear in this book are to (a) nurture an avid interest in the young about those social issues facing society, *and* (b) prepare them to confront and deal with them in thoughtful and constructive ways.

As teacher educators—who variously prepare future teachers and school administrators, work with experienced teachers and administrators in the schools, and guide the study of doctoral candidates—the contributors to this book have undertaken (and continue to undertake), individually and in small groups, a host of efforts vis-à-vis the incorporation of social issues into the school curriculum. Such efforts, for example, include: (a) developing theories, models and approaches for incorporating the study of social issues into the school curriculum; (b) conducting research into the most effective ways to engage students at the elementary and secondary levels of schooling about social issues; (c) publishing articles, chapters, and books about diverse aspects of teaching about social issues; and (d) promoting the teaching of social issues in our nation's schools via different venues. In doing so, they are dedicated to providing teachers and schools with well thought out, systematic, and practical ways to incorporate the in-depth study of social issues into the extant curriculum. Key terms here are *well thought out, systematic* and *in-depth.*

While there are many similarities amongst the various contributors' approaches to the incorporation of social issues into the curriculum, there are also marked distinctions. That is natural and to be expected as they are, first and foremost, unique individuals (i.e., with various make-ups in relation to gender, race, ethnicity, religion, geography, and education). Concomitantly, they have had vastly different experiences in relation to family life, community life, schooling, and beyond; studied under different professors with vastly different philosophies and approaches to education and the study of social issues; read and been influenced by different authors/literature; and, ultimately, have seen, and continue to see, the world from their own perspective.

Based on their reputations as outstanding educators who have an avid interest in seeing that our nation's schools educate the young about social issues, invitations were extended to 35 U.S.-based teacher educators to contribute to this book. In the end, 23 of the 35 contributed to the book. They are a fairly eclectic group (race and ethnicity being a striking exception).[1] More specifically, there are fifteen males and nine females. Two contributors are in their 80s, at least two others are in their 70s; a majority in their 50s and 60s. The youngest are in their early 30s. At least one contributor is gay. While most are Caucasian (20), two are African American and two are Hispanic. As far the disciplines represented by the 23 contributors, fourteen are in social studies education; two are in science education; four are specialists in the field of curriculum and instruction; three are critical theorists; and one is an "educator-historian."[2]

## The Focus of the Pedagogical Creeds

In order to make the contributions as interesting, thought-provoking, and valuable as possible (and to ensure a certain consistency throughout the book), each contributor was asked to do the following:

• Write a two to five page introductory autobiographical statement in regard to the genesis and evolution of (a) your interest in social issues and (b) the incorporation of the study of social issues into the school curriculum.

• Spell out your pedagogical creed in relation teaching and learning about social issues. Please divide this part into sections. For example, John Dewey divided his pedagogical creed into the following sections: I. What Education Is; 2. What the School Is; 3. The Subject Matter of Education; 4. The Nature of Method; 5. The School and Social Progress. (Note: The aforementioned breakdown should *not* be interpreted as *the* division one must follow. Rather, it is provided simply as food for thought. Unlike your contribution to this book, Dewey's pedagogical creed did not solely focus on the incorporation of social issues into the school curriculum, and thus your division may be radically different from his.)

## Commonalities/Distinctions

While a large number of contributors addressed a host of similar issues (e.g., the importance of preparing the young to take an active part in the democracy/republic in which they reside; the imperative of providing ample time for authentic discussion and debate amongst the students vis-à-vis the issues they are examining and debating; and the immense value in incorporating reflection during such a study), their approach to such concerns were often quite distinct. To do justice to all of the variations—that is, to attempt to delineate and analyze them here—would require a dissertation-length essay.[3] Thus, the discussion will be limited to several of the more interesting and significant examples.[4]

A majority of the authors (17 out of 24) comment, in one way or another, on the significance that students in the United States live in a democratic state and will, ultimately, have the opportunity to vote (both in regard to leadership positions within one's local community and state, as well as the nation, and, in various cases, how certain social issues should be addressed by the government on the behalf of the people). Concomitantly, many speak to what it means to educate students in a democracy and what that should entail (including, for example, a clear understanding by the students regarding the rights and responsibilities of citizens in a democracy).

A mere listing of the contributors' comments/assertions regarding the above should provide readers with a solid sense of the diversity of thought amongst the contributors:

- "I believe that the teaching and learning of social issues is the foundation of American democracy. In 1816, Thomas Jefferson advised, "If you expect a nation to be ignorant and free and in a state of civilization, you expect what was never was and never will be" (Thomas Jefferson's letter to Charles Yancey, 6 January 1816; Graham, 2005, p. 3). Democracy depends on an educated populace. Understanding the nation's history and government as well as those of other countries is vital to human relations and advancement."
- "Education can and should serve societal goals—whether it is to sustain them or revise them to be more inclusive and reflective of the democratic ideal we tout in this country."
- "I believe that democratic education centers on learning and teaching about social issues in a way that recognizes multiple perspectives and hierarchies of oppression. Harding (1993) writes, "An effective pursuit of democracy requires that those who bear the consequences of decisions have a proportionate share in making them" (p. 3). The effectiveness of education for democracy requires that students and teachers recognize that social issues are viewed differently depending upon a person's positionality."
- "I believe that public schools exist to make democracy possible. Government by the people cannot succeed unless it operates with an educated electorate—educated in the empirical knowledge available and imbued with the values necessary for large-scale cooperation."
- "While I support the inclusion of controversial political issues discussions in schools for multiple reasons, none is more important than the reality that an intrinsic connection exists between a healthy and well-functioning democracy and the ability of people to engage with one another productively in deliberations about what 'we' should do in response to important public problems. Discussion is a proxy for democracy itself. Put another way, a democracy cannot function without discussion."
- "I believe—and teach—that democracy, as Dewey said, is a not just a form of government but a way of living and being with other people. The way we talk to each other and solve problems in this country must be based on that shared understanding."
- "In agreement with Rugg, Engle and Ochoa, and Evans and Brodkey, I believe that in an avowedly democratic society, in order to encourage thoughtful citizen participation, we need a social studies curriculum focused on active inquiry, rational discourse, and persistent and 'troubling' issues."
- "Reflection, evaluation, and judgment about what is being learned . . . are closely tied to the social, democratic, and moral dimensions of education in a democracy. As a Pragmatist, I believe that education ought to produce consequences, and these consequences ought to go beyond words to action. We need to apply our ideas shaped by education in the public sphere, by carrying out our obligations to the fellow members of our community and to the broader communities of which we are a part. Social education ought to

be about developing knowledge and ethical commitments to living in a way that demonstrates integrity and the importance of putting knowledge into practice."

- "I believe that teachers are the "guardians of democracy" (Gould, 2003), and schools should be places in which students are regularly engaged in democratic behavior. Unfortunately, Dewey's dream of schools as democratic institutions has fallen short. Students, of course, do learn about "democracy," but the concepts are generally not practiced in schools, for most school administrators and teachers, oddly, see such as a challenge to their place in the system. In this situation and milieu, controlling student behavior by limiting the type of knowledge that will reduce student cynicism and create a more manageable classroom environment (Leming, 1989) is seemingly of utmost concern, almost to the point at which a calm classroom is more greatly desired than true student learning. Until those inside and outside the educational arena mobilize to propel school reform toward the establishment and implementation of a true democratic model for schools, we will continue to pay lip service to the latter through our rhetoric and contrived actions (Beane and Apple, 1995, pp. 1–25).

- "I believe that classrooms should be viewed as sites of deliberation in which the practice of democratic citizenship skills is paramount. Greater voice and control should be placed in the hands of the students, especially in the areas of curriculum selection, which, hopefully, will help them to see and make relevant connections between their school work and their lived lives (Van-Sickle, 1990). Students have been anesthetized by traditional social studies practices, and, more often than not, they do not perceive the relevance of what they are studying. Hence, it is the responsibility of the teacher to evaluate the applicability of the subject matter to be presented in relation to the life experiences of the pupil.

  The tradition of socializing students with this nation's time honored traditions and values has been persistent, and rightly so as it serves a vital function within our school system, and that is to teach students the political, economic, social, and religious tenets that have withstood the test of time in our turbulent history. But that only constitutes half the job; teachers must also incorporate the process referred to as "countersocialization—the process of expanding the individual's ability to be a rational, thoughtful, and independent citizen of a democracy" (Engle and Ochoa, 1988, p. 29).

- "I believe that Dewey's (1936) words still ring true today, in the 21st century: 'Today, freedom of teaching and learning on the part of instructors and students is imperatively necessary for that kind of intelligent citizenship that is genuinely free to take part in the social reconstruction without which democracy will die' (pp. 16–166)."

- "[I believe in bringing] the promises of democracy from the ideal to a true reality in the lives of students."

- "I believe that the school must serve as a laboratory of democratic practice if students are to become effective participants in a society that upholds democratic ideals as the foundation of civic life. Too often, schools are governed autocratically, with little or no commitment to democratic practices, and the contradictions between civic ideals and the reality of civic life in schools are endemic. Schools can change this pattern by placing social issues at the center of the curriculum, particularly in social studies, and using the school itself as the focus of issues-based study. Students can be *encouraged* to challenge their exclusion from governance, to study how resources are distributed and employed within schools to advance specific interests or goals, and to investigate how the overt and hidden curricula are designed and delivered, along with their impact on student access to higher education and related societal resources. In doing so, young people can be taught the skills of political engagement, and then develop strategies and campaigns to make schools more democratic and responsive to their needs."

- "I believe the purpose of teaching social issues is to allow students the opportunity to become effective decision makers . . . .So is the recognition that reasonable compromise is often an important part of the democratic decision-making process" (NCSS, 2007)."

- "Social issues education should develop breadth and depth of understanding, problem-solving skills, and the capacity for political action. Democracy is at risk unless citizens learn constructive, intelligent, democratic forms of inquiry, problem-solving decision-making, and political action.

  Given the historic function of education in preparing enlightened citizens for a democracy, social issues education should be the priority of public schooling. Using contemporary rhetoric, students should graduate from high school "citizenship-ready." The school is the institution best suited to developing social issues education competencies in students because it possesses the resources to do so. Multiple school goals of academic, vocational, civic, and personal development can be integrated and realized through social issues education (Goodlad, 1984). Because social and personal growth are the key tasks of democracy, social issues education should especially contribute to the development of civic capacities of students and to the personal development of students as autonomous individuals (Kelly, 2009).

- "In a democracy, citizens have the right to make up their own mind about anything and everything. Period. The most critical consideration in regard to the use of methods in social issues education is that the resolution of and subsequent political action on any social issue that students arrive at should be neither predetermined nor dictated by the teacher."

- "Social issues education manifests a commitment in American culture to individual and collective pragmatic thought and action and serves the historical national education goal of preparing students to act as enlightened citizens of a democracy. To avoid social issues education is to leave democracy to whim, the vagaries of emotion, knee jerk reactions, mob thinking, the influence of special interests promoted at the expense of the social or individual good, and the manipulation of the powers-that-be. Social issues education should function as a constituent part of the education of all children and youth, enabling schools to achieve their role of preparing enlightened citizens for a democracy. This is the social issues education imperative."

- "Along with Dewey, I value citizens willing to question and take on challenges of an imperfect democracy, not citizens who mouth the platitudes and scrubbed patriotism fed to them by public authority or private interests. In sum, thinking citizens are essential to a democratic system, and inquiry is essential to digging and searching for some semblance of truth."

- "I believe that those schools, teachers, and curricular programs that avoid teaching about so-called controversial issues are contributing to a narrow-mindedness that is antithetical to providing a sound education in a democratic society. Indeed, I believe that schools and teachers that avoid teaching about controversial social issues are potentially damning our young to lives of apathy, a lack of serious participation in our democracy, and a listlessness about issues that can, and certainly will, at least at times, seriously (and often adversely) impact them, their children, and the nation in which they live. This, I believe, does not bode well for the health and life of the body politic."

- "I believe it is imperative that students gain an in-depth understanding (versus one that is perfunctory, as most students, unfortunately, receive in their high school education) of the U.S. Bill of Rights and U.S. Constitution *in a way that resonates with them*. One way of accomplishing the latter is tying the documents/protections/rights to the study of key social issues and social movements from the past and present. In that way, individual rights shimmer with significance versus appear as something static, dry, and unimportant. Only in this way, it seems, will students truly come to understand what rights they have, how such rights can be abrogated, and what they can do to address the latter. Simply reading these documents is not likely to have half the punch of tying them to actual cases in which citizens were denied rights but fought for them and were successful in doing so."

- "Ultimately, then, it is about helping students to understand that, as a citizen in a democracy, it is their job, as much as anyone else's, to see to it that the government, and those in government, abide by the Constitution, and that it is absolutely critical that officials at all levels—locally, state, nationally—be held accountable for their actions and inactions when they abrogate such rights."

One can readily ascertain how the comparison and contrast of such insights/positions could lead to a rich discussion by professors and teacher education students. The discussion and debate of other central concerns found in the pedagogical creeds in this book could lead to equally rich learning experiences.

## Research into the Efficacy of Teaching and Learning about Social Issues

Of paramount significance in regard to strengthening the incorporation of social issues into the school curriculum is (a) the need to conduct more solid research into teaching and learning about social issues, and (b) making use of such research to inform one's pedagogical efforts. Without solid research into what is and is not most effective when teaching and learning about social issues, pedagogical efforts become scattershot. Likewise, without access to research findings one can only guess as to what the short and the long-term impact is of using one model or approach versus another.

Over the past 100 years or so, there has been far greater activity around the development of approaches and curricular units of study and their implementation than there has been research into the efficacy of such. Be that as it may, the good news is that there has been much more research around the teaching and learning of social issues over the past 30 years than there had been in the previous 70 years. Furthermore, the relatively small number of researchers who have conducted research (and those who continue to do so) into various aspects of teaching and learning about social issues have been fairly prolific in their efforts.

A simple listing of some of the more significant topics that have been studied by researchers provides a good sense of the activity along this line:

- The impact of nationalistic political education on the curriculum (Jack Nelson);[5]
- Academic freedom and censorship vis-à-vis teaching "controversial issues" (Jack Nelson);
- Censorship and censure aimed at those attempting to teach about social issues (Ronald Evans);
- Preservice teachers' knowledge about politics and current events (Wayne Journell),
- Preservice teachers' understanding of democracy (Elizabeth Yeager Washington);
- Preservice teachers' conceptualization of academic freedom and teaching controversial issues (Thomas Misco and Nancy C. Patterson);
- Democracy in the classroom (Diana E. Hess);
- Students' civic negotiation of the public space of school, which includes such tactics such as avoidance, dissent, and incivility that reshape space (Sandra J. Schmidt);
- Class climate and the study of controversial issues (Carole Hahn);
- Controversial issues and democratic discourse (Diana E. Hess);
- The significance of the need for high quality classroom discussions and political discourse and what that entails (Mcavoy and Hess);

- The teacher's role in discussing controversial issues (Thomas E. Kelly);
- The examination of race and racism/constructions of racial dialogue (Tyrone C. Howard);
- How high school students experience and learn from the discussion of controversial public issues (Diana E. Hess);
- Principled thinking and tolerance for conflict and controversy (Janet Eyler);
- Critical reasoning vis-à-vis civic issues (Walter Parker);
- Negotiating dissonance (Nell O. Houser);
- Culturally responsive teaching, principles and effects (Geneva Gay);
- Discussions of race in a predominantly white high school classroom (Elizabeth Yeager Washington);
- The use of literature to develop a framework for understanding social action (Cynthia A. Tyson);
- Investigating the use of narrative in affective learning on issues of social justice (Nancye McCary);
- Gender equity (Margaret Crocco);
- Political socialization, tolerance, and sexual identity (Patricia Avery);
- Infusing the discussion of sexuality and homophobia into social studies teaching (Margaret Crocco, Heather Oesterreich, Brian Marchman);
- "Identity, discourse, and safety in a high school discussion of same-sex marriage" (Terrence A. Beck);
- Instructional outcomes with Science/Technology/Society (Robert Yager); and
- Ideological diversity in the classroom and its impact on controversial issues discussion (Diana E. Hess).

As positive as all that is, *and it is*, there remains a dearth of solid research into a host of other issues, all of which could possibly shed important light on how to make the teaching and learning of social issues much stronger and more effective than it has been up to this point in time. Among such issues are, for example, the following:

(a) knowledge and attitudes about locally-based social issues;
(b) knowledge and attitudes about social issues at the national level;
(c) knowledge and attitudes about global issues;
(d) the impact of parents' political attitudes on their children;
(e) student attitudes towards studying about social issues;
(f) student attitudes towards controversy (meaning, student willingness to engage in totally honest discussions and debates on issues over which different students hold vastly different thoughts, opinions, and beliefs);
(g) students' tolerance for conflict and controversy;
(h) students' processing skills in studying about social issues;
(i) students' beliefs about citizenship in a democracy;

(j)  students' openness to the consideration of various positions around an issue;

(k)  change in student thinking about a controversial issue in particular (and/or controversial issues, in general);

(l)  students' development of civic attitudes;

(m)  students' civic commitment;

(n)  students' sense of political engagement;

(o)  student self-efficacy in regard to addressing social issues individually;

(p)  student self-efficacy in regard to addressing social issues as part of an organized group; and

(q)  students' sense of efficacy vis-à-vis civic action.

## Concerns to Seriously Consider as One Prepares to Incorporate a Study of Social Issues into the Classroom/ School Curricular Programs

One needs to inform oneself—through wide reading and study—of those models and approaches (and learning activities) that contribute to deep (versus perfunctory) learning by students about social issues. As noted above, many scholars/ teacher educators have put in enormous amounts of thought and time into developing various models and approaches and/or into conducting research into what works and does not work vis-à-vis teaching and learning about social issues, and it only makes sense to thoroughly familiarize oneself with the latter while preparing to undertake one's own pedagogical efforts. *If nothing else*, through such study, one is likely to learn about potential pitfalls to avoid. More likely, though, one is likely to come across a host of revelatory insights and ideas that will assist one to start off on a strong and positive foot.

Key questions that anyone who is keen to incorporate the study of social issues into the school curriculum must ask oneself are: Am I making solid use of research to inform my pedagogical efforts so that they are as effective as possible? If not, why not? And, if not, how do I *really* know whether I am reaching my stated goals and objectives or not?

It is also highly advisable for those planning to teaching about social issues to seriously ponder the distinctions between the following: education versus indoctrination; academic freedom versus the appearance of such (the latter of which might include some type of censorship, including self-censorship by the teacher); a progressive versus a critical approach to pedagogy; the most effective type of classroom discussion versus the appearance of such, etc.

Concomitantly, the following questions are worthy of serious consideration by anyone preparing to incorporate the study of social issues into the extant curriculum:

1)  What is/are my main goal(s) in regard to incorporating a study of social issues into the school curriculum?

a)  To nurture students' interest in such concerns?

b)  To nurture students' interest in such concerns and provide them with the skills to intelligently analyze social issues in order to ascertain their personal stance/position?

c)  To prepare students to be social activists who actively confront key social issues and work to ameliorate them?

d)  To transform society; that is, to actively work to transform what is perceived by some/many as an inherently oppressive and elitist society that is unjust, classist, racist, etc.? In other words, to commit oneself to addressing systemic issues in society that ostensibly create "us and them," "the haves and have nots," the disenfranchised, et al.

e)  Or . . . .?

2)  Is there one goal over all others from the above list that is most *ideal*/appropriate for inclusion in our nation's schools? If so, which one, and why? And who is to make that decision, and based on what rationale?

3)  Are there one or more goals in the initial list that are insufficient/unsatisfactory for inclusion in our nation's schools? If so, which one(s), and why? And again, who is to make that decision, and based on what rationale?

4)  Is there one (or more goals) in the list above that I believe might verge more towards indoctrination than education? If so, which one(s), and why?

5)  While the goal(s) and objectives to which I adhere may prepare students to analyze and weigh social issues in an intelligent and constructive manner, now and into adulthood, are my students more likely to be concerned with social issues in the future or not? If not, is that a problem with my approach? Why or why not? Put another way: If, in the end, the incorporation of the study of social issues results in little more than the acquisition of knowledge by students about current social issues, is that satisfactory? And put yet another way: If students learn how to make sense of various positions vis-à-vis a social issue but never apply that beyond the classroom, is that satisfactory? Why or why not?

6)  Is it even the place of the school to prepare students to become social activists? Why or why not? And, again, who is to make that decision, and based on what rationale?

7)  Is it the place of schools to prepare students to become "critical activists"—that is, those who have the sense of agency to create social change with an aim at transforming society in order to attempt to rid it of social inequities (racism, classism, poverty, oppression, et al.) and to liberate all members of society so that they are able to lead free lives in a fair and just society?[6] Why or why not? And, again, who is to make that decision, and based on what rationale?

8)  Does the goal of preparing students to be social activists verge more along the lines of indoctrination versus education?[7] Why or why not?

And, finally:

9)  Does the goal of preparing students to be "critical activists" verge more along
    the lines of indoctrination versus education?[8] Why or why not?

Some may find one or more of the questions highly uncomfortable, but, as the
editor of this volume, I firmly believe that such questions must be asked *and*
answered.

## Conclusion

For close to a century now, a relatively small number of educators in the United
States have worked assiduously to incorporate social issues into the school curriculum. The effort has been anything but smooth. Time and again, conservative
forces, both inside and outside schools, have pushed back, attempted to stifle and,
sometimes, outright prevented a host of efforts. Certainly, two of the more notable
cases include the following: the controversy surrounding Harold Rugg's textbook
series (see, for example, Ronald Evans' [2007] *This Happened in America: Harold
Rugg and the Censure of Social Studies*. Charlotte, NC: Information Age Publishers) and the controversies spawned by the 1960's New Social Studies movement,
which centered on inquiry, issues, and social activism (see, for example, Ronald
Evans' [2011] *The Tragedy of American School Reform: How Curriculum Politics and
Entrenched Dilemmas Have Diverted Us from Democracy*. New York: Palgrave).

The debates, conflicts, and controversy surrounding the history of incorporating social issues into the school curriculum have not solely been one of conservatives versus liberals. In not a few cases, conflict arose between so-called neoliberals
and radicals—and the conflict did not end there. Tellingly, not all progressives
preferred the same approaches and thus questioned one another's goals, objectives, and, yes, pedagogy. The same has been true amongst those who considered
themselves conservatives or on the radical left. Of course, when serious differences abound, consensus is extremely difficult to come by.

Unfortunately, more than a few who have developed models and programs
have had a propensity to shoot themselves in the proverbial foot. In a good
number of cases, the models and programs developed by researchers and teacher
educators proved to be overly complicated—to the point where teachers had
great difficulty implementing them and, in the end, simply gave up trying. Furthermore, some of the aforementioned models/programs were extremely time-
consuming to implement and thus resulted in great frustration for teachers facing
over-packed curricular demands, relatively short class sessions (45 to 50 minutes),
and overwhelming class size vis-à-vis the number of students taught (both in a
single class as well as over the course of a day).

It is also true, of course, that wave after wave of new governmental and educational policies have constantly buffeted our nation's schools. Old and not-so-

old policies, standards, goals, and standardized tests have been replaced by new policies, standards, goals, and standardized tests, only to see the lattest iterations replaced time and again in a maddening merry-go-round that imposes ever-increasing constraints on teachers' professionalism, freedom, and course/class schedules.

And yet, through it all, many educators have stood firm in the belief that, in a democracy such as ours, it is imperative for the young *to be prepared* to take an active part in societal debates, discussions, and decisions, and that the best way to do that is to engage them in the study of social issues while they are still in school. Only in this way, they believe, are we, society as a whole, likely to nurture in our nation's young a keen interest in and concern about the social issues that buffet society and impact the lives of both groups and individuals. And not only that, but also to help them (the young) become adept at examining an issue from various angles, to analyze and ascertain why different parties/actors hold vastly different positions, to appreciate the various nuances inherent in various arguments vis-à-vis a social issue, to issue counter arguments that are reasoned and objective, and, finally, if need be, to come to a compromise that is as fair and just as possible for one and all.

## Notes

1   Information not readily available to the editor about the contributors includes religion or religious status; political leanings (though a safe guess would be that most probably lean towards the liberal side of the liberal-conservative spectrum); and wealth.
2   Several of the individuals work in two or more disciplines, and at least one of the social studies experts is also a critical theorist.
3   Over and above that, including such herein might curtail a reader's interest in and/or willingness to conduct his/her own analysis of the various pedagogical creeds and/or undertake a synthesis of the similarities and differences between and amongst the various pieces.
4   It is also worth noting that various contributors emphasize concerns/factors that no one else does, but which they believe are absolutely essential when teaching about and/or incorporating social issues into the school curriculum.
5   The names in parentheses following an issue/topic are those of the researcher(s) who has/have conducted studies into such concerns.
6   A slew of fascinating, and, granted, not so fascinating, books, chapters, and articles have been written about critical pedagogy. All of the following works, I believe, are clearly written, well-argued, and worthy of serious consideration by those who are either new to critical pedagogy, have questions about its strengths and weaknesses and/or its practicality or lack thereof as it applies to our nation's classrooms: Ira Shor's (1992) *Empowering Education: Critical Teaching for Social Change* (Chicago, IL: University of Chicago Press); the (2013) 41(4) Special Issue ("Critical Studies and Social Education") of *Theory and Research in Social Education* co-edited by Jack L. Nelson and William B. Stanley; and (2014) *Critical Pedagogy: Educating About Social Issues in the 20th and 21st Centuries: A Critical Annotated Bibliography: Volume 4* edited by Samuel Totten and Jon E. Pedersen (Charlotte, NC: Information Age Publishers). Three articles that educators at both the secondary and university levels should find particularly informative and highly thought-provoking are: Nicholas C. Burbules and Rupert Berk's "Critical Thinking and Critical Pedagogy: Relations,

Differences and Limits." In Thomas S. Popkewitz and Lynn Fendler (eds.). (1999) *Critical Theories in Education: Changing Terrains of Knowledge and Politics* (pp. 45–65) (New York: Routledge); "Adventures in Critical Pedagogy: A Lesson in U.S. History" by Deborah Seltzer-Kelly at (2009) 36(1) *Teacher Education Quarterly*, pp. 149–162); and "Preface: Reflections on Critical Theory in Education" by Ronald W. Evans in Samuel Totten and Jon Pedersen (eds.). (2014) *Critical Pedagogy: Educating About Social Issues in the 20th and 21st Centuries: A Critical Annotated Bibliography* (Charlotte, NC: Information Age Publishers).

7  An equally uncomfortable question, which, I realize is likely to create cognitive dissonance for many, is: If an educator is not in favor of preparing his/her students to be activists in relation to addressing social issues impinging on individuals and society, is he or she merely another cog in the proverbial machine and thus really more interested in the study of social issues as an intellectual and academic exercise versus preparing his/her students to be thinking and active members of the democratic society in which he/she resides?

8  While critical theory is purportedly predicated on questioning the status quo and the systemic dispositions, policies, and actions of national, state, and local governmental agencies and leaders (including our nation's schools and classrooms), do critical pedagogues really encourage students to questions the essential tenets and positions of critical theory and critical pedagogy?

# References

Beane, James A., and Apple, Michael W. (1995). "The Case for Democratic Schools." In Michael Apple and James A. Beane, eds., *Democratic Schools* (pp. 1–25). Alexandria, VA: Association of Supervision and Curriculum Development.

Dewey, John. (1897). "My Pedagogical Creed." 54 *School Journal*, pp. 77–80.

Dewey, John. (1936). "The Social Significance of Academic Freedom." 2(6) *The Social Frontier*, pp. 165–166.

Engle, Shirley, H. (1960). "Decision-Making: The Heart of Social Studies Instruction." 27(4) *Social Education*, pp. 301–304.

Engle, Shirley H., and Ochoa, Anna (1988). *Teaching for Democratic Citizenship: Decision Making in the Social Studies*. New York, NY: Teachers College Press.

Gould, Jonathan (ed.). (2003). *Guardian of Democracy: The Civic Mission of Schools*. Philadelphia, PA: The Leonore Annenberg Institute for Civics of the Annenberg Public Policy Center at the University of Pennsylvania and the Campaign for the Civic Mission of Schools.

Graham, P.A. (2005). *Schooling America: How the Public Schools Meet the Nations Changing Needs*. New York, NY: Oxford University Press.

Greene, Maxine. (1977). "Toward Wide-Awakeness: An Argument for the Arts and Humanities in Education." 79(1) *Teachers College Record*, pp. 119–125.

Harding, S. (ed.). (1993). *The "Racial" Economy of Science: Toward a Democratic Future*. Bloomington, IN: Indiana University Press.

Hunt, Maurice P., and Metcalf, Lawrence E. (1955). *Teaching High School Social Studies: Problems in Reflective Thinking and Social Understanding*. New York, NY: Harper.

Jefferson, Thomas. (1816). Letter to Charles Yancey. Accessed online at *Thomas Jefferson Encyclopedia*. http://wiki.monticello.org/mediawiki/index.php/Quotations_on_Education.

Kelly, A.V. (2009). *The Curriculum: Theory and Practice*. London, UK: Sage.

Leming, James S. (1989). "The Two Cultures of Social Studies Education." 53(6) *Social Education*, pp. 404–408.

National Council for the Social Studies (NCSS). (2007). "Academic Freedom and the Social Studies Teacher." Retrieved online at: http://www.socialstudies.org/positions/academicfreedom.

Newmann, Fred. (1988). "Can Depth Replace Coverage in the High School Curriculum?" 69(5) *Phi Delta Kappan*, pp. 345–348.

Thoreau, Henry David. (2012). *Walden and Civil Disobedience*. New York, NY: Signet Classics.

VanSickle, Ronald L. (1990). "The Personal Relevance of the Social Studies." 54(1) *Social Education*, pp. 23–27, 59.

Whitehead, Alford North. (1967). *The Aims of Education and Other Essays*. New York, NY: The Free Press.

# PART I
# The Imperative

# 1

# THE IMPERATIVE TO INCORPORATE A STUDY OF SOCIAL ISSUES INTO THE SCHOOL CURRICULUM

*Samuel Totten*

PROFESSOR EMERITUS, CURRICULUM AND INSTRUCTION,
UNIVERSITY OF ARKANSAS, FAYETTEVILLE

My interest in social issues was sparked while in high school (Laguna Beach High School, class of 1967). Many of the teachers at LBHS were outstanding, and not a few engaged us, their students, in discussions/projects dealing with various social issues. My biology teacher, Mr. Art Robertson, who walked a good distance to work everyday, not only for the exercise but also for the sake of the environment, constantly spoke to us about the beauty and value of the environment and what individuals could do to preserve it. He was not didactic or preachy but rather approached us in a way that was more contemplative (in a quiet voice), almost as if he was simply sharing his deepest thoughts with us.

One of the most profound lessons I experienced in relation to the environment was when Mr. Robinson (who ultimately left Laguna High to earn his doctorate in biology in order to teach at the university level) took a small group of students to a local tide pool, paired us up with a partner, and asked us to collect as many different specimens as we could within a two-hour period. Even though I had romped around tide pools during my many days at the beach while surfing, body surfing, skin diving, and fishing, I had little to no idea just how rich and alive tide pools were. In the end, our group of thirteen students or so located 56 different items from the tide pools, including such fascinating specimens as the following: a sea anemone, striped shore crab, hermit crab, kelp, starfish, California mussel, acorn barnacle, surf grass, chiton, sandcastle worm, owl limpet, periwinkle snail, sea lettuce, gooseneck barnacle, feather boa (brown algae), coralline algae, black turban snail, purple sea urchin, and owl limpet. Ultimately, from this single lesson, I learned to truly appreciate the richness in nature, the symbiotic nature of flora, fauna, and the settings in which they live—and that, in turn, led to my becoming more appreciative of the critical need regarding the conservation and protection of nature.

Another incredibly powerful lesson I gleaned in high school vis-à-vis social issues took place in my U.S. History course during my junior year. Our teacher, Mr. Walter Lawson, a recently retired officer in the U.S. Marine Corps, required each of us to read and review a book from a list he provided. The latter assignment served as a supplement to the regular coursework. I chose Upton Sinclair's *The Jungle*. Not only was I deeply moved by the conditions that the workers in the stockyards faced and the horrific treatment of the animals, but I was also deeply impacted by a particular message in the Preface to the book. Therein, I discovered that Sinclair's book had been read by President Theodore Roosevelt and, as a result of having read the book, he pushed through the Pure Food and Drug Act. (Many years later I read that this was an apocryphal assertion.) What really hit me at the time, though, was the ostensible power of "the word," the power that a writer could have, and that one's words could truly change the world. It was at that point that I began to yearn to become a writer whose words would impact the world in a powerful and positive way.

Upon graduating from college (California State University, Long Beach) with a degree in English, I intended to write a novel. To that end, I moved to San Francisco where, for thirteen dollars per week (yes, per week), I took up residence in a single residency occupancy hotel that bordered Chinatown and North Beach. Each morning I would catch a trolley car out to San Francisco State University, where I would write for five or six hours. Then, each evening, after a cheap but substantial dinner in a tiny Chinese joint, the Ding Ho Cafe, I would head to Lawrence Ferlinghetti's City Lights Bookshop, where I would pull the same four or five books off the shelf and read the night away. One evening, as I sat down at my usual table in the basement, I noticed a journal, amongst several books and other journals sprawled across the tabletop, with the words "Torture in Chile" scrawled across the front cover. My interest piqued, I read the article, and in doing so I was shocked: shocked at the barbaric use and types of torture against so-called "enemies of the state," the pervasiveness of torture across the globe, and the fact that I had never heard or read about such atrocities and horrific human rights violations in high school or college.

This incident virtually changed my life, and from that point forward I became increasingly immersed in issues germane to the protection of international human rights, including the issue of genocide, which I've conducted research into and written about for the past 25 years.[1]

At the very outset of my teaching career as a student teacher at Costa Mesa High School in Costa Mesa, California, where I taught Freshman Composition and American Literature, I was pretty much locked into what Freire (1985) refers to as a "banking system of education." That is, I was a stickler for detail and insisted that students learn specific literary definitions, concepts, theories, etc., not only to be tested on them but to apply them to their study of literature. Still, the way in which I set the tests up meant that the students pretty much had to memorize the material and regurgitate the answers. The one saving grace,

I suppose, is that I purposely incorporated into the curriculum topics, issues, themes, and readings (along with a few unique learning activities, though not many) that were rather unusual and out of the ordinary. Each of these was tied to social issues-related topics. For example, there was a month-long theme on African American history and literature, during which the students read Richard Wright's *Black Boy* and *Native Son*, short stories by Wright and James Baldwin, and Ernest Gaines' *The Autobiography of Miss Jane Pittman*, and listened to and engaged in discussion with an African American pastor from a nearby city who spoke about parishioners who lived in homes with dirt floors and without running water. The students even took a facsimile of an actual exam that African Americans in the South were forced to take in order to qualify to vote. In the process I attempted to prod students to be more aware of their lived lives and the world around them. Unfortunately, there was more prodding than assisting and nurturing them to thoroughly analyze or reflect upon their lived lives in comparison to those of others in the world—and the ramifications of such.

Later, after becoming immersed in the field of human rights and volunteering with Amnesty International, I began incorporating even more diverse readings into my English classes (in Australia, in California, at the Walworth Barbour American International School in Israel, and at the U.S. House of Representatives' Page School), along with research projects tied to the readings. As a result, various students in those settings read and discussed, for example, such fictional and nonfictional works as Solzhenitsyn's *One Day in the Life of Ivan Denisovich*, Elie Wiesel's *Night*, John Howard Griffin's *Black Like Me*, and Arthur Miller's "The Crucible."

Gradually, I added projects on other social issues, including but not limited to apartheid, child and spousal abuse, the pervasive use of torture by various governments around the world, censorship, and totalitarian states. Some topics were suggested by my students, others by me. All potential topics were voted on by the students.

It was not until my fourth year of teaching that I even realized that there were other educators who were keenly interested in engaging their students in a study of social issues. Our superintendent at the Walworth Barbour American School in Israel saw to it that faculty had ready access to educational journals and encouraged us to read them. It was during that time that I came across both *Social Education* and *Educational Leadership*, each of which periodically included articles related to educating students about one social issue or another. Over time, I gradually became familiar with the writings and efforts of such scholars as Richard Gross, Donald Oliver, James Shaver, Fred Newmann, and Carole Hahn, among others.[2] My introduction to the aforementioned scholars' work, and the history of the National Council for the Social Studies' efforts vis-à-vis the incorporation of social issues into the extant curriculum, vastly altered my own efforts, in that they became more in-depth, more systematic and, ultimately, more sophisticated.

## My Pedagogical Creed

### Dispositions Apropos to Studying and Coming to Care About Social Issues

I believe that both experienced and prospective teachers need to be conversant with, and ponder long and hard, the ideas found in Herbert Spencer's *What Knowledge is of Most Worth?* (1884) Indeed, it is one that all teachers need to ask themselves throughout the school year and whenever they are planning their units and lessons. This is just as true for those teachers who find themselves boxed in and constrained by curricular programs and state standards that ostensibly leave little wiggle room for any deviation from the "set" or "standard" curriculum. In that regard, I firmly believe that even those teachers who face a top-down curriculum driven by state and/or federal standards, textbooks, and/or standardized tests have the wherewithal, if they choose to take it, to infuse key social issues and radically different perspectives into the extant curriculum. It, of course, takes more energy, thought, imagination and work—not to mention gumption—but, in the end, it is what the most professional and creative teachers do in order to provide their students with the best education possible.

I believe in Socrates' dictum, "The unexamined life is not worth living." I believe that individuals who do not probe their own lived lives (why they think, believe, and act the way they do, etc.), who are not well informed about the world they live in (locally, regionally, nationally, internationally), and who do not take the time and effort to thoroughly think about and wrestle with key social issues and problems are less than fully alive intellectually and hardly the type of citizens so essential to a healthy democracy.

I believe that helping to nurture "wide-awakeness" in students is critical to the educational endeavor. In regard to the critical need to be "wide-awake," Thoreau (1963) eloquently asserted the following:

> Moral reform is the effort to throw off sleep. Why is it that men give so poor an account of their day if they have not been slumbering? They are not such poor calculators. If they had not been overcome with drowsiness they would have performed something. The millions are awake enough for physical labor; but only one in a million is awake enough for effective intellectual exertion, only one in a hundred million to a poetic or divine life. To be awake is to be alive. I have never yet met a man who was quite awake. How could I have looked him in the face?
>
> *pp. 66–67*

More apropos to the study *and* confrontation of social issues, Maxine Greene (2008), one of my professors at Teachers College, Columbia University, comments as follows:

The only way to really awaken to life, awaken to the possibilities, is to be self-aware. I use the term *wide-awakeness*. Without the ability to think about yourself, to reflect on your life, there's really no awareness, no consciousness. Consciousness doesn't come automatically; it comes through being alive, awake, curious, and often furious.

*pp. 1–2*

I believe that it is imperative that teachers, in conjunction with the curriculum that is taught, nurture and sustain curiosity in the mind of each and every student. If teachers truly aspire to assist their students in becoming life-long learners, then nurturing curiosity seems to be the first step in that direction: curiosity about the world in which they live, curiosity about their place in it, curiosity about why things are the way they are and how they possibly could be different, and how significant change has been, and can be, undertaken. This is where students begin to learn that a "taken-for-grantedness" view of life is not only limiting but intellectually and morally vacuous. Here, I think, for example, of all those whites in the U.S. who accepted Jim Crow as a given (i.e., "the way things have 'always' been, how they are, and how they should always be"). The same, of course, is applicable to those South African whites who accepted apartheid as "a given" or those "good Germans" who accepted and lived according to the beliefs and dictates of the Nazis.

Given that complex social problems do not simply disappear over time (that is, it often takes Herculean efforts over the long haul by individuals and groups working together to ameliorate them), and that the appearance of new social issues is inevitable, I believe that life-long learning is critical to both the health of individuals and the nation.

I believe that students need to be taught the value of being a reflective thinker *and* citizen. While one can often be swayed by facts presented in a particular light, it is also important to weigh the issues against what is fair and just when supporting one side of an issue or another. Without deep reflection about as many possible sides of an issue as possible[3]—as well as the many ramifications, positive, negative, or otherwise, that might result from one's support of a particular side or another—one can hardly consider oneself to be a truly conscientious citizen.

## Incorporating the Study of Social Issues into the School Curriculum

I believe that teachers in most curricular areas should strive to incorporate the examination and discussion of social issues in order that it constitutes an integral part of the daily curriculum. It should not be a stretch to do so, for numerous social issues/problems are germane to topics studied in social studies, history, government, English, the sciences (general science, biology, chemistry, and physics) and even mathematics. Moreover, it is not merely contemporary social issues that are important: it is vitally significant for students to learn how certain social issues arose and were dealt with in the past (e.g., women's right to vote, "separate but equal," the testing of atomic bombs in, for example, Utah and the South Pacific). Concomitantly, the study of those social issues from the past *that continue to impact society* today is not only warranted but very much desired (e.g., racism, the spread of nuclear energy, the nuclear arms race, the fact that women frequently earn less than men despite doing the very same job).

I believe that in many ways the "null curriculum" (Eisner, 1985) is as important as the extant curriculum, and that teachers need to seriously consider the null curriculum when designing lessons and units of study. Eisner (1985) defined the null curriculum as follows: "The options students are not afforded, the perspectives they may never know about, much less be able to use, the concepts and skills that are not part of their intellectual repertoire" (p. 107). If the study of social issues ends up constituting part and parcel of a school's or a class' null curriculum, the list of *options* (e.g., use of the Freedom of Information Act and the fact that individuals can, if need be, contest a lack of justice all the way to the U.S. Supreme Court), *perspectives* (e.g., not all laws are just; one individual can make a world of difference; and individuals banding together can, and have, changed society for the better in many significant ways), *concepts* (e.g., critical theory), and *skills* (e.g., thoroughly examining complex social issues, and cogently debating controversial social issues) of which students are left ignorant (or are incapable of undertaking) are not only many in number but have the potential to significantly limit the important role a student could play as a citizen in a democracy.

I believe that an education bereft of a systematic study of key social issues (local, regional, national, and international) and how they can be addressed by individuals, alone or in cooperation with others, is sorely incomplete. Knowledge can be, and often is, a window onto the world and its various (social, political, religious, economic, etc.) complexities. Ignorance can, and often does, leave one bereft. Examples of the latter, unfortunately, abound: the dangers inherent in building and purchasing homes atop waste dumps (e.g., Love Canal); the dangers inherent in building nuclear reactors in tsunami-prone areas (e.g., the Fukushima I nuclear accident in Japan); and the many and different dangers that result from contact with lead-based paint, and the fact that lead-paint (despite being outlawed) continues to cause grievous harms to individuals.[4]

I believe that those schools, teachers, and curricular programs that avoid teaching about so-called controversial issues are contributing to a narrow-mindedness that is antithetical to providing a sound education in a democratic society. Indeed, I believe that schools and teachers that avoid teaching about controversial social issues are potentially damning our young to lives of apathy, a lack of serious participation in our democracy, and a listlessness about issues that can, and certainly will, at least at times, seriously (and often adversely) impact them, their children, and the nation in which they live. This, I believe, does not bode well for the health and life of the body politic.

I believe that teachers must make a genuine effort to address what Hunt and Metcalf (1983) refer to as "closed areas" (including, for example, systemic causes of racism, sexism, disenfranchisement, and the ramifications of such), *and* to engage their students in reflective thought about such issues—including why and how such areas and topics become closed due to their controversial nature. As Hunt and Metcalf (1983) put it:

> It has come to be granted that American culture is beset with problems. Problems seem to accumulate at a rate faster than we can solve them. It is our contention that this problematic suspect has not been well understood. It has not been understood that problems of social conflict exist not only as issues between individuals and groups, but also as sources of confusion within individual personalities. Neither has the existence of closed areas as one of the attributes of a problem area been widely recognized. It is one thing to say that American culture includes a "race problem." But it says a great deal more to observe that this problem exists not only between Negroes and white, but within each, and that rational solutions are difficult to achieve because race is treated in the culture as a closed area. In our curriculum proposals, we argue for reflective studies of the problematic aspects of American culture, including elements of personal and social conflict that are sometimes closed to rational examination. The closure may rise from community taboos or personal prejudice.
>
> *p. 98*

## Approaches

I believe that schools, department programs and teachers should strive to incorporate, when possible, extended studies of social issues (i.e., week-long, two-week-long, month-long, and quarter-, semester- and/or year-long) into the curriculum.

Furthermore, I firmly believe *that any effort to address social issues in the curriculum that requires at least some substantial thought by students is worthwhile.* Put another way, even those efforts that are not predicated on a theoretical model, are not part of a sustained effort to incorporate social issues throughout the curriculum over the course of the school year, etc., are valuable. I believe that even, for example, having students read a book of their choice (based on the recommendation of their teacher or at least okayed by the teacher) which deals with a social issue can pay huge dividends.[5] (Please see my comments in the introduction vis-à-vis my reading of Upton Sinclair's *The Jungle* in my junior U.S. History course.)

I believe that the concept of "depth over coverage" (Newmann, 1988) should be at the heart of teaching, and that such a concept is particularly germane to any study about a social issue. As Fred Newmann (1988) has cogently stated:

Knowledge is thin or superficial when it does not deal with significant concepts of a topic or discipline—for example, when students have a trivial understanding of important concepts or when they have only a surface acquaintance with their meaning. Superficiality can be due, in part, to instructional strategies that emphasize coverage of large quantities of fragmented information.

Knowledge is deep or thick when it concerns the central ideas of a topic or discipline. For students, knowledge is deep when they make clear distinctions, develop arguments, solve problems, construct explanations, and otherwise work with relatively complex understandings. Depth is produced, in part, by covering fewer topics in systematic and connected ways.

*pp. 9–10*

Ultimately, superficial coverage leads to superficial knowledge and, in the end, information that is largely forgotten.[6] This is part and parcel of what I have deemed "the perfunctory curriculum."

I believe that it is a teacher's job to play the devil's advocate when engaged in teaching about social issues, and to teach students how to play the devil's advocate in a constructive and intellectually sound manner. In this way, students are more likely to engage in a healthy and deep dialectic (i.e., a thesis/antithesis/synthesis-like approach) vis-à-vis the issue at hand.

Concomitantly, I believe that, to fully challenge students to think deeply about important social issues and to move them to construct their own understanding of them, it is imperative for teachers to create cognitive dissonance in their students and to assist them in reaching clarity.

I believe that it is critical to engage students in writing-to-learn activities (that is, learning activities in which students are encouraged to write out any questions they might have about an issue; respond in writing to an article or chapter or book about an issue; clearly state in writing their position vis-à-vis an issue and a rationale for their position; spell out any changes in their thinking about the issue as they learn more about it; and delineate in writing their new understanding about an issue, etc.) during the course of study of social issues. By engaging the students in well thought-out writing assignments, it will likely enhance student thinking, deepen their understanding of what they are attempting to learn, and contribute to their long-term memory of the issue. By engaging the students in such writing it is not only more likely that they will express *their own* ideas, questions, and concerns, but also dig more deeply into the complexities and dilemmas of the issues and construct their own understanding.

I believe it is critical to engage students in sustained authentic discussion throughout the study of social issues. Just as when students engage in writing-to-learn activities, engaging in sustained authentic discussions in the class provides significant opportunities for them to express their own ideas and concerns, posit their own questions, and, as above, dig more deeply into the complexities and dilemmas of the issues at hand, *and* construct their own understanding.

I believe that it is critical that students come to understand the value of being reflective and have ample practice in class of doing so. As Dewey (1933) commented, reflective thought entails "active, persistent, and careful consideration of any belief or supposed form of knowledge in the light of the grounds that support it and the further conclusions to which it tends" (p. 9).

Cognitive dissonance, writing to learn, engaging in sustained authentic discussion, and becoming a reflective thinker/individual are all likely to contribute to higher-order thinking, a greater depth of knowledge about the issues at hand, and, hopefully, a deeper connectedness to the world beyond the classroom.

I know that individuals and organizations that have confronted seemingly intractable social issues have made a profound and positive difference in society. I believe that it is critical to teach students about such individuals, organizations, and social movements, and what they accomplished. In doing so, students are likely to learn why and how social issues bubble up and become the focus of serious concern to the so-called "average person" or "common citizen." Likewise, students are likely to learn about how small but highly focused groups of activists have had an impact far outweighing their number and/or have come together to form much larger and more powerful movements that have frequently overcome—at least what appeared to others to be—insurmountable barriers to influence positive change.

Teachers need to provide ample and powerful examples of these efforts (that is, it is not enough to simply comment on such efforts). Even more valuable, teachers ought to seriously consider having their students conduct their own studies into activists' efforts. For example, even if one limits the study to what has taken place in the United States and only as far back as, for example, the beginning of the twentieth century, it is incredibly impressive what the so-called "common" person/people have accomplished, including the suffragists' efforts to gain the right to vote for women; the civil rights movement's indefatigable efforts to end Jim Crow and "separate but equal," while also helping blacks gain the right to vote; and the environmental movement's efforts to push through the passage of (a) The Clean Air Act of 1970, (b) The Marine Protection, Research and Recovery Act of 1972, and (c) The Endangered Species Act of 1973. Such efforts are ripe for examination and analysis, and it seems as if such a study would likely be highly informative, thought-provoking, and even hopeful.[7] If nothing else, and this is not insignificant, such a study will enable students to begin to understand that positive change *is possible*, that individuals and/or groups/organizations of "average" citizens *can and have made an incredible difference in addressing complex and critical social issues impacting individual lives and society*, and that, while social issues are complex and cannot be solved "overnight," they *are solvable when there is the determination, commitment, and energy to do so.*

I believe that it is extremely worthwhile to educate students about the vast differences between life in a democracy and life in totalitarian states. Too many people—and not simply the young—in the United States seem to readily accept life in a democracy as a given, while not fully appreciating the fact that such freedom is precious and must be protected, lest it slip away, either all at once at the hands of outside enemies or slowly, in dribs and drabs, at the hands of those within our own government who think they know what is best for the "commonwealth." This is particularly important today, when more and more of our freedoms in the United States are in danger of being eroded due to actions by such organizations as the National Security Agency.

I believe it is important to engage students in reading and discussing both fiction and nonfiction works about totalitarian societies. George Orwell's *1984* and *Animal Farm*, Ray Bradbury's *Fahrenheit 451*, Alexander Solzhenitsyn's *One Day in the Life of Ivan Denisovich*, Aldous Huxley's *Brave New World*, and/or Lois Lowry's *The Giver* are all outstanding fictional works that would be ideal for such a study. These works, among many others, provide readers with a solid sense of what it means *to not be free* to voice one's concerns about one's society and government, *to not be able to* assemble peacefully and carry out protests, and *to not be able to* vote in and out one's national, state, and local leaders, and so forth.

I believe it is imperative that students gain an in-depth understanding (versus one that is perfunctory, as most students, unfortunately, receive in their high school education) of the U.S. Bill of Rights and U.S. Constitution *in a way that resonates with them*. One way of accomplishing the latter is tying the documents/protections/rights to the study of key social issues and social movements from the past and present. In that way, individual rights shimmer with significance versus appear as something static, dry, and unimportant. Only in this way, it seems, will students truly come to understand what rights they have, how such rights can be abrogated, and what they can do to address the latter. Simply reading these documents is not likely to have half the punch of tying them to actual cases in which citizens were denied rights but fought for them and were successful in doing so.

I believe students must be given ample opportunity to address, in school, in their local community, and beyond, those social issues of concern to them. In this regard, I am in agreement with John Dewey when he asserts, in his pedagogical creed, that "I believe that the only way to make the child conscious of his social heritage is to enable him to perform those fundamental types of activity which makes civilization what it is."

Ultimately, then, it is about helping students to understand that, as a citizen in a democracy, it is their job, as much as anyone else's, to see to it that the government, and those in government, abide by the Constitution, and that it is absolutely critical that officials at all levels—locally, state, nationally—be held accountable for their actions when they abrogate such rights.

Finally, I believe that there is no place for propaganda in our nation's classrooms. In that regard, I think it is imperative that teachers help students to understand how to detect propaganda and how to combat it. Those who do not know how to detect such, or how to combat it, open themselves, and the larger society, up to being duped by those who use propaganda to gain control of others.

## Conclusion

I believe that teachers who are not conversant with key social issues of the day are remiss in that they can hardly consider themselves truly educated, let alone fully prepared to even begin to strive to be an outstanding educator. Teachers who do not stay abreast of the news of the day, let alone make an effort to understand the complexities of such, are extremely poor role models as to what it means to be a well-informed citizen. Of course, no person can be well informed about all issues everywhere but that is no excuse for not being as well informed as possible about as many of the most pressing issues of the day as possible—particularly those that directly impact one's community, state, nation—*and/or* are germane to one's academic discipline. Ultimately, it is the responsibility of both parents and educators to prepare our youngest citizens to take an active and positive part in keeping our democracy healthy and strong and to be proactive in addressing those social issues that impinge upon society and the lives of individuals.

## Notes

1   Over the past 25 years I have, for example, served as an investigator with the U.S. State Department's Atrocities Documentation Project in Chad, where the 24 investigators with the project conducted interviews with refugees from Darfur, Sudan. The data in the interviews were used by U.S. Secretary of State Colin Powell to make the determination that genocide had been perpetrated by the Government of Sudan against the black Africans of Darfur. I have conducted additional field work in Chad, the Nuba Mountains in Sudan, and in refugee camps in South Sudan; co-founded a journal, *Genocide Studies and Prevention*; and have written and co-edited more than a dozen books on genocide, including, for example, *Genocide by Attrition: Nuba Mountains, Sudan* (Transaction Publishers, 2011); *We Cannot Forget: Interviews with Survivors of the 1994 Rwandan Genocide* (Rutgers University Press, 2010); *An Oral and Documentary History of the Darfur Genocide* (Praeger Security International, 2010); and *The Darfur Genocide: Investigating Atrocities in the Sudan* (Routledge, 2006).

2   Somehow, though, for a good many years I remained ignorant of the critical theorists. Because of that I was not even cognizant of Paulo Friere's (1985) pronouncement that (and here I am paraphrasing) education serves one of two purposes—to domesticate or liberate. In fact, I was not introduced to the thoughts and works of Freire, Michael Apple, Jean Anyon, and Henry Giroux, among others, until I began graduate school at Teachers College, Columbia University in 1980.

   While there was much about critical theory (and its various offshoots over the years, i.e., critical feminist theory, critical race theory) that I found (and continue to find) intriguing, persuasive, and vital, I never could, and thus never did, completely embrace critical pedagogy. There were numerous reasons for that. First, it took me quite a while to gain a firm grasp of the theoretical constructs of critical pedagogy. Second, while I gravitated towards certain aspects of critical pedagogy, there were other aspects that I looked askance at. In that regard, *my reading* of critical pedagogy suggested that major aspects of it leaned rather heavily towards indoctrination versus education, and I was very much put off by that. Third, while I greatly desired to "adopt" and buy into certain aspects of critical pedagogy, a voice at the back of my brain suggested that one was either a critical pedagogue or one was not: that it was not a piecemeal endeavor. Fourth, I readily admit that I never gained a solid grasp on how to approach the curriculum in order to create learners who skillfully learned the content, became critical thinkers, *and* developed an understanding and appreciation of what it meant to be a citizen with a critical perspective (Shor, 1992). Fifth, I believed in the curriculum that I was teaching: how to prepare students to become solid writers, the need for students to become conversant a wide range of literature through the ages (which moved me to teach works that I considered vitally significant) and the need for them to have appreciation of those social issues that impact both individuals and society as a whole. Sixth, and to be totally honest, critical theory just had too radical of a feel for me. Seventh, and, again, to be totally honest, I allowed the ostensible power of the "system" to intimidate me (meaning, I sensed that there would likely be a real push back by the powers that be—administrators, school board members, department chairs, deans) and thus took the easy route out. On that weasel-like and sour note, I should say, believe it or not, that ultimately I do believe, along with John Dewey, that "all education proceeds by the participation of the individual in the social consciousness of [humanity]."

3    It is a common misunderstanding that a controversial or social issue has only two sides.

4    "There are many ways in which humans are exposed to lead: through air, drinking water, food, contaminated soil, deteriorating paint, and dust. Airborne lead enters the body when an individual breathes or swallows lead particles or dust once it has settled. Before it was known how harmful lead could be, it was used in paint, gasoline, water pipes, and many other products. . . . Old lead-based paint is the most significant source of lead exposure in the U.S. today. Most homes built before 1960 contain heavily leaded paint. Some homes built as recently as 1978 may also contain lead paint. This paint could be on window frames, walls, the outside of homes, or other surfaces. Harmful exposures to lead can be created when lead-based paint is improperly removed from surfaces by dry scraping, sanding, or open-flame burning. High concentrations of airborne lead particles in homes can also result from lead dust from outdoor sources, including contaminated soil tracked inside, and the use of lead in certain indoor activities such as soldering and stained-glass making.

"Lead affects practically all systems within the body. At high levels it can cause convulsions, coma, and even death. Lower levels of lead can adversely affect the brain, central nervous system, blood cells, and kidneys. . . . The effects of lead exposure on fetuses and young children can be severe. They include delays in physical and mental development, lower IQ levels, shortened attention spans, and increased behavioral problems. Fetuses, infants, and children are more vulnerable to lead exposure than adults since lead is more easily absorbed into growing bodies, and the tissues of small children are more sensitive to the damaging effects of lead. Children may have higher exposures since they are more likely to get lead dust on their hands and then put their fingers or other lead-contaminated objects into their mouths." United States Environmental Protection Agency (2012). "Lead-Based Paint." Remodeling Your Home? Have You Considered Indoor Air Quality? Accessed at: www.epa.gov/iaq/homes/hip-lead.html?.

5    While such a hit and miss approach is far from the ideal, there is always the possibility that once a teacher begins postholing or assigning individualized assignments/projects centered around the study of social issues and discovers his/her students' enthusiasm for such (that is, their keen desire to discuss issues in class, their unsolicited comments in regard to their individual findings and/or the excitement of talking to individuals outside of the school who are attempting to address social issues in the local community and beyond), then he/she may be more prone to taking the next step towards incorporating the study of social issues into the curriculum in a more systematic manner. In doing so, there is always the possibility that he/she will seek out the ideas of others about how to do so, about what works and doesn't work and why, and/or

come across the names and ideas of key individuals (e.g., Harold Rugg; Maurice Hunt and Lawrence Metcalf; Donald Oliver, James Shaver and Fred Newmann; Shirley Engle and Anna Ochoa-Becker; Ron Evans; Diane Hess; Henry Giroux; and Michael Apple, among a host of others) who have thought long and hard about the imperative to engage students in a study of social issues. And that, in turn, could lead to a move from being a traditional teacher who has been locked into the mandated curriculum to being one who branches out and incorporates more opportunities for his/her students to examine, discuss, and debate social issues. Pie in the sky? A certain naïveté? No, I don't really think so. Will most teachers travel down such a road? No, probably not. But some, I believe, will—and that could, in some cases, make all the difference in the world to that particular teacher's students.

6    See also Fred Newmann's (1988) "Can Depth Replace Coverage in the High School Curriculum?" 69(5) *Phi Delta Kappan*, pp. 345–348.

7    The ultimate purpose of such an approach is not to create social activists, per se, but rather to simply inform students about how various individuals in society at various points in time have chosen to have their say about key social issues impacting society, have refused to accept the status quo, and have moved from working on an individual basis to a more organized basis to attempt to enact change in society.

## References

Dewey, J. (1933). *How We Think: A Restatement of the Relation of Reflective Thinking to the Educative Process*. Boston, MA: D.C. Heath and Company.

Eisner, E. (1985). *The Educational Imagination: On the Design and Evaluation of School Programs*. New York, NY: Macmillan.

Freire, P. (1985). *The Politics of Education: Culture, Power, and Liberation*. South Hadley, MA: Bergin & Garvey.

Greene, M. (2008). "The Importance of Personal Reflection." April 12. Accessed at: www.edutopia.org/maxine-greene-daring-dozen

Hunt, M.B., and Metcalf, L. (1983). *Teaching High School Social Studies*. New York, NY: Harpers.

Newmann, F.M. (1988). "Can Depth Replace Coverage in the High School Curriculum?" 69(5) *Phi Delta Kappan*, pp. 345–348.

Shor, I. (1992). *Empowering Education: Critical Teaching for Social Change*. Chicago, IL: University of Chicago Press.

Spencer, H. (1884). *What Knowledge is of Most Worth?* New York, NY: John L. Alden Publisher.

Thoreau, H.D. (1963). *The Variorum Walden*. New York, NY: Washington Square Press.

# 2

# THE SOCIAL ISSUES EDUCATION IMPERATIVE

*William G. Wraga*

PROFESSOR, EDUCATIONAL ADMINISTRATION AND POLICY,
THE UNIVERSITY OF GEORGIA

## Introduction

Because preparing students to act as enlightened citizens of a democracy is the historic national goal of education in the United States, social issues education should comprise the heart and soul of public schooling. In what follows, a biographical statement precedes a discussion of what social issues education is, my perception/beliefs of what (a) the role of the school in social issues education is, (b) the content and method most ideal for carrying out social issues education, and (c) the integral connection between social issues education and social progress.

The social issues education imperative came to me through the field of curriculum theory and development. As an undergraduate at Rutgers College, before I decided to teach, I studied the cultural history of the United States under the mentorship of the extraordinary cultural and intellectual historian Warren Susman (1984). The master's level pre-service teacher education program I completed in 1980 at the University of Chicago, prepared me to convey subject matter to students, which was what initially attracted me to teaching. At Chicago, William Pattison (1964) oriented me to geography education and Mark Krug's (1967) *History and the Social Sciences* influenced my approach to teaching history.

My original career goal was to teach a high school elective on the cultural history of the United States. I thought the opportunity to do so would not arrive for years—until I had seniority in a social studies department. So I began my career in New Jersey public high schools teaching subject matter in United States history, world history, and American and British literature courses. Fortuitously, my second teaching job was in a high school with an exhausted faculty and a new principal who gave me almost *carte blanche* to develop new courses. During my fourth year as a teacher I developed and taught a course called Cultural History of

Modern America, which examined, within a historical context, cultural patterns that emerged from developments in literature, music, art, and popular culture.

Ultimately, it had become disappointingly apparent that the subject matter was more interesting to me than to my students. In order better to engage them, I began to build into units consideration of debates among historians about the causes of historical events. For example, in addition to establishing the events typically identified as precipitating the Civil War, in class we would also consider the views of perhaps three or four historians as to the main cause of the war. Some textbooks featured brief but useful sidebars summarizing such interpretive debates. Students identified what they thought was the main cause of the war, and defended their position in an essay, in which they would use historical facts as evidence to support their case. Some students were stunned that a teacher was actually interested in their opinion on something; others were intimidated because they had no experience articulating any kind of coherent argument. A typical comment was, "You can't grade us on this because it's our opinion, right?" To which I enjoyed responding, "You will be graded not on the position you take, but on the argument you make." At any rate, this was a nascent disciplinary form of issues-centered education, adopted to encourage students to engage with subject matter.

I decided to return to graduate school at Rutgers University, in order to pursue further study in history and also to obtain certification as a school supervisor. Having developed my own courses, I thought it would be interesting to coordinate the program of a whole social studies department. So, in the fall of 1983, I found myself in a graduate course taught by Daniel Tanner (1980) about developing curricula and instruction. Among many other things, Tanner emphasized that there were three principal sources for the curriculum: the subject matter, the student, and society. It became clear to me that I had totally exploited the first source, barely begun to consider the second source, and completely neglected the third source. Tanner also showed me that the subject-centered curriculum, however pervasive in schools, was only one of a number of ways to organize the curriculum. I realized that acquiring more subject matter knowledge through further study of history would not expand my thinking and teaching in the way that learning more about curriculum development would.

Most of the professional literature in the field of curriculum development that I read in my doctoral studies placed greater emphasis on the nature of the student and of society as sources for the curriculum, than on subject matter. It was largely through this literature that I developed an understanding and appreciation of the importance of the role of the public school in preparing students for life in society. And, in the U.S., an obviously important aspect of social living was democratic citizenship. It was quite impressive how classic curriculum works consistently emphasized the role of the schools in preparing future citizens in a democracy to be able to tackle complex social issues: the *Cardinal Principles* report (Commission on the Reorganization of Secondary Education, 1918); the statement of the National Society for the Study of Education's (1926) Twenty-Sixth Yearbook Committee; the publications of the Eight-Year Study (Aikin, 1942); the Educational Policies Commission reports (e.g., 1953); the Harvard Report (Committee on the Objectives of General Education, 1945); the general education literature (Hock and Hill, 1960); the core curriculum literature (Lurry and Alberty, 1957); even James Bryant Conant's (1959) *The American High School Today*; and numerous other works identified issues-centered education, if not in name, as an imperative component of the public school curriculum. Social issues education seemed an effective way to synthesize the three sources of the subject matter, the student, and society.

I began incorporating consideration of social issues into my teaching, and in the position of supervisor worked with interested teachers and principals to develop activities and units that addressed social issues, a course that integrated American history and literature, and a capstone course at the high school level that expressly engaged students in an examination of social issues and problems (Wraga and Zimmerman, 1993; Townsend and Wraga, 1997; Wraga, 1996). As I conducted this work, and read beyond readings in my doctoral program, I also began to attempt to contribute to the professional literature about interdisciplinary curriculum and social issues education, a project I continued to pursue after I left K-12 schools for a position in academia (Wraga, 1989, 1992a, 1992b, 1993, 1998, 1999, 2001).

## What Social Issues Education Is

Social issues education should foster in all students the abilities, dispositions, and inclination to analyze, evaluate, and act upon common social problems.

Social issues education should prepare students to participate in foundational activities of collective democratic living.

Social issues education is imperative for achieving the fundamental purpose of education in a democracy: to establish an enlightened citizenry that can serve as a check against the powers that be. Thomas Jefferson (1785/1961) contended: "Every government degenerates when trusted to the rulers of the people alone. The people themselves therefore are its only safe depositors . . . . And to render even them safe, their minds must be improved to a certain degree" (p. 97). George Washington (1796/1966) urged the nation to "Promote . . . as an object of primary importance, institutions for the general diffusion of knowledge. In proportion as the structure of a government gives force to public opinion, it is essential that public opinion should be enlightened" (p. 222). And, in *Brown v. Board of Education*, the Supreme Court (1954) established "the importance of education to our democratic society" which the court considered "the very foundation of good citizenship" (p. 493).

A democratic citizenry should not only be enlightened, but also must possess the capacity and willingness to engage in common social problem solving. As

John Dewey (1937/1991) put it, democratic living is a form of collective problem solving. What this means, in short, is that as a community faces common social problems, community members should be encouraged to propose possible solutions; these are then tested in experience to determine which proposed solutions contribute to the resolution of the problem. Every member of that community has the right to propose solutions to common problems. Education must maximize each citizen's capacity to solve common problems so that collectively a community may optimize the quantity and quality of potential remedies. Social issues education should directly develop such capacities.

Social issues education should develop breadth and depth of understanding, problem-solving skills, and the capacity for political action. Democracy is at risk unless citizens learn constructive, intelligent, democratic forms of inquiry, problem-solving decision-making, and political action.

## Role of the School in Social Issues Education

Given the historic function of education in preparing enlightened citizens for a democracy, social issues education should be the priority of public schooling. Using contemporary rhetoric, students should graduate from high school "citizenship-ready." The school is the institution best suited to developing social issues education competencies in students because it possesses the resources to do so. Multiple school goals of academic, vocational, civic, and personal development can be integrated and realized through social issues education (Goodlad, 1984). Because social and personal growth are the key tasks of democracy, social issues education should especially contribute to the development of civic capacities of students and to the personal development of students as autonomous individuals (Kelly, 2009).

Because social issues transcend disciplinary boundaries, social issues education must be both multidisciplinary *and* interdisciplinary. Indeed, *every subject in the school curriculum should contribute to social issues education*; social issues education should animate the whole curriculum.

Following the recommendations of the Commission on the Reorganization of Secondary Education (1918), every school should have a designated Citizenship Education Director to coordinate social issues education throughout the programs and the daily operation of the school.

## Content of Social Issues Education

The content of social issues education should be comprised of the following:

- Social issues past, present, and anticipated.
- Methods of identifying and analyzing social issues.
- The application of disciplinary subject matter to the analysis of social issues.
- The application of non-disciplinary sources, such as journalistic analyses and

policy analyses to the examination of social issues.
- Strategies for integrating these sources.
- Skills of problem-finding, problem-solving, critical thinking, decision-making, and cooperative group work.
- Rules of logic and evidence.
- Ability to detect and counter logical fallacies.
- Political action skills.

Social issues education employs subject knowledge not for its own sake, but as evidence. Social issues education should focus on making students knowledge-able: capable of using knowledge to analyze social issues.

## Method of Social Issues Education

In a democracy, citizens have the right to make up their own minds about any-thing and everything. Period. The most critical consideration in methods of social issues education is that the resolution of, and subsequent political action on, any social issue that students arrive at should be neither predetermined nor dictated by the teacher. In that regard:

- Social issues education should privilege logic and evidence.
- Social issues education should dignify the integrity of the learner.
- Social issues education should provide students with experience developing convictions that are based upon logic and evidence.
- Social issues education should engage students in the substantive analysis and evaluation of all sides of social issues.
- Social issues education curricula should be developed for particular students in particular communities.
- Students should participate in developing social issues education curricula.
- Students should be evaluated not on the position they take, but on the argu-ment they make.
- Classroom evaluation forms should be based upon and should enhance the experiences students have with social issues education.
- Teacher participation in the continuous development of issues-centered cur-ricula and instruction should function as a form of professional development for teachers.

## The School, Social Issues Education, and Social Progress

Social issues education occurs in schools that are situated in communities. Social issues education can be an unsettling thing for many parents, whose concerns range from having their children just learning the basics and academic subjects, to fear that their children will disagree with them at the dinner table, to the fear that they will develop convictions at odds with their own cherished opinions. Social issues education curricula should be developed in connection with the local community.

As students engage with real social issues, as students learn through the experience of seeking resolution to social problems, as social issues education contributes to the development of students' personhood, and as social issues education enables students to function as citizens who can contribute to the improvement of their society, social issues education is a manifestation of American pragmatism in education (Childs, 1956).

## Conclusion

Social issues education manifests a commitment in American culture to individual and collective pragmatic thought and action and serves the historical national education goal of preparing students to act as enlightened citizens of a democracy. To avoid social issues education is to leave democracy to whim, the vagaries of emotion, knee jerk reactions, mob thinking, the influence of special interests promoted at the expense of the social or individual good, and the manipulation of the powers-that-be. Social issues education should function as a constituent part of the education of all children and youth, enabling schools to achieve their role of preparing enlightened citizens for a democracy. This is the social issues education imperative.

## References

Aikin, W.M. (1942). *The Story of the Eight-Year Study*. New York: Harper.

*Brown v. Board of Education*, 347 U.S. 483 (1954).

Childs, J. (1956). *American Pragmatism and Education*. New York: Henry Holt.

Commission on the Reorganization of Secondary Education. (1918). *Cardinal Principles of Secondary Education*. Bulletin 1918, No. 35, Department of the Interior, Bureau of Education. Washington, DC: U.S. Government Printing Office.

Committee on the Objectives of a General Education in a Free Society. (1945). *General Education in a Free Society*. Cambridge, MA: Harvard University Press.

Conant, J.B. (1959). *The American High School Today*. New York: McGraw-Hill.

Dewey, J. (1937/1991). "Democracy and Educational Administration." In J.A. Boydston, ed., *John Dewey: The Latter Works, 1925–1953, Volume 11* (pp. 217–225). Carbondale: Southern Illinois University Press.

Educational Policies Commission. (1953). *Education for ALL American Youth*. Washington, DC: National Education Association.

Goodlad, J.I. (1984). *A Place Called School*. New York: McGraw Hill.

Hock, L.E., and Hill, T.J. (1960). *The General Education Class in the Secondary School*. New York: Holt, Rinehart, and Winston.

Jefferson, T. (1785/1961). "Notes on the State of Virginia." In G. C. Lee, ed., *Crusade Against Ignorance: Thomas Jefferson on Education* (pp. 92–97). New York: Teachers College Press.

Kelly, A.V. (2009). *The Curriculum: Theory and Practice*. London: Sage.

Krug, M.M. (1967). *History and the Social Sciences: New Approaches to the Teaching of Social Studies*. Waltham, MA: Blaisdell Publishing.

Lurry, L.L., and Alberty, E.J. (1957). *Developing a High School Core Program*. New York: Macmillan.

National Society for the Study of Education. (1926). *The Foundations of Curriculum-making*. 26th Yearbook of the National Society for the Study of Education, Part II. Bloomington, IL: Public School Publishing.

Pattison, W.D. (1964). "The Four Traditions of Geography." 63 (May) *Journal of Geography*, pp. 211–16.

Susman, W.I. (1984). *Culture as History: The Transformation of American Society in the Twentieth Century*. New York: Pantheon Books.

Tanner, D., and Tanner, L.N. (1980). *Curriculum Development: Theory into Practice*. New York: Macmillan.

Townsend, R., and Wraga, W.G. (1997). Implementing an Interdisciplinary Unit on the Holocaust. In S. Totten and J. E. Pedersen, eds., *Social Issues and Community Service at the Middle Level* (pp. 43–59). Needham Heights, MA: Allyn and Bacon.

Washington, G. (1796/1966). "Farewell address." In D. Boorstin, ed., *An American Primer* (pp. 211–229). New York: Mentor.

Wraga, W.G., and Zimmerman, S. (1993). "Fostering Participatory Citizenship: The Liberty Corner Student Committee." 13(1) *Educational Viewpoints* (New Jersey Principals and Supervisors Association), pp. 34–35.

Wraga, W.G. (1989). "Political Literacy: Teaching Active Citizenship." 68(1) *Educational Horizons*, pp. 46–49.

Wraga, W.G. (1992a). "The Core Curriculum in the Middle School: Retrospect and Prospect." 23(3) *Middle School Journal*, pp. 16–23.

Wraga, W.G. (1992b.) "Crusade of Ignorance: Democratic Citizenship and Education Goals." 56(3) *The Educational Forum*, pp. 257–267.

Wraga, W.G. (1993). "The Interdisciplinary Imperative for Citizenship Education." 21(3) *Theory and Research in Social Education*, pp. 201–231.

Wraga, W.G. (1996). "Teaching Societal Issues Across the Secondary Curriculum." In R.W. Evans and D.W. Saxe, eds., *Handbook on Teaching Social Issues* (pp. 265–275). Washington, DC: National Council for the Social Studies.

Wraga, W.G. (1998). "Implications of Issues-centered Education for the Social Studies Curriculum." 13(1) *International Journal of Social Education*, pp. 49–65.

Wraga, W.G. (1999). "Organizing and Developing Issues-centered Social Studies Curricula: Profiting from Our Predecessors." 90(5) *The Social Studies*, pp. 209–217.

Wraga, W.G. (2001). "Democratic Leadership in the Classroom: Lessons from Progressives." 14(2) *Democracy & Education*, pp. 29–32.

Wraga, W.G., and Zimmerman, S. (1993). "Fostering Participatory Citizenship: The Liberty Corner Student Committee." 13(1) *Educational Viewpoints* (New Jersey Principals and Supervisors Association), pp. 34–35.

# 3

# AUTHENTIC TEACHING IS VENTURING INTO UNCERTAINTY

*Geneva Gay*

PROFESSOR, CURRICULUM STUDIES AND FACULTY ASSOCIATE OF
THE CENTER FOR MULTICULTURAL EDUCATION, UNIVERSITY OF WASHINGTON

## Introduction

I don't recall as a young child desiring to be a teacher, or any other specific profession. My elementary school teacher was mean, punitive, and dictatorial. She had taught my mother and all her other siblings, and my age mates' parents as well, in the little school in rural eastern Georgia that served the African American community. She was feared rather than admired. Throughout my elementary grades she was the only image of "teacher" that I experienced, and I certainly did not dream of being like her when I became an adult.

In the larger community my life was situated in a sociopolitical environment that was racially divided between Blacks and Whites, and engaged in deeply entrenched racist practices that oppressed and contained African Americans. In high school I had caring and competent African American teachers, but at the time I didn't think about eventually becoming one of them. They seemed far beyond my reach and my imagination socially, economically, and professionally. Those teachers were more like celebrities or exotic figures to be admired from afar, not to be considered as reasonable models to emulate. There was no one else in my immediate environment to provide alternative options of aspiration. My family background of long-term poverty, racial discrimination and oppression, rural living, and limited education created seemingly impenetrable obstacles of isolation. Yet, even as a young child I loved to read and repeatedly read the one or two tattered "readers" left over from the school days of my younger aunts and uncles. The folkloric and fictional content of those books were fascinating and captivating; they stimulated my imagination, and offered a welcomed retrieve (although momentarily) from the drudgery and harsh realities of my daily life.

Although I don't recall as a small child actively *planning* to be anything or anyone different to what and who were available in my immediate environment, I did think that there must be a better way to live, and I just wanted to be different. I always had problems with my human worth being determined by other people's criteria of quality and normalcy, especially those set by a dominant mainstream society that questioned the fundamental humanity of African Americans. This desire to be different has been, and continues to be, a constant presence in how I engage in teaching. Simply stated, I just don't want to be like everyone else, or the way I am supposed to be according to some rules and regulations established by some external agents or organizations, especially if these represent ways of being that are "normative for everyone." Nor do I think there is, or should be, a "universal standard" for everyone. Instead, I am continually asking, "Why can't the quality of different human beings be determined by the contexts and conditions of their own socialization?" "What's the merit of making the unreasonable demand in education that all people believe, value, and behave alike in socio-political communities and countries when diversity is an inherent attribute of humanity?" "Why judge everyone in a group, community, or nation as if they were clones of each other?" This questioning of prevailing educational assumptions and social customs and claims is a determining influence in how I teach and my chosen areas of concentration (multicultural education and culturally responsive teaching).

As a child, I was never quite "in sync" with the prevailing customs, traditions, and/or practices of the people I lived with and the places we inhabited. While my difference (or "oddness") was tolerated, it was not honored, encouraged, or facilitated. My crude self-constructed strategies for claiming the right to be different were crafted and conducted without much assistance from family members or schoolteachers. The early efforts were somewhat like looking for that proverbial needle in the haystack, or trying to chart a course of action without knowing exactly where you are going and without a definitive map to help you get there. I knew that I didn't want to be and behave as Blacks were expected to (because it was demeaning), but I wasn't sure what the alternatives were. Consequently, much of my early efforts at validating and normalizing my difference were various forms of escapism, such as reading, silence, and withdrawal from activities that were routine for my family and community. I became an outsider within! It wasn't until I was in graduate school taking courses in cultural anthropology that I received some formal instruction about dealing with difference, both for my own racial and cultural identity, and for people and experiences in general. I actually went to graduate school in search of myself, and in the process also found my professional commitment. I learned that my difference was normal for me, and nothing to be ashamed of or apologetic for. This revelation was truly psychologically, intellectually, and socially liberating. If cultural and ethnic self-knowledge and self-discovery could do this for me, they could probably also do similarly for other students from marginalized groups of color at other levels of education. It was then that I began to formalize and actively pursue my advocacy of cultural diversity, equity, and multicultural education for African American students, and ultimately for other under-achieving and marginalized groups of color as well.

I believe there is truth to the adages that our careers often choose us rather than us choosing them, and that teachers teach themselves, meaning how we teach is strongly influenced by who we are as persons—that there is a strong personal nuance to our professional personas and practices. This is certainly true for me. I did not deliberately desire or plan to be a teacher. For a time I thought I became a teacher by default. In my impoverished, racially separated childhood community the only professional careers readily evident among African Americans was the ministry, teaching, nursing, and funeral directors. Of these, only teaching and nursing were considered appropriate for females. Nursing did not seem feasible since all the nurses and doctors at the time in our nearby town were White, and I couldn't qualify racially. Yet, I did not *plan* to go to college to become a teacher. I fantasized about going to college because that's what members of my high school social network said they were going to do. I was a good student academically and took college prep classes because if you were intellectually smart that's what you did. Academically I was in a high status ranking, but I was a social misfit and uncomfortable with my ethnic and racial identity. As my peers aspired to be doctors, ministers, and lawyers, I felt obligated to declare an aspiration of similar stature. So, I said I was going to college to become a lawyer, but I had no idea how I was going to make this happen financially or experientially. Privately, I didn't even believe my own public declarations, but I did want to be different to my current conditions, and was willing to fantasize the possibility. No one in my immediate family had ever completed high school, not to mention going to college, *and* they were poor tenant farmers. Where was the money for college going to come from?! I couldn't even expect to receive any realistic guidance and encouragement from my family, since the academic world was alien to them. Miraculously, and due in part to my relocation to a city in northern Ohio and a federal government student loan program which allowed me to attend a local college, I ended up with a teaching degree after taking pre-law undergraduate courses.

My desire to be different has served me well over the years. It is the catalyst for me seeking new experiences and new exposures, and my willingness to allow new adventures to shape themselves without too much pre-planning and pre-expectations on my part, beyond the beliefs that "this will be a different experience and as such it will have some kind of inherent value. I will be different after having experienced it than before because it is new to me." This is my approach to experiencing life, whether I am reading a book, taking a trip, or teaching a class. I am excited and stimulated by differences rather than being intimidated by them, and easily bored by similarity and routinization. I seek out differences and invite their presence into my life, but I am not reckless or capricious in doing so. Every new experience is an invitation for me to extend my personal repertoire of difference. And, while some experiences may at first look like they are repeats of earlier ones, they never are, since I have never done that exact thing before. I think this disposition toward difference is a highly valuable complement for good teaching.

Some people believe deeply that teaching is a calling. I can't say for certain but maybe that is why I became a teacher without deliberate intentionality. I do know that I love to teach, and I engage in the enterprise as a continually evolving act of discovery, adventure, and learning; a moral mandate to put forth my very best effort in every teaching endeavor; and an acceptance that difference is a valuable attribute to be honored and a resource to be developed. I believe high quality teaching and learning involve moral, social, personal, civic, psychological, emotional, and cultural, as well as academic knowledge and skill development. I was motivated early in my career to do explicitly for students of color what was not done for me. At least my high school teachers were African Americans and they did exhibit ethnic and cultural affiliation in some of their personal behaviors and classroom social capital—but they did not incorporate African American cultural content in their formal curriculum and instruction. I don't remember my elementary teacher in the little country school I attended ever mentioning anything about African American history and culture, other than what was negatively portrayed in textbooks of the times, although all of the students were African American. I want to be very deliberate and transparent in all aspects of my teaching that ethnic, racial, and cultural diversity are fundamental to high quality and effective teaching and learning.

Undoubtedly, all of these experiences, whether positive or negative, intentional or not, have influenced my perceptions of teaching, and how I engage in the process.

## My Pedagogical Creed

To name my pedagogical creed, I borrow a statement from William Ayers. Several years ago, in speaking about an essential characteristic of teaching, he declared that good teaching is at best an imprecise and uncertain endeavor, and it is never exactly replicated from one occurrence to another. This statement captures the essence of my beliefs about teaching and how I engage in the process. It is explicated further in my delineation of my pedagogical creed below.

I believe teaching is always a work in progress, a leap of faith, and a continuous venture in trial and error—in hopeful experimentation. A teacher is never certain that what he or she plans to do will, in fact, be done as planned and anticipated. Regardless of how long one teaches or how skillful one is, there is always something else to learn about the craft; yet another technique to try out, another class or student to challenge a teacher's ingenuity, imagination, creativity, and competence, and/or demand a reconstruction of what one assumes to be his or most effective efforts. Because teaching is a perpetually evolving process, it is never finished; never completely mastered. Therefore teachers have to always be evolving, too—that is, they have to be actively refining their craft and how they cultivate and carry it out. For these reasons and more, teaching is incredibly invigorating and demanding, and sometimes very aggravating and even frustrating.

I believe teaching is both intuitive and a systematically learned and well-planned behavior. Good teaching takes more than waiting for flashes of inspiration, although this does factor into the equation. It requires knowledge, skills, observations, and reflections perfected over time; therefore, teaching is both artistic and scientific. Just as artists invest foresight, preparation, and planning into a project before putting anything on a canvas, and continue to study their subject as the vision takes shape and form, so do teachers. Teachers must be skillful and astute observers of their own and their students' presence and participation in the teaching and learning process, and use the insights gained to reconstruct the teaching dynamics as they are unfolding. Because of these demands, I believe teachers have to have the ability to function somewhat like ethnographic participant-observers, in that they are consciously monitoring and modifying their teaching process as they are immersed in it. Thus, teachers must be competent and diligent observers and analysts of themselves who are able to multi-task *as* they are teaching. Curiously, while this multi-leveled engagement in action may sound chaotic or impossible in description, it can be perfected to the point of being habitual, once teachers get to the point of doing it without conscious pre-thought.

I believe teaching is very personal and idiosyncratic, to the extent that it is an exercise in futility to invest much time and energy into looking for universal best practices (as some educators are currently doing). While general principles and features of teaching may be identifiable and valuable, they still have limited utility for action with particular teachers in specific contexts. At the point and place where actual practice prevails over theoretical conceptualizations, teaching is a very context-specific enterprise, and a critical factor in that context is the person who inhabits the role of teacher. Therefore, I believe, as some other scholars have declared, that teachers teach who they are. That is, they always put a personal stamp on their teaching habits and behaviors. Consequently, if teaching is routinely and habitually staid and devoid of exuberance then the teacher is likely an uptight, highly controlled, and uninteresting person. If teaching is heavily regulated by rules and regulations, then the teacher is probably one who likes a lot of order in his or her life and is not inclined toward adventure, experimentation, and playfulness. Conversely, individuals who consider teaching to be exploratory, adventurous, and enjoyable are likely to incorporate humor, mystery, novelty, surprise, joy, and discovery in their teaching. They focus more on learning how to know and discovering uncommon sources of knowledge than on what to know from more conventional depositories. This, I believe, is a hallmark feature of powerful pedagogy.

I believe good teaching always involves the performance of loosely structured scripts. As such, teaching as performance operates somewhat like improv theater. Good teachers know their craft thoroughly, including both subject matter content and pedagogical skills, and easily nuance their delivery such that they are responsive to the unique needs and characteristics of varying groups of students. Since no two audiences are exactly the same (nor, for that matter, does any audience (or group of students) function identically at all times and in all contexts), teaching processes need to be nuanced somewhat differently to accommodate these circumstances. Additionally, teaching as performance adds to the mixture of content knowledge and pedagogical skills large dosages of improvisation, intuition, playfulness, and a willingness to trust the guidance of "on the spot insight" about what to do to capture the attention and engagement of student audiences. Like theater, the motivational intentions and action styles of teaching as performance are to entice involvement from students holistically—intellectually, emotionally, socially, physically, ethically, and even spiritually (in a secularly way)—but more dialectically and organically than linearly and sequentially. What may appear to be impulsiveness or effortlessness is, in fact, the execution of a thoroughly learned craft that is in continuous stages of refinement.

Good teaching extends beyond technical mastery and creative ingenuity, even though these two dimensions of the enterprise are intellectually, physically, and imaginatively demanding.

I believe effective teaching is a moral endeavor. There are so many things teachers should do simply because they are the ethically right things to do, and others that should not be done because they are fundamentally wrong, unfair, and unjust. Among the right things to do is working diligently to ensure that all students have the highest quality opportunities possible to achieve academically to the best of their ability, and doing so without compromising or demeaning, denying, and ignoring their ethnic, racial, cultural, and gender identities and heritages. At the heart of teaching as a moral endeavor is the fundamental belief that the humanity of teachers and students are important factors and influences in teaching and learning, and a fundamental anchor of humanity is cultural socialization. At their most essential human level, students and teachers are always cultural beings, and in reality they are culturally different since they are socialized into and through different cultural systems. Therefore, to be minimally adequate (not to mention excellent), methodological difference must be an inherent part of teaching, and the process should always be reflective of and responsive to ethnic, racial, cultural, and social diversity. This is a moral imperative, as well as a human reality and a pedagogical must.

Closely connected to morality is my belief that teaching is a venture in caring. Here I am not talking about caring as warm-fuzzy emotionalism, or the glibness with which many declare, "of course I care *about* my students," and "I love all children." My conception of caring is much more complex and demanding than the aforementioned type of fantasized and romanticized bonding among human beings. It is better described as caring *for* rather than *about* students, because it focuses on what teachers *do* to help students build their intellectual, personal, performance capacities. I believe teachers who genuinely care *for* students engage in action-driven partnerships with students to ensure maximum success for everyone. They do not necessarily have to even like all of their students or agree with them. But, caring teachers do respect students, honor them, and advocate for them and their right to a high quality education. These teachers realize, and act accordingly, that school success is multidimensional for each individual and quite different for everyone. It encompasses building intellectual, moral, ethical, personal, social, political, and cultural knowledge, values, and skills. Caring teachers are, as some scholars have declared, "warm demanders"—that is, they always insist on high performance of all kinds for all students, and they are very diligent about facilitating and assisting in these accomplishments.

Unlike some teachers who issue performance demands and then leave students to accomplish them on their own, caring teachers do the reverse. They make "the learning journeys" with students, and when the need arises they are the trailblazers, mediators, navigators, and negotiators of the processes. They model learning as collaborative engagement and reciprocal relationships among teachers and students. They readily concede that sometimes students must teach and teachers must be learners, and both must share resources to achieve maximum outcomes. Caring teachers also demonstrate that they do not necessarily have to be masters of all the resources (and support) that students need to learn, but, when learning is occurring under their tutelage, they use all of their ingenuity and networking skills to make supports available for students. Additionally, caring teachers convey personal attitudes and create classroom climates in which success is both normative and taken-for-granted; it is so habitual as to not merit any special attention. Yet, they know the value of celebrating self, and because the self of each student in their care is deserving of high honor and appreciation, it is worthy of note as part of the process of students and teachers being the best they can in all that they do. With these attitudes and associated behaviors, failure is not an option for teachers who genuinely care for their students.

I also believe teaching is political. For me, the essence of politics is distributing power and negotiating values, ideologies, and other valuable resources. Teaching fits this description because knowledge is power, and teaching involves the distribution of knowledge and the navigation of different variations of intellectual property. Teachers are perpetually engaged in deciding what constitutes knowledge, and what knowledge is worth knowing, by whom, and under what conditions. In so doing, some forms of knowledge (and the people who generate them) are recognized and validated while others are ignored, denied, and/or devaluated. These decisions are never based solely on logic and rationality; rather, they are value-driven since knowledge is socially constructed, and some people's conceptions of knowledge are perceived to be more valuable than others. A case in point is how the funds of knowledge of peoples of color in the United States have been devalued while those of European Americans have been elevated to canonical status. These choices and distributions of intellectual resources are equivalent to the empowerment of some ethnic individuals and sociocultural groups, and the disempowerment of others—a fundamental attribution of political behavior!

I believe good teaching is reflectivity, reflection, and responsiveness. However well instructional intentions are preplanned, they never unfold in action as they were intended. Part of this is due to the fact that, although good teachers know their students well, they cannot ever predict student behaviors in all circumstances with absolute certainty. Therefore, teachers have to be astute observers of both their own and their students' behaviors in the moments of occurrence, and, at one and the same time, be capable of making necessary adaptations. This requires well-developed observational skills, flexibility, and fluidity in teaching. Inherent to these processes is the need for teachers to be self-confident, yet open to change; the ability to "read" their student audiences for cues and gaining insights about how well (or not) the instructional process is going; and possession of a wide repertoire of teaching techniques for use in different circumstances.

Communication and relational skills are at the center of these needs and capabilities. Teachers who relate well with students and see themselves first and foremost as advocates of students are always attuned to the "feel" of their classroom dynamics. They know, almost intuitively, when instruction is going well and when it is not; when students understand or are confused; when students are interested and motivated, or are bored and disengaged. They depend as much on nonverbal cues as on verbal comments (if not more so) to obtain this information, make the assessments quickly, and adjust their instructional behaviors accordingly. Amazingly, all of this is done *in real time, as teaching is taking place*. To be this attuned to the flow of their classroom dynamics, teachers have to be closely connected to and invested in their students, intellectually and personally; in other words, they cannot teach from a physical and emotional distance. Even the language and actions of teaching have to be up close and personal. Sometimes, academic language and actions alone simply will not suffice. Outstanding teachers know this and are not above developing and using a wide repertoire of linguistic skills (such as mixing colloquial, informal, and cultural styles of speech with academic and professional language) to facilitate student learning. Nor do they see doing so as compromising academic standards. In other words, these kinds of teachers know that academic success involves more than academics; that personal, social, and emotional factors contribute to learning as well, and they evoke them in their efforts to expedite maximum learning for all students.

I believe teaching involves perpetual learning, especially when teachers accept the fact that students have valuable contributions to make to the teaching-learning process. For this to work best, teachers must value and accommodate this reciprocal relationship. Teaching provides infinite opportunities to acquire new knowledge and skills; to examine the adequacy of existing values, perspectives, and assumptions; and to question claims of truth. These opportunities are available to teachers as well as students. Teaching culturally diverse students is a graphic example of such. There is no way possible for teachers to be experts on all ethnic and cultural groups that comprise the student populations present in U.S. schools. Yet, more and more teachers encounter this diversity on a daily basis. Without allowing themselves to be taught, at least partially, by the diverse students they encounter regularly in their classrooms, teachers will miss golden opportunities to expand their repertoires of knowledge and skills. Students from diverse backgrounds are capable of conveying a great deal of valuable information for improving teaching by simply being their cultural, ethnic, and racial selves. This information is indispensable for teachers who are committed to providing educational equity and excellence for students from diverse ethnic, cultural, and social backgrounds.

Teaching also provides self-study opportunities for teachers to learn about themselves and how they perform their role functions. There often are significance differences between what teachers think they do and what they actually do while teaching. Learning to be critically reflective about their own teaching can help to bridge gaps between thought and action, and improve the quality and effects of actual performance. This pursuit of continuous improved performance is integral to both good teaching and high quality learning.

I believe teaching constitutes a blend of general beliefs and values actualized in particularized behavior. Consequently, teaching can never be an entirely objective process; nor at the level of action, can it be purely technical, or totally devoid of some kind of personal bias. Individuals who teach have beliefs about how the process should unfold, about what is significant or not, and about how best to impact students. These beliefs and concomitant behaviors may vary somewhat according to different student populations, subjects, and skills taught, and the environmental settings in which teaching occurs, while maintaining some persistent orientations.

I believe that mediating is integral to the act of teaching. This mediation has many different forms and effects. One of the most common and obvious forms of mediation is a teacher intervening between the known and the unknown for students, making knowledge accessible, or making the unfamiliar familiar for students. This apparently simple task of teaching becomes complicated when it is examined in relation to who the students are; that is, in order to make knowledge accessible for students from different ethnic, racial, cultural, and social backgrounds, teachers have to make many different border crossings in their various efforts at mediating. Sometimes they have to mediate teaching and learning styles so that the acquisition of knowledge is not unduly obstructed by procedural misfits. Sometimes teachers have to mediate the language of academics to make it understandable to out-of-school settings. Other times, teachers have to mediate between conflicting sources and perceptions of knowledge, and the interpretations of events such as the views of insiders compared to outsiders. And sometimes they need to determine whose versions of events and meaning are most valid. Sometimes these "insiders and outsiders" are the students and teachers themselves, and teachers are then called upon to mediate these differences. Mediation demands that teachers' instructional skills and interactional styles that go far beyond merely telling students the "right" answers or how to behave; indeed, instead it may involve problem-solving and/or conflict resolution, which means helping students develop their own skills in these domains. Teaching as mediation also involves teachers resolving conflicts between the current stage of their own teaching skills and other possibilities—that is, acting on the realization that however one's good teaching is, it is never as good as it potentially could be. Therefore, this mediation is about seeking continuous growth and improvement. This need is always there regardless of how long a teacher teaches.

I believe teaching is elusive and mystifying, yet incredibly engaging. It is difficult (if not impossible) to descriptively characterize the salient features of teaching beyond broad generalized ideas, because it is so contextually specific. The impermanent and evolving nature of teaching complicates efforts to capture its nature precisely. Terms such as relevant, personal, planned, student-centered, flexible, energizing, and captivating—while worthy attributes—do not, in reality, adequately convey the actual behavioral attributes of teaching.

Another reason why teaching is mystifying is because it is always changing. What works in one setting and time is not guaranteed to be equally successful in another; nor from one teacher to the next. This elusive nature of teaching demands that those who teach be able to tolerate a high degree of ambiguity, uncertainty, and flexibility as a natural part of their professional lives. Rather than being troubling or disconcerting, though, this is the very reason why I find teaching to be so personally and professionally captivating, invigorating, enjoyable, and enriching.

# 4

# ROOTS, BRANCHES, AND SHOOTS

*Margaret Smith Crocco*

PROFESSOR, SOCIAL STUDIES EDUCATION, MICHIGAN STATE UNIVERSITY

## The Temper of the Times

As almost anyone who has studied American history knows, many characterize the 1960s as a tumultuous period. Those who lived through the decade have varying opinions about whether the tumult ought to be viewed favorably or otherwise. Undoubtedly, a great deal of what happened during those years—especially the assassinations of John Kennedy, Robert Kennedy, and Martin Luther King—represent tragedies of the first order, ones that shook many citizens to the core at that time.

Concurrently, urban riots across the nation created recognition that the yawning divide between the circumstances of blacks and whites, middle class and poor, and inhabitants of inner cities and prosperous suburbs needed to be acknowledged and addressed. Likewise, as the decade wore on, the Vietnam War increasingly intruded into American life in the form of the draft or the nightly news broadcast. As a student interested in politics, history, and the world during my high school years, 1964 to 1968, these events contributed to a lifelong interest in what today we call matters of "social justice."

Two events stand out—one local, the other global—in raising my consciousness about social issues.

In the summer of 1967, two cities near my hometown of Westfield in New Jersey were among the places that exploded in race riots: Newark and Plainfield. The violence was far worse in Newark, resulting in the deaths of dozens of individuals, destruction of millions of dollars worth of property, and the looting of businesses in certain areas. In both cities, the National Guard was called out to restore calm. My family, along with many neighbors and friends, followed the situation closely, wondering whether the violence would spread to our bucolic suburban town.

On Palm Sunday 1968, three days after the murder of Martin Luther King, my parents and I participated in a "Walk for Understanding" in Newark. Sponsored by the Queen of Angels Church in Newark to bring white suburbanites into the city to demonstrate solidarity with its citizens, the march had been scheduled weeks before King's assassination. Because of that tragedy, concerns arose over whether the news would incite another round of riots. Instead, 25,000 people— white and black—from city and suburb alike, formed a human phalanx of ten abreast that extended over a mile and a half to signify their shared concerns about poverty and injustice.

Besides the racial injustice brought to national attention so vividly by the civil rights movement and the urban riots, geo-politics offered another set of lessons regarding social issues. During my senior year in high school at Oak Knoll School, I took a full-year course on East Asian history, and began to wonder whether the United States could be victorious in what seemed a Vietnamese struggle for liberation from colonial oppression. Despite my parents' disagreement with my anti-war stance, my father offered to put me in touch with a business colleague who was a prominent liberal Democrat in New York City supporting Eugene McCarthy's bid to wrest the Democratic presidential nomination from the incumbent president, Lyndon Johnson. With the agreement of my school's principal, I invited this individual to address the school about why he opposed the War. His speech solidified my conviction of the importance of dissent in the face of injustice, whether national or global. When I went off to college in Washington, D.C., six months later, I became involved in an attempt to remove the ROTC (Reserve Officers' Training Corps) from campus, volunteered for the Hubert Humphrey campaign, and marched against the Vietnam War.

Although many factors undoubtedly account for my commitment to teach social issues, the momentous national and world events of my high school years and the personal connections I made to these events from the platform of my small high school and suburban hometown played a critical role in orienting my teaching career. My pedagogical creed developed out of an evolving understanding of how to best effectuate the aim of student engagement in social issues that had so stimulated my own educational experience.

## Roots

"Actions not words": This expression of the mission of the Society of the Holy Child Jesus (SHCJ) influenced my years as a student at Oak Knoll School in Summit, New Jersey, from grades 6 to 12. Despite some Catholics' negative recollections of their education by nuns, my experiences were largely positive. Oak Knoll was (and remains) coeducational in grades K-6, and all-girls in grades 7–12. This single-sex arrangement during the adolescent years provided an environment in which young women could assume leadership positions and take academic achievement seriously. In those days, and perhaps even today, young women often believed that appearing smarter than boys would make them less appealing to potential suitors. If this sounds archaic to readers, then we've made some progress.

Based on Cornelia Connelly's vision of what schools should be and do, Oak Knoll provided a strong foundation for my developing views about teaching and learning. Connelly established her first schools in England during the mid-19th century, long before Dewey wrote his pedagogic creed. Nevertheless, broad similarities exist between his principles and her ideas.

Besides the SHCJ commitment to "actions not words," several other phrases ingrained in us capture key aspects of Connelly's approach. Education should "meet the wants of the age"; promote a "spirit of joy and happiness"; develop the "whole child"; and prepare young women to take "an active place in society." Launched at a time when the Lancastrian system of education in England dictated an approach to schooling modeled on factories, Connelly's classrooms diverged markedly from a system focused on rote learning, narrow curriculum, and self-control. Moreover, advocating women's contributions to society beyond the confines of home and church was an unusual perspective for Victorian England, not to mention the first decades of the 20th century when Connelly's followers established schools in the United States.

Connelly called for a "solid education" for all girls. In England, she introduced new approaches that would make schooling available to poor working class girls, for example, by teaching at night and on Sundays. She advocated the same liberal education for all girls that boys from the middle and upper classes received. Her curriculum emphasized reading, writing, math, history, geography, the arts, and "physical science." Outdoor recreation as well as activities associated with imagination and celebration played important roles in the school year. Connelly believed in a rhythm to school life. She encouraged her teachers to create a positive physical environment in their classrooms that would promote a "spirit of joy and happiness," which was considered critical to a positive educational experience.

Connelly inveighed against education for women that fostered only superficial knowledge of a narrow set of topics; she stressed the need to teach for understanding and judgment. Her methodology was inductive, beginning with the life experiences of her students and moving through graduated levels of understanding ("line by line, and step by step in all learning and in all virtues") towards discernment of "truth" and development of strong character. Although Connelly encouraged teachers to adapt their teaching to students, she cautioned against underestimating their ability to learn, whatever their social class or background.

Then, as now, nuns who challenged conventional ways of doing things, especially regarding women's place in society and religion, created friction with men in power. Connelly's life had its own share of episodes that might have produced conflict but instead prompted her acquiescence to male authority. Connelly lived her life in conformity with 19th century notions that women were the property of their husbands and that obedience to men was required of women. She agreed to her husband Pierce's decision to become a Catholic priest (he had been an Episcopalian priest when they married), even though it meant she had to take a vow of "perpetual chastity" and would become a nun. Later, she adopted a similar posture towards the dictates of the Catholic hierarchy, acquiescing to an English bishop's demand that she send two of her young children away to boarding school. When Pierce renounced the Catholic priesthood and returned to being an Episcopalian priest, he took their young children out of boarding school to live with him, with only infrequent visits to their mother. One can only wonder at her willingness to put aside her familial obligations in pursuit of a sense of religious duty. Despite these questions about her personal choices, her legacy, as it manifested itself in my experiences at Oak Knoll, provided a compelling vision of teaching and learning long before I became acquainted with the ideas of John Dewey.

## *Branches*

At Georgetown University in Washington, D.C., I majored in philosophy with a focus on American Pragmatism. In graduate school at the University of Pennsylvania in Philadelphia, I pursued the study of intellectual history more deeply as a path to understanding American education. The quintessentially American platform of Pragmatism, surprisingly perhaps, harmonized with my educational experiences at Oak Knoll: William James's insights into psychology; the Pragmatist idea of truth as manifest through the consequences of a proposition; and myriad aspects of Dewey's philosophy, including his approach to "art as experience" and education of the "whole child" all seemed to provide a philosophical warrant for my own experiences of schooling. This may seem ironic to some readers, since many Catholic educators of the 1960s inveighed against progressive education and perceived Dewey's "Godlessness" as anathema. Perhaps it is just one measure of the differences between conventional parochial schooling of the 1950s and 1960s and the education I received from the Holy Child nuns that the ideas of progressive education seemed more familiar than foreign to me. That said, there was far less explicit attention to ideas of "citizenship" at Oak Knoll than was found in public schools, undoubtedly due to the often strained relationships between advocates of the two systems since the parochial schools were first established in the United States in the 19th century.

Dewey's writings on education return again and again to central themes of the intertwined relationships across school, society, and child. His "Pedagogic Creed" reflects concerns about the impact of industrialization, immigration, urbanization, and social stratification on American society during the late 19th century. As he reflects on the tensions between the psychological and the sociological within education, he highlights the need for equilibrium. Dewey promotes the notion that schooling is not preparation for life, but is life. He views schools as a mode of social life, with moral and communal concerns as part of the civic socialization the schools ought to provide. Since he also considers democracy to be a form of associated living, rather than merely a political system, the school plays a critical role in preparing citizens. Both Dewey and Connelly believed activity to be an essential aspect of schooling, albeit with different emphases in terms of the purpose of such engagement.

Dewey strongly advocated for what we today call the social studies, in particular, geography and history. However, he also acknowledged the importance of a curriculum that included the arts and physical education, science and literature. Since the Deweyan framework places so much emphasis on the child's interest, it would seem to follow that students should have the opportunity to cultivate a wide variety of interests as a facet of their school experience.

Some contemporary scholars identify Dewey as the original constructivist theorist of education, even going so far as to call him a "social constructivist." Clearly, Dewey believed that inquiry and discovery should be central processes of the educational enterprise. He advocated active learning in the form of problem solving and project-based approaches. Dewey recognizes that learning is a sensory as well as cognitive experience; he reminds readers of his "Pedagogic Creed" that the image and the object as well as the word must be investigated within the teaching and learning experience.

Unsurprisingly, Dewey is far more explicit than Connelly about the notion that education is essential to social progress in a democracy. Dewey writes within a very different political and social context than Connelly did. As a result, he considers the community's duty to education in ways that go well beyond the orientation towards community Connelly brought to schooling. But, to the degree that both saw the purposes of education as tied to social amelioration, one through democracy and the other through religious suasion, their perspectives are not entirely dissimilar. Both consider the aim of education as something more than providing one's own children with a competitive advantage in an economic rat race. Instead, they see education as a means of advancing social welfare by providing all children with a "solid education." In that sense, they share a conviction that the fates of school and society are yoked together.

## New Shoots

By approaching this project as a reflection on the development of my own pedagogic creed, I have thus far provided a sense of the ideas that have informed this development. Let me now offer a note of clarification about certain aspects of this development in light of contemporary ideas about teaching and learning.

In focusing thus far on action and activity, I do not wish to ignore the importance of reflection as part of the educational process. Reflection, evaluation, and judgment about what is being learned, along with "meta-cognition," are critical pathways to consolidating the learning process so that it "sticks." But they are important for other reasons as well, chiefly, in my judgment because they are so closely tied to the social, democratic, and moral dimensions of education in a democracy. As a Pragmatist, I believe that education ought to produce consequences, and these consequences ought to go beyond words to action. We need to apply our ideas shaped by education in the public sphere, by carrying out our obligations to the fellow members of our community and to the broader communities of which we are a part. Social education ought to be about developing knowledge and ethical commitments to living in a way that demonstrates integrity and the importance of putting knowledge into practice.

Since Dewey was a contextualist and an empiricist, he would surely expect that a writer of a pedagogical creed circa 2013 would add some points to his 1897 formulation. We know a great deal more today than we did then about the psychology of learning, human motivation, and the important role played by the ecologies of learning, whether they are families, schools, or informal learning settings.

What I have tried to do in the following list is to address issues that are muted, or non-existent, in Dewey's formulation of his pedagogic creed or Connelly's writings about education. Together, these principles comprise the "new shoots" that I would add to the root and branches of the ideas discussed above. I have structured these as belief statements that resemble the approach Dewey used in his declaration. Some derive from my reading of the educational research literature, but much of it must be considered convictions for which I have no evidentiary warrant other than the values I bring to my teaching.

- I believe that education needs to go deep into subject matter, that teachers ought to try to uncover misconceptions in students' understanding, aim for the "big ideas," and, ideally, help them make connections across their subjects and between what they learned yesterday and what they are learning today.
- I believe that education ought to be purposeful in attending to civic engagement, for example, drawing upon pedagogies such as service learning, internships, and projects that connect school to society in explicit and constructive ways.
- I believe that education ought to provide, in the words of Emily Style, both a mirror that reflects one's own experience and a window into the experiences of others. We need to be mindful of the differences of race, class, gender, religion, sexual orientation, etc., as powerful forces shaping the social dynamics of the classroom as well as society. These are differences that often have an effect in communities; we cannot ignore their potential impact on learning, classroom dynamics, school and society.
- I believe that teachers ought to be caring, as Nel Noddings reminds us. Caring means having high expectations for all students and not settling for something less than high expectations based on accidents of birth and their various manifestations in our students.

- I believe, with Dewey and Connelly, that education ought to develop cognitive capacities, perspective-taking, a sense of empathy, an appreciation of the complexity and ambiguity of human existence, the capacity for persistence in the face of failure, for creativity and risk-taking, and a willingness to take a stand in the face of injustice. All of these are dimensions of one's character and related to what we call "social-emotional learning."

- I believe that education is not only career, professional, or workforce preparation, although these are important. The essence and effects of education are not always easily measured, and certainly not measured exclusively through multiple choice tests, but they are nevertheless profound and far-reaching, especially if the teacher is conscious of his or her role in helping subject matter serve, as Dewey said, to "reconstruct experience."

- I believe that education ought to attend both to mind and body: *mens sana in corpus sanum* (a healthy mind in a healthy body), as the ancients put it. Physical activity, especially when it takes children outdoors and puts them in touch with nature, or in dance or drama, is all too often overlooked these days, especially as "virtual" and "digital" representations become so addictive for many people. Mediated reality has its charms, and the power of the image is as compelling as that of the word, but education of the "whole child" through firsthand experience of the natural world as well as the mediated and manufactured world ought to be a more prominent feature of educational experience than it is in many places today.

- I believe that education ought to prioritize new ways of thinking about the student's place in the world. Education must continue to be both psychological and sociological, but it also needs to be ecological as well as global in its consciousness formation. We are increasingly citizens of the world as well as citizens of a community and a nation. Education that ignores the global will soon come be seen as narrow, parochial, and unsuited to the demands of 21st century living.

- I believe that education for sustainability should become a more prominent feature of social education. Education that ignores the threats to our planet and does not problem solve for solutions to the threats we face from consumption, population growth, and the burning of fossil fuels will doom future generations to a deteriorating, if not dangerous, quality of life.

- I believe that education ought to help us understand how to use technology effectively, in ways that do not diminish our humanity but enhance it. Technological tools can be powerful auxiliaries in the teaching and learning process. They offer real possibilities for opening up opportunities for education for those who currently have little access to it. Understanding what is gained and what may be lost as a result of our devotion to—indeed, in some cases, absorption in—these tools will be important to the pedagogical process going forward.

- I believe, with Connelly, that education ought to inculcate a spirit of joy, of play, and of enthusiasm for the learning process. Teachers and administrators need to help create this culture in schools, however difficult that is these days.
- Finally, to restate a central tenet of Connelly's and Dewey's views, I believe that education ought to lead to action, attention to, and engagement with the world. It ought to make a difference in the lives of students and the lives of others. Education ought to lead students to question why the world is the way it is and how it might be made better. Education can certainly begin in contemplation, but it lies inert and unfulfilled if it ends there—if ideas are not put to the test of their truth through their consequences in action, wherever that might lead, but most importantly, towards social justice.

# 5

# A CREED FOR THE NON-RELIGIOUS

## Intellectual Freedom

*Jack L. Nelson*

PROFESSOR EMERITUS, SOCIAL STUDIES EDUCATION, RUTGERS UNIVERSITY

Ideas about school, teachers, knowledge, society, and life come from a variety of sources, all experiential. Some are direct, some vicarious, some imagined. A few can be traced by recall to specific events or circumstances, though most come by accumulation and modification.

I was fortunate to have lived my childhood and youth in a place (Denver, Colorado) and time where progressive ideas were viewed as positive and schools and teachers tried to be happy and encouraging. Given the Depression, it was not an auspicious time in the United States for the economy, for life in and below the middle class, or for protecting children from a variety of illnesses or happenings. The Depression, though I did not realize it as a child, was actually very depressing. Yet, there was an undercurrent of positive notions such as the ability to overcome adversity, personal grit, group adhesion, and better things ahead. Education was obviously a primary means to improvement, one of the few available and severely limited for too many people.

Franklin D. Roosevelt was elected president the year (1933) I was born and reelected for most of my elementary school years. Denver schools in the 1930s and 40s were in the progressive mainstream, and I had some excellent teachers, along with a small number who should have been in another line of work. At South Denver High School, my favorite teacher was Mr. Erb, who taught history and advised the Senate Club and the International Relations Club. He was provocative and engaging, relying on student inquiry.

Erb ran for Congress later, while I was an undergraduate at Denver University, and the Denver newspaper published his ideas on world affairs and global interchange. His ideas were controversial among some important figures in the isolationist and anti-UN movement of the 1950s, and he was fired by the otherwise decent Denver Schools. He appealed under the state tenure rules, and was reinstated after a hearing—but the district forced him to teach English rather than history, and he left after a couple of years, a disappointed man. His example, and others I encountered in later times, contributed to my thinking about the need to provide better protection—academic freedom—for real educators to teach.

Over the course of my career I encountered several other serious infringements of intellectual freedom. I discovered later, while reading an anti-communist book, that one of my graduate education professors had apparently been fired by Northwestern University after he was accused in that book of being "sympathetic" to Communist ideas.

As a new secondary school social studies teacher, I was called to the principal's office because parents had complained I was teaching about evolution and they were offended. A couple of years later, when I was a young college professor at California State University, Los Angeles, I worked with student teachers in a California school district in which the School Board had passed a policy that all teaching materials that mentioned "Russia" or "Soviet Union" were to be banned from the schools. The dean of our college was among those accused in a California legislative document, like the national HUAC committee, of doing a doctoral dissertation at UC Berkeley that was tainted by "leftist ideas," though the study was about school administration.

Years later, as chair of a school board in Highland Park, New Jersey, I was faced with a group of citizens who wanted all sex education taken out of schools, and another time I was shown a sample of a classroom set of books, Solzhenitsyn's *A Day in the Life of Ivan Denisovich*, that a teacher had marked up to cover up swear words. When serving on an ACLU board, I attended a school board meeting at which a student newspaper had been censored by the principal because it included slightly controversial news from outside the school.

Some of my research during my years at Rutgers, based on in-school interviews, showed how widespread and insidious the fear of censorship is among teachers, with a result of sterile classes to avoid controversy. One of my own books, *Population and Progress* (Prentice-Hall, 1972) was banned in Miami, Florida, because it contained a clearly labeled segment from Jonathan Swift's satirical essay, "A Modest Proposal," on boiling babies to limit population growth.

I could cite many more examples in my personal experience, and myriad more in the literature about censorship and freedom, but the point has been made. From these, I began to recognize that the improvement and protection of intellectual freedom for competent teachers and their students is the central element in education. Without it we have training or indoctrination. Misused by incompetent teachers, it is proselytizing or indoctrination. Such freedom is fragile, and in need of constant vigilance.

That position relates directly to ideas about individuals, society, knowledge, and education. Academic freedom assumes that individuals can learn, that learning requires personal involvement, and that learning depends upon critical thinking. Critical thinking, in turn, requires freedom to inquire and test ideas. Academic freedom assumes that societies evolve and that progress is possible. Education is the place where experience in intellectual/academic freedom can be practiced and improved, offering individual and social progress. School should be a relatively safe place with resources to find and challenge ideas and information. The primary work of teachers is to develop and maintain competence and to provide opportunities for students to engage in critical thinking. Knowledge is not static, but cumulative, depending again on the freedom of minds to explore and examine and test.

## My Pedagogical Creed

John Dewey's remarkable 1897 pedagogic creed states a long list of beliefs in a short three pages. I read it many years ago as an undergraduate student in social science teacher education at the University of Denver, and later as a doctoral student in education at the University of Southern California, but had not returned to it until invited to draft one of my own for this publication. Dewey's list starts with his beliefs on education, and continues through the topics of school, subject matter, teacher method, and social progress. My list is shorter, presents "acceptable ideas" rather than "beliefs," and is organized differently.

Mine is shorter because I agree with the substance of most items on Dewey's list. I do not, however, use "beliefs' to start each item as he did, because I follow other Dewey writings in which critical inquiry is encouraged, and those of Bertrand Russell, who counsels skepticism. The standard meaning of beliefs did not seem to fit that very well.

The one area in which I most question Dewey's Creed is in his final statement, which reads: "I believe that in this way, the teacher is always the prophet of the true God and the usherer in of the true kingdom of God."

As an agnostic and supporter of critical thinking and evidence-based argument, I do not see religion or a god as the basic grounding or source for human knowledge, society, education, school, and teaching. Concomitantly, this part of Dewey's Creed seems inconsistent with much of Dewey's other published works, where he is known for nontheistic or rational atheistic views. Nor does it comport with his being one of the 34 original signatories to the *Humanist Manifesto*, which challenges religious dogma. Dewey's 1934 *A Common Faith* (Yale Press) defines God in a "naturalistic" form, in which God is merely an ideal for human consideration and unrelated to a specific theology. In the same book, he also claims that traditional religion was drifting, was being supplanted by science, and would only be of interest to historians. Neither his view of God nor of the demise of religion has become as popular as he thought. In contemporary society, I think Dewey's idea of "God" is open to facile misunderstanding and thus I do not use it in my statement as a guiding force.

Finally, I do not think a creed is necessarily religious. The most common definition of creed is "fundamental beliefs," usually illustrated as a document of religious dogma, but another acceptable definition offers the idea of guiding principles. My creed uses acceptable ideas to serve as a guide to principles and to incorporate the opportunity to disprove or modify them as new evidence develops. Mine is also organized differently from Dewey's because I think the flow should be from views of knowledge, society, and social progress, to education, schools, content, and teacher methods.

## Acceptable Ideas

### Knowledge

1. Knowledge is a human construct, and is basic to the identification, organization, evaluation, and expression of ideas about self, others, society, education and progress.
2. Knowledge is the continuing result of cognition, accumulation, testing, and alteration of ideas and information from a variety of sources, including experience, sensory organs, and experimentation.
3. Knowledge relies on evidence and reasoned thinking, though intuition may offer immediate insights that subsequently can be evidentially tested.
4. Knowledge is an interrelated set of tested ideas that offers reasoned explanation of and for phenomena.

### Society and Social Progress

1. Society is a set of relationships among individuals and groups that establishes, maintains, and alters expected behaviors and expressed values.
2. Society is continually subject to tensions among tradition, reform, reaction, and revolution.
3. Societies exist as fluid structures, resistant to change but always changing, albeit slowly.
4. Individual identity is a fluid composite of social norms and self-perception, both conditioned by personal experiences and social pressures to conform or rebel.
5. Progress is movement toward an ideal state, defined by reference to a given society within the current state of acceptable knowledge.
6. Social progress is largely determined by the beholder, or victor, and is conditioned by cultural and traditional factors that serve as markers of progress.
7. My markers of social progress represent a cultural perspective that incorporates improved life conditions for increasingly larger numbers of people, e.g., health and longevity, freedom, justice, and personal well-being—ideas that can be tested evidentially and which serve to identify progress in civilization.

## Education

1. Intellectual freedom is a necessary condition to develop and improve individual, group, and social knowledge—progress.
2. The key element in developing knowledge and social progress is education, whether in the home, the school, or society at large.
3. Education incorporates learned habit, tradition, behavior, knowledge, and systems of critique.

## School

1. Schools offer a socially organized, moderately efficient system for conveying accumulated knowledge and social values.
2. Schools are one location for education, but can be miseducative to the extent that intellectual freedom for teachers and students is unnecessarily or inappropriately restricted.
3. Schools also offer opportunities to relatively safely challenge and test that knowledge and those values.
4. Schools need continual public scrutiny and critical evaluation to maintain a focus on individual and social progress.

## Subject Matter

1. The subject matter of education is knowledge and its development.
2. Specific subjects (disciplines) are traditional efforts to organize topics within knowledge to facilitate learning or ease investigation, but they are neither sacrosanct nor independent from each other. They should be viewed with skepticism when they become rigid or overly professionalized.
3. The focus of school subject matter should be to assist students to understand the interrelationships and dynamics of current knowledge, and to participate in the rational critique of information, ideas, and forms of knowledge.

## Teachers and Teacher Methods

1. The teacher's primary role is to stimulate and encourage learning.

    Good teaching methodology incorporates serious interest in and respect for the individual student, thoughtful diagnosis of individual and group academic strengths and weaknesses, provision of current knowledge in forms that stimulate the intellectual interest of students, promotion of critical and creative thinking, and comprehensive evaluation of intellectual growth.
2. Teachers have other professional responsibilities, including self-improvement through continuing study and critical thinking, advocacy for and protection

of academic freedom for teachers and students, ethical conduct, and concern for the welfare of students and the school as a progressive enterprise in society.

3. The teacher should actively participate in society, not only as a demonstration of civic involvement but to assist in educating, and being educated by, the public.

# 6

# OPENING UP TO INQUIRY

*Jack Zevin*

PROFESSOR, SOCIAL STUDIES EDUCATION, QUEENS COLLEGE,
THE CITY UNIVERSITY OF NEW YORK

## Introduction

I started out on the south side of Chicago, in a fairly tough environment: a nice but boring elementary school and a rather terrifying high school (Hirsch High School) experience, in the sense it was dull, anti-intellectual, and bound up with sports to the detriment of accomplishment in academic subjects. I just went along for the ride and was saved by a really annoying English teacher, who gave us fun stuff to read, and a wacky science teacher who hid all the bright kids doing science fair projects from the hoodlum element. I went on to win a science fair scholarship because of his ministrations, and then went to the University of Chicago because my counselor at the school said I should.

Mother had no money, so this was entirely on scholarship. I really felt out of place for my first year, since I was a poor kid and unused to being surrounded by intellectuals, but then emerged into a wonderful new feeling of confidence in my skills, due mostly to the wonderful teachers I had at the college. It was really tough going but so stimulating that I had never had an experience like that before, and it was also socially conscious. We argued issues, allegiances, rights, and developed life-long commitments to causes. My allegiances and commitments varied from time to time, but because of the poor economics of my childhood I have always felt for those who are underdogs, the low wage earners, particularly since my mother was a saleslady (as they called it) and I had to work to make my own spending money and help her out. Father was out of the picture due to extended psychological illnesses and was also a burden on us in terms of care and finances as well as the terrors of mental disturbances. Nevertheless, I managed to survive the University of Chicago and prosper, took up a number of commitments to environmental protection, as we would call it now, and supported the work of various organizations (i.e., the Sierra Club, the Audubon Society, the ACLU, and SDS). When I became a public school teacher, I was an avid union supporter and activist, helping others join and support the wide variety of causes that were available to support in Chicago. Then and now, Chicago is a pretty tough place to be poor, and a pretty dangerous place to inhabit, with active gang life that has got tougher as neighborhoods changed almost overnight from white to mixed to black.

I was happy as a secondary school teacher in a tough Chicago school environment, working and debating ideas with an unusually creative and quirky group of relatively new teachers. The influences that carried with me into the classroom were many, although I did not appreciate them fully at the time. These included, as alluded to earlier, a rich and varied University of Chicago classical curriculum, university mentors who were active proponents of the "inquiry method," social scientists creating new National Science Foundation funded materials for classroom use, and the field-testing of unusual and provocative material.

Dr. Byron Massialas, a strong proponent of inquiry teaching, was my primary professor and supervisor at the University of Chicago, and later my Ph.D. advisor at the University of Michigan. He recognized my instructional skills early on and encouraged experimentation when I began teaching. We wrote a book together, *Creative Encounters in the Classroom* (Wiley, 1967), based on my field-testing of various ideas suggested by theorists and curriculum innovators.

Added to these influences and innovations was a sense of excitement and experimentation inspired by America's race to compete with and top the Soviet Union's achievement of Sputnik, the launch of the first space satellite during the Cold War epoch. Activity in American education was fermenting, accompanied and supported by generous funding, approval for alternative models of education, and a rethinking of the rationale for and philosophy of education, particularly within the sciences and social sciences.

The year I graduated with my Master's degree from the University of Chicago, the work of Jerome Bruner was becoming popular among educators and there was a great deal of new language in the field of education, with talk of "discovery learning," "inquiry method," "problem-solving," "critical thinking," "values education," "conflict resolution," "simulation gaming" and "role play." Education was awash in ideas, competing for attention at all levels and raising consciousness for many who sought new, active, and imaginative ways to stimulate students to engage with a wide range of subjects.

The leaders were largely in the sciences, but the social sciences were not far behind. Serendipitously, I landed on multiple projects, almost without seeking them out and found each incredibly stimulating. Within these '60's curriculum movements nestled the heirs to a pedagogic creed that encompassed Deweyan progressivism with significant updating by noted psychologists such as Jerome Bruner and L. S. Vygotsky.

There were, of course, many other scholars, thinkers, and researchers who contributed ideas and strategies, but for me their ideas were embedded in the wave of curriculum innovation that I took part in as a graduate student and beginning teacher. These included the Anthropology Curriculum Study Project, Sociological Resources for Secondary Schools, and, later, The Human Sciences, an interdisciplinary social/biological science fusion program.

I started out with the Anthropology Project as a field-test teacher in Chicago and found myself awash in rich and varied resources the likes of which I had never experienced. This included a set of stone tools, reproductions of prehistoric skulls, and lessons on the beginnings of language and writing, the agricultural revolution, and more. Part of the enjoyment of this program were trips to various destinations for intensive training and discussion by those social scientists who were deeply interested in changing instructional practice and who paid attention to the details of teaching, our teaching. As a young teacher I found this personalized attention incredibly helpful in building confidence and bolstering subject matter knowledge.

At the time, I was teaching anthropology as part of a world history course at Bowen High School on the south side of Chicago, and I used the aforementioned approach/materials to engage my students, much like a hands-on approach in science classrooms with labs. I was suddenly one of the most popular teachers in the high school: even the "cutters" would arrive on time waiting to get into my classroom. Every time a box arrived, there was a thrill of anticipation about what sort of "weird" material I would pull out to share with students. As well as the aforementioned stone tools and skulls, this included pottery fragments, ancient codes, weird objects, films about chimpanzees in the wild, and cave paintings.

There was never a dull moment, and my experience with the NSF project solidified and focused my lifelong commitment to the importance of play and discovery as keys to capturing and directing student interest.

I also helped design and test curricula for The Sociological Resources for the Social Studies project at the University of Michigan, and was later an NSF project director with The Human Sciences Project (melding history, social science, and biology) in a school in a "disadvantaged" area of Queens. Participation in these alternative curricula waves shaped my views and philosophy of instruction and bolstered my skills of curriculum writing and design using creative problem-solving and discovery strategies.

Already a convert to what is often in graduate school called the "inquiry method," my involvement with school improvement and curriculum invention solidified and strengthened my commitment to a pedagogic creed of creativity and imagination (Zevin, 2013). At the University of Michigan I also met another inquiry teacher and member of the National Council for the Social Studies who became my wife. All in all, the evolution of my pedagogic creed had many productive side effects, resulting in a life centered on the art and science of teaching, teaching about teaching, and research on teaching.

Throughout my career, from beginning teacher in Chicago through graduate student at the University of Michigan and on to Professor of Education at Queens

College, I have maintained a deep interest in and commitment to Dewey's and Bruner's approach to pedagogy based on a concept of experience that promotes interest, raises provocative questions, and is open to experimentation.

I've added what I hope is my own sense of playfulness and whimsy to the proceedings.

## Influences on my Pedagogic Creed: Dewey, Bruner, and Beyond

I approach the delineation of My Pedagogic Creed with a deep sense of humility before the renowned thinkers who influenced my development and growth as an educator. At the time I became interested in teaching and absorbed many ideas, techniques, and philosophies there was not even an inkling what my future held: to become a professor who not only practiced inquiry but also contributed to the literature.

My view of teaching has been shaped by early encounters with the work of John Dewey, and, a bit later, Jerome Bruner, who was also influenced by Dewey's work. Several works, especially *How We Think* by Dewey (1997), and *The Process of Education* (1962) and *Toward a Theory of Instruction* (1967) by Bruner, deeply altered my views of both theory and practice in education and shaped my own approach to a theory of instruction.

A central idea vis-à-vis inquiry, a key idea, was that the teacher was a partner, a guide, a democratic leader, but not a walking encyclopedia, authority, or petty autocrat. In practice this meant that teachers acted as stimulators and challengers rather than authorities providing all the answers and "truths." Data, information, knowledge is viewed as subject to questioning and criticism, not simple acceptance. As Dewey (1916) put it roughly a century ago in *Democracy and Education*:

> The teacher is not in the school to impose certain ideas or to form certain habits in the child, but is there as a member of the community to select the influences which shall affect the child and to assist him in properly responding to these. Thus the teacher becomes a partner in the learning process, guiding students to independently discover meaning within the subject area. This philosophy has become an increasingly popular idea within present-day teacher preparatory programs.
>
> *p. 32*

The idea of "independent discovery" and the "teacher as a partner" seemed eminently adaptable to my instructional setting and student audience because they certainly were not interested in me lecturing to them or, as they put it to me, "at them." Tellingly, they certainly had no experience of ever being treated as "independent" learners.

The students' major problems were a lack of engagement with teachers or materials, and (in my opinion) a deep-seated lack of confidence in their abilities. My treatment of them as partners, as inquirers whose interpretations mattered, and as creatures with whom I was willing to play and work, and (above all) make work seem like play, resulted in learning becoming a voyage of discovery.

The point is that teachers should be discussion starters, idea rousers, devil's advocates, but NOT propagandists, witting or unwitting, and certainly not purveyors of pre-packaged goods.

## My Pedagogic Creed: Central Values and Judgments about Pedagogy

My pedagogic creed, my principles of teaching and learning, are based on a view of experience as a vital component to learning. Direct experience is to be valued over virtual reality or third-hand narratives where at all possible.

After years of practice and research it is my judgment that the best experiences are those that stir interest, draw us into mysteries, and attract our detective skills. In a classroom that is theater, everyone can play with each other to solve problems. Everyone can switch sides and play teacher or student, or both. *Within this instructional dyad, all participants should feel free to express, explain, and expand on ideas and interpretations however odd, unpopular or upsetting.*

Feelings and judgments ought to be as much a part of the process as content. Strangely, emotion is very often missing from teaching and learning (lessons, units, and courses) even in such a potentially emotional subject as history and civics. From an "advanced" inquiry viewpoint, there is a range of attitudes, feelings, and knowledge from simple data to sophisticated judgments that characterize the inquiry classroom.

Growth, the cornerstone of education, certainly depends on engagement. As Dewey (1916) noted:

> There is no paradox in the fact that the principle of continuity of experience may operate so as to leave a person arrested on a low plane of development in a way that limits later capacity for growth. On the other hand, if an experience arouses curiosity, strengthens initiative, and sets up desires and purposes that are sufficiently intense to carry a person over dead places in the future, continuity works in a very different way. Every experience is a moving force.
>
> *pp. 37–38*

From the theory comes the practice, and from the practice comes a refinement of theory. After many years of working with the guiding progressive principles of Dewey (and others) and the provocative educational psychology of Bruner (and others) I have evolved, field-tested, and refined a "creed." I think the guiding principles still hold up well, even in the face of an onslaught of 21st-century teacher evaluation schemes and student assessments, generated by so-called "reformers," most of whom I suspect have never taught, let alone studied the fields of teaching and learning.

So, I hereby offer a summary of my principles, the values and judgments that have sustained my view of teaching and learning.

## Motivation and Knowledge

*Above all, I value curiosity and initiative as the soul of personal and public educational advancement*, forming the basis for creative classrooms now, and in the future. *I value drawing out feelings, emotions and attitudes as the heart of motivation and decision-making in a democratic environment.*

I value conversation, thinking out loud that is legitimated by whoever is playing the teacher role, where students come to understand that they are seeking to discover answers by using their minds and skills in understanding and making sense of evidence.

I value evidence, content, data, as open to discussion, argument, analysis, and alteration. May the best interpretations and arguments win out! May interesting creative ideas be expressed freely, and without following a scripted lesson "to get to the 'right' answer(s)." May judgments be offered and challenged.

In my view, knowledge is not there to be memorized but to challenge; as food for thought; and all questions and the responses to such should be open and negotiable. In fact, in this pedagogy, the fun is in the debate and negotiation of answers, not in the answers themselves, a very different view of classroom goals and life than is commonly found in schools. Furthermore, "we" like our content raw, from the original sources, and not spoon-fed to us like infants.

## Growth and Query

In my judgment, growing beings (and we can grow until our very last moment) need to exercise their own skills and thought processes, learning how to observe, apply, understand, define, and reason on the way to their own discoveries and conclusions.

I value questions as perhaps the most vital tool in our pedagogical arsenal, for they are the avenue to opening up problems, sparking a really good intellectual brawl with lots of muscular give and take of ideas and arguments, generating more questions and, yes, coming to an answer, tentative as those ideas may be and with the understanding that they are certainly open to more and deeper exploration.

In my judgment, teachers should provide weird, odd, funny, and mysterious challenging data that rivets student attention. *They should value imagination, creativity, insight, and intuition as the top of the taxonomy, not rote-learning and memorized lists.*

## Thinking about Thinking

Thinking about experience while learning *how* to think about thinking is a key component of my pedagogical creed.

I believe we should work to build citizens who can make judgments based on their own interpretations of the information presented, resulting in thoughtful decisions and debates on both the content itself and the issues inherent in private and public controversies.

Along with Dewey, I value citizens willing to question and take on the challenges of an imperfect democracy, not citizens who mouth the platitudes and scrubbed patriotism fed to them by public authority or private interests. In sum, thinking citizens are essential to a democratic system, and inquiry is essential to digging and searching for some semblance of truth.

## Classroom as Theater

In my judgment, teaching is a form of theater. Teachers and students play roles, and the way these are played, especially the plot, characterization, and dialogue, make a great deal of difference in the atmosphere created. If the teacher views herself as an actress/actor with a sense of drama, then the result will be a much livelier classroom than one in which the teacher views herself as a delivery agent of prepackaged goods.

Interpretation is the heart and soul of experience. Students need to grasp the classroom as a drama to which they can contribute; in which they are part of the action—and the best dramas from a pedagogic point of view are rich in emotion and ideas.

Invention and improvisation in the classroom are what builds participation and a sense of direct experience and excitement in learning.

In my judgment, many teachers are actually directors of a theater of the absurd in which students are more or less memorizing set scripts for history, math, science, language, that require little or no personal input and very little freewheeling interpretation. An ideal classroom is one more like street theater, where the audience and the actors are mutually interchangeable. The dramatic process is far more important than the ending.

## The Value of Uncertainty and Confusion

In my judgment, and thus a key component of my pedagogical creed, promoting uncertainty is a pedagogical must. Yes, that's right, UNCERTAINTY. To my way of thinking, uncertainty is one of the most powerful forces at the disposal of teachers to bring about great lessons and contribute to great units and courses. Inquiry grows out of problems, and problems, *real ones*, engage (students) because there are missing pieces that need discovery, or unexplained causes to parse, or internal contradictions and inconsistencies that are noticeable and must be dealt with and explored.

I value problems that offer unknowns and cry out for solutions. I value multiple interpretations of people's positions and actions, places, and events because perspectives demand comparison and contrast in order to work out a reasonable (tentative) conclusion.

I value social and philosophical issues that may be disturbing or even nearly irreconcilable, even confusing and difficult to debate, precisely because they invite reflective argument.

## The Raw and the Cooked (Content as Food for Thought)

In my judgment, raw data is lovely precisely because it is undigested and requires care in preparation. We might not even know what we have in our grasp. It may be inedible or undecipherable. It may be sweet and juicy or ambiguous. The point is that learners, observers, gourmands must come to terms with the raw before ingesting, much less digesting, its contents.

Cooked food is already done, a take-out, prepared by an invisible force or person we may not even know. We don't even necessarily know what the basic ingredients were, or how these were put together. It might be very tasty indeed but we, the consumers, did nothing to assist in its preparation.

I value learning that results from effort. Naturally, based on experiential learning, "raw" data is much preferred to "over-cooked." Deep observation and examination of data (for example, historical sources) provides learners and teachers with the opportunity to dig into the details, allowing us, the participants, to construct meaning and significance, not to mention attach emotions to our findings.

## Discovery of Discovery: The Power of Play, Imagination, and Intuition

I value the power of creative play as a key element of pedagogy. Creative play forms a basis for experimentation and discovery that can be pleasurable.

I value creative play as natural. Teachers who know how to turn work into play and play into work shape and construct learning environments that are rich in stimuli, varied in activities, and attractive for discoveries. Creative play helps learners to engage with evidence, think about observations, solve mysteries, and work out problems for intrinsic reasons: for the fun of it.

## A Summary of the Creed

My pedagogic creed may be summarized with a series of concepts that express the values of inquiry and discovery, problem solving and creativity. In an age of geometrically increasing data, widespread availability of lessons, both terrific and terrible, and, often, distracted students, each of these is a lot easier to list than to realize as part of direct experience.

1. Orientation: participatory democracy
2. Approach: curious
3. Attitude: skeptical
4. Content: scrutiny
5. Skills: query, query, query
6. Process: discovery
7. Projection: playful
8. Role: guide/provocateur
9. Presentation: balanced
10. Strategy: mysteriousness

I think Dewey would say that, above all, collect evidence and think for yourself, while Bruner would agree by adding that you should have fun playing, discovering, and testing ideas built on experience.

To my distinguished forebears, I would add that a spark of interest, a dollop of emotion, a sense of judgment, and critical- mindedness might be added as standards for everyday success in the classroom.

## References

Bruner, J.S. (1962). *The Process of Education.* Cambridge: MA: Harvard University Press.

Bruner, J.S. (1967). *Toward a Theory of Instruction.* Cambridge, MA: Harvard University Press.

Dewey, J. (1916). *Democracy and Education.* New York, NY: Macmillan.

Dewey, J. (1997). *How We Think.* New York: Dover Publications.

Massialas, B.G., and Zevin, J. (1967). *Creative Encounters in the Classroom.* New York, NY: John Wiley & Sons.

Vygotsky, L.S. (1962). *Thought and Language.* Cambridge, MA: MIT Press.

Zevin, J. (2013). *Creative Teaching for All: In the Box, Out of the Box, and Off the Walls.* Latham, MD: Rowman and Littlefield.

# 7

# TEACHING ABOUT SOCIAL ISSUES AND CONCERNS NEED NOT BE AN "ALL OR NONE" CIRCUMSTANCE

## O.L. Davis, Jr.

PROFESSOR EMERITUS, CURRICULUM AND INSTRUCTION,
UNIVERSITY OF TEXAS AT AUSTIN

A military convoy of young American soldiers stopped in my hometown to have lunch before continuing to an embarkation port. The time was mid World War II. I was 15 years old. Lometa, Texas, in those days was, as it continues to be 70 years later, a one blinking-red-stop-light cluster of buildings that straddled US 183 some 90 miles from Austin.

My father and I sat in the town's single café that day. It had a capacity of maybe 45 patrons, but business that day was slow and only a few of us locals were seated. Soon, the first soldiers from the convoy entered and took places at empty tables.

Immediately, the café owner faced a problem.

Two of the soldiers were Black. Lometa had no Black residents and the owner likely had never served a meal to Black persons. Very quickly and quietly, the owner told the two Black soldiers that he would not serve them in the regular eating area with the white soldiers and the regular customers. They were welcome to eat in the kitchen, however. These two Black GIs knew very well the too-familiar story. But they were hungry and had several hundred miles to ride to their destination. They arose and headed toward the kitchen.

These Black soldiers had taken only a couple of steps when my father, not uttering a word to anyone, stood up, picked up his plate and glass and walked with the soldiers into the kitchen. As he did so, he asked if he might eat with them, and they nodded "yes."

Dad later told me that they had an interesting, pleasant conversation. They were farm boys from the South, just as he once had been. Their meal completed, Dad paid for all three meals and the two soldiers thanked him. Soon afterward, all the soldiers boarded their trucks and the convoy departed.

Several local men, all of them white, stared in near shock throughout this unfolding scene. Their town's Superintendent of Schools had not only eaten with Black men, he had deliberately joined them in their forced isolation in the kitchen. One of the men said to my dad, "Prof, you didn't need to eat with those Nigras."

I'll never forget my dad's soft, firm reply: "Friends, those men are Americans just like you and I are. We are staying home, but they probably are headed to combat in North Africa. Within weeks, they will be fighting German soldiers and they may be wounded or killed. Those American men are first class in every way. They should not have to eat by themselves. We should live together."

This dramatic incident highlights the influence of my father on many of my ideas and sentiments about human beings, social issues, and particularly about justice and peace. That he was a New Dealer until Franklin Roosevelt ran for a third term did not mean that he was a flaming liberal. Nor did it mean that he was a stiff-necked conservative when he voted for Dwight Eisenhower and other Republicans afterward. From time to time, I thought that he was consistently inconsistent, but I eventually decided that he, too, was continuing to seek clarity and to un-learn sentiments that he had developed as a boy. These processes had been underway since he was a young adult and continued as long as he lived. And I learned from him, but not only from him.

## Ups and Downs and Forwards and Backwards

I grew to adulthood in a deeply segregated society. No Blacks lived in our rural area; in fact, not one Black person lived in the entire county. Additionally, only a few families of Mexican descent lived in or near Lometa and the male adults worked mainly for Anglo ranchers, stereotypically as "cedar choppers," who felled cedar trees and trimmed their trunks and some limbs into fence posts. Three German-American families ranched near the Colorado River, but they still carried the burdensome reputation of "draft dodgers" from the World War I era. All the churches, except for a single Catholic chapel with an itinerant priest, were protestant Christian denominations. When local preachers spoke of the "brotherhood of man," they were essentially referring to white people and, in certain instances, possibly to some non-white people who lived in foreign lands (e.g., China, African colonies, South American countries) to whom their church or denomination sent missionaries

When I left home to attend North Texas State Teachers College in Denton, Texas, I began to realize that the racially and culturally segregated society in which I had lived continued in my legally segregated college and in the social structures in the surrounding towns and cities. The absence of Blacks, Hispanics, and other "minorities" in my experience had left me a "racist," even though I wasn't even aware of the term at the time. I realized, however, that I needed to change in order that I could understand more fully what it meant to live in a diverse and conflicted society.

Some of the courses that I took in college helped me undertake that journey. Some, but very few. More important than courses was the influence of a few professors, notably economist Rosser B. Melton. Interactions with classmates helped me also. A few touted their ugly, racist attitudes whereas most appeared to be similar to me, an older teenager trying to reconcile the incongruities of civic declarations and private and public behavior.

I remember supporting Henry A. Wallace, the Progressive candidate for U.S. President in 1948. With two other students, I picketed and heckled Dixiecrat J. Strom Thurmond's presidential campaign speech in Denton. I confess that I was happy, however, that Harry "Give 'em Hell" Truman won the election. I presume that Office of Naval Intelligence investigators found my young adult behavior sufficiently non-threatening to U.S. security to grant me a Top Secret clearance, a designation that I held for more than 35 years of active and reserve naval service.

Without setting down in writing my developing notions about racial diversity, abolition of the poll tax, welcome of Blacks and Hispanics by my church, school desegregation, and similar matters, it is notable that I became known as my family's "radical," the one who frequently was out of step with the others. What I had learned, much of it over time, certainly influenced me, including, for example, all about "the powers that be" (Wink, 1992): those institutions, structures, and systems that exert such immense control over the lives of persons in our society. As well, I came to understand, certainly too slowly, the powerful privilege enjoyed by white persons in our society, particularly white males.

My transition away from my racist past seemed always to take sharp and largely unexpected turns, never to follow a straight line. During those years and since, I realized that I was, and still am, now at age 85, a recovering racist.

Upon my release from active military duty, my three member family moved to Nashville, Tennessee, and I entered the doctoral program at George Peabody College for Teachers. Not at all coincidentally, I accepted the position of eighth grade homeroom teacher in the Peabody Demonstration School. My good fortune was to follow Gordon Vars in that post.

Gordon was an outstanding core curriculum teacher. He was comfortable in teaching about personal pre-adolescent concerns as well as social and economic problems within the United States. He organized his instruction very carefully, but he offered considerable flexibility to his students to follow their "gleam" in personal and group projects within the scope of the larger study. In his preparation to teach a class session/course, he read widely, was well informed, and, consequently, was a fount of information for his students for whom he could, and did, suggest additional sources of information. It was obvious that he continued to learn additional "content" as he taught and as his students engaged the questions that framed their individual and small group inquiries. I quickly decided that Gordon was a master teacher. When I took his place the following fall, I did not *adopt* his ideas or plans or topics. I did *adapt* a number of his ideas and procedures with which I was comfortable and used them for a number of years. I admit, however, that I did not adapt his emphasis on personal adolescent concerns. My

"Davis-type core" experience, however, enabled me to move deliberately and with increased confidence into additional and deeper studies of social issues with my students.

During my years at the Dem School, my students and I developed several memorable units. One focused on proposals to merge the city of Nashville with the surrounding Davidson County. Perhaps the students' and my favorite unit developed out of the class' intense interest in learning about the Soviet Union and Communism.

As with all our major units, I invited parents of my eighth graders to meet with me several weeks before our class was scheduled to begin its study of the USSR. Not one parent objected to the study itself nor any of the reading materials that I had gathered, some issued by the USSR and the Communist Party of the U.S.

Most parents asked to be kept informed about the study and the students and I did just that. The school principal, although he did not rule that our study could not proceed, urged caution, but several of my Peabody College professors surprisingly suggested that this topic might be too controversial for the times and, therefore, could have unfortunate consequences. Our class undertook the study. Years later, those eighth graders still remembered this study as one of the most informative and motivating of anything that they had studied in school.

Subsequent to my Ph.D. program, a number of my colleagues stimulated my continued progress in opening up previously closed areas of curriculum development and teaching, especially social concerns and issues. I recognize the prominence of senior colleagues Harold D. Drummond, my major professor, William Van Til, Harold Benjamin, Jack Allen, Henry H. Hill, Alexander Frazier, Rodney Tillman, William M. Alexander, Alice Miel, and L. Thomas Hopkins. Several of my contemporaries, particularly David Turney, Kaoru Yamamoto, Norman Bowers, Jim Macdonald, Jack Frymier, Louise Berman, Gordon Cawelti, and my English cousins, Bill Reid and Maurice Holt, seemed routinely to contribute fresh ideas, mindful criticism, and provocative questions. The generation of scholars that followed us, including Walter Parker, Bill Ayers, Margaret Crocco, Bill Schubert, William Wraga, Jim Banks, Bill Watkins, Nathalie Gehrke, and Samuel Totten added immensely to the expansion of my views. Whereas quite a number of my 165 doctoral advisees merit mention, I will hazard to identify only a few whose special contributions to my increasing sensitivity to social concerns and teaching about social justice and peace were substantial. They include Francis P. Hunkins, Drew C. Tinsley, George L. Mehaffey, Marcella L. Kysilka, Virginia Rogers Atwood, Christine Bennett, Geneva Gay, Cathy Dueck (Skau), Gerald A. Ponder, Sherry Field, Gary J. De Leeuw, Lynn M. Burlbaw, Ronald W. Wilhelm, Stuart J. Foster, Mark J. Reid, Karen Riley, Elizabeth Yeager Washington, Chara H. Bohan, and Mindy Spearman. I am particularly pleased to recognize Matthew D. Davis, my son and colleague, for his successful insistence that I attend to critical race theory as well as a host of other theoretical constructs that have contributed impressively to the development of my ideas.

## Toward the Enunciation of My Basic Pedagogic Beliefs

Because I am not a creedal person, in religious faith and practice or in other aspects of my life, I ordinarily have exempted myself from contributing to a creed related to teaching. John Dewey found that his "Pedagogic Creed" (1897) enabled him to focus major ideas and sentiments about teaching and learning and his Creed surely must have positively impacted hundreds of thousands of American teachers. On this occasion, however, I struck a bargain with myself. I will identify several very important beliefs in the form that I now express them, ones that have guided and altered both my practice and theorizing about curriculum and teaching, especially that which has to do with teaching with a focus on social issues. These beliefs, to be sure, constitute a work in progress, to be modified by addition and subtraction, mainly, as I continue to seek, by conversation and deliberation, increased clarity and perspective.

1. **Persons are important.** When I prepared to teach, the socially appropriate word in our discussion and planning was "individuals," as in "Individuals are unique." A few years later, primarily through a column in *Educational Leadership* named "The Importance of People," the word's fresh usage and the plural meaning hooked me. "People" appeared to emphasize the nature of democratic citizenship in those early post-World War II years, and highlighted the possible contributions of teachers to resolve common teaching concerns by working cooperatively with their colleagues in small discussion groups. In recent years, through the influence of John Macmurray, the prominent 20th century Scottish philosopher, I have begun to use "persons" rather than "people" in my thinking. I believe that Macmurray (1961) is correct in noting that the term "persons" is especially powerful in educational discourse. It seems more robust than "people," is more inclusive of the range of human capacities, and more decisively emphasizes the fullness of human potentiality. Furthermore, it offers a freshened currency to meanings of democracy as it is most dynamically conceptualized and practiced.

2. **Persons in society are important.** The understanding that persons ordinarily do not exist alone seems to be an essential meaning. Not only are persons born into a society (e.g., a family of families and of friends), they typically join with others in different social groups throughout their lives (e.g., clubs, sporting groups, military units, recreational dancing, coffee-and-conversations, political parties, religious groups). To be sure, persons must learn how to "be a member" of these variously purposed groups with varying qualifications for initial and continuing membership, as well as to learn to shift the appropriateness of personal behaviors when holding memberships in different "societies" at the same time. School curricula, particularly in the social studies, commonly focus attention on governing bodies, executives, administrative units, and groups that socially distribute economic

and social benefits. This attention is proper, but remains seriously insufficient. What is also absolutely necessary is to focus attention on the nature and constitution of "the powers that be" and their effects on persons in society.

3. **Persons in relation in communities are especially important.** Fundamental to understanding this idea is that "communities" are *not* "societies," although common usage too frequently conflates the terms (Fielding, 2012). Communities sometimes are described as having special geographic and sociological characteristics. In specialty study, such usages make sense. On the other hand, Macmurray has characterized a "community" as typically much smaller than a society, a group composed of members who intend both to enhance the work and yields of another and/or others in expression of common commitments and intense personal relationships sometimes approaching the notion of "love." Communities are not leaderless, but their leadership commonly is less hierarchical than that of societies. The experience of "communities" in school settings at this point in time is unsettled, although, admittedly, some "teams" in sports and groupings related to performances in music, science projects, and social action initiatives (e.g., service learning) may come close to the mark.

4. **The study of issues and concerns of social justice has a justifiable place in the program of social studies education in schools.** "Study" is the operative term. It clearly is *not* "Friday Current Events." It also is *not* "solving" a pressing social problem in the city or town (e.g., need for increased water in a metro area or use of tax abatements to recruit a high tech industry). On occasion, but irregularly, it might be undertaken as a part of a larger effort to educate the adult citizenry about a serious public issue (e.g., homelessness). This study focus, if anything, must be rigorous in terms of time, effort, and commitment. It certainly is *not* tasking students to confront and propose solutions to a civic or international concern that adults have so far been unable to unravel.

   In most situations, students are ineligible by law from such decision making; to lead them to believe that their conclusions based on their research will even be considered by appropriate authorities is a "fool's errand," a kind of "dressed up masquerade" with no place to go. Studying social problems or issues is *not* solving these problems or concerns. To be sure, students' studies on occasion can and frequently should result in *action* beyond the classroom. Such actions, indeed, may contribute to measures to alleviate problems in other places, e.g., construction of water wells in a drought-plagued region such that residents can have fresh, uncontaminated water.

5. **The responsible study of social issues must draw on students'** prior **knowledge as well as insist that they search for knowledge particular to their current study.** Study of social issues must *not* be seen as a substitute for attention to substantive and procedural knowledge in history and other social science offerings. To be negotiated is the time, intensity, comprehensiveness, and estimated value of *both* foci.

6.  **Teaching about social issues and concerns requires** more **rather than fewer instructional materials and resources.** Thus, the development of an expanding collection of books, pamphlets, posters, and other references likely will be time consuming and possibly more expensive than the routine assembly of resources for teaching regular history or social science courses.

7.  **Experience indicates that teachers who focus attention on social issues and concerns commonly need some extra background in history and other social science course work as well as additional attention to pedagogy and curriculum as continuing preparation for teaching.** These teachers need to keep abreast of contemporary, vexing, and sharply argued proposals and counter-claims about a variety of social issues in a range of political contexts. Such personal involvement requires—or, at least, strongly suggests—that conspicuous attention be focused on an expanding panoply of theoretical and substantive methodologies. Critical race theory, for example, is vital to uncovering understanding about the treatment of minority and immigrant groups, as are multiple examples of local and state opposition to federal laws (e.g., school desegregation) throughout the course of American history.

    I must confess to my early failure to know satisfactorily the work of some prominent scholar-practitioners such as Maurice Hunt and Lawrence Metcalf and their lucid and practical theorizing and teaching suggestions. When I discovered their work, however, it added insight to my planning and confidence in my teaching. Although the work of Donald Oliver, James Shaver, Shirley Engle, Anna Ochoa, and others came to my attention too late to use in my teaching in schools, I found their practical scholarship important contributions to my efforts in teacher education and curriculum development.

8.  **Teaching about social issues and concerns need** not **be the province of one teacher or a group of "Lone Ranger" teachers.** Many individual and independent instructional schemes fail to acknowledge the reality that widened participatory involvement of teachers in a department and even an entire small school tends to develop increased understanding and support of varying teaching plans and idiosyncratic procedures. Nevertheless, the social and bureaucratic reality in most schools, particularly in this era of common core requirements and high stakes testing, appears to severely restrict individual teacher decision-making about choice of studies and of procedures (i.e. content and activities). Recent "push-backs," however, should increase the opportunities for individual and/or collaborative teaching that may differ strikingly from the majority of instruction at various levels and in specific courses. But, then again, it may not. The need for a "community" of teachers, along the lines of Macmurray's suggestions, seems to be a potentially important development. Such a community could encourage or support individual teacher actions that are discrepant from those of most other teachers in the group/community. Prospects for teaching about social issues and concerns, in such a situation, need not be an "all or none" circumstance.

## Continuing to Learn to Teach

Critically important to the aforementioned views of teaching is the keen awareness that education focuses on the development of human beings, of persons (Macmurray, 1964). This truth is evident in the consideration of the roles of both pupils and teachers. I invite teachers and other educators *to consider* my beliefs, to discuss them seriously, and then *to adapt*, not *adopt*, only those that seem seriously attractive to the prospects of improved teaching about social issues in their particular settings.

## References

Dewey, John. (1897). "My Pedagogic Creed." 54 *School Journal*, pp. 77–80.
Fielding, Michael. (2012). "Education as if People Matter: John Macmurray, Community, and the Struggle for Democracy." 38(6) *Oxford Review of Education*, pp. 675–692.
Macmurray, John. (1961). *Persons in Relation*. London, UK: Faber.
Macmurray, John. (1964). "Teachers and Pupils," 39(1) *The Educational Forum*, pp. 17–24.
Wink, Walter. (1992). *Engaging the Powers: Discernment and Resistance in a World of Domination*. Minneapolis, MN: Fortress Press.

# PART II
# Underpinning Democratic Society

# 8

# THE CHALLENGE OF TEACHING ABOUT AND FOR DEMOCRACY WHEN DEMOCRACY IS SO TROUBLED

*DIANA E. HESS*

PROFESSOR, DEPARTMENT OF CURRICULUM AND INSTRUCTION,
UNIVERSITY OF WISCONSIN, MADISON

Like all students, I learned a lot about teaching from my "apprenticeship of observation." Dan Lortie defined this concept in his 1975 book *Schoolteacher: A Sociological Study*:

> Teaching is unusual in that those who decide to enter it have had exceptional opportunity to observe members of the occupation at work; unlike most occupations today, the activities of teachers are not shielded from youngsters. Teachers-to-be underestimate the difficulties involved, but this supports the contention that those planning to teach form definite ideas about the nature of the role.
>
> *p. 65*

Like a much smaller number of teachers, I was also the child and grandchild of teachers. My mother taught English and American Government and sponsored the student newspaper at Sycamore High School, a small town 70 miles west of Chicago, and my father taught communications at Northern Illinois University in DeKalb, a larger town close to Sycamore. Consequently, I learned about teaching not only from being a student, but also from listening to my parents talk about their work lives.

I became a public school teacher in 1979 in a well-funded and large high school (with a student body of more than 4,000). My social studies colleagues were an intellectually lively group who paid significant attention to educational theory and research. I later learned this was not typical. Even though I taught a variety of classes, including government, constitutional law, U.S. history, and global geography, I recognize now that in all those classes I was in fact a civics teacher because the entire focus of the social studies scope, sequence, and curriculum at this high school was on preparing students to participate in democratic life; in part through classroom discussion of issues of various kinds. I know now how unusual this was, and I am exceedingly thankful that, by some miracle, I launched my teaching career surrounded by experienced and committed mentors who knew how to help young people develop the knowledge, skills, and dispositions needed to engage in discussions of society's most important and contentious issues.

I was also quite involved in the teacher union—becoming president in my last two years of teaching there. To this day, I don't think anything has had as much impact on my thinking about the work of schools and teachers as that role. In particular, it was in this role that I began to grasp how incredibly important the overall ethos of a school was to the ability of teachers and students to do their best work, and how policies and practices of school administrators would either enhance or diminish the amount of "academic press" that existed in a school and the very conceptions of what school was for in the first place. Moreover, it was in this role that I realized the positive relationship between the power of teachers to influence what constituted high quality curriculum and pedagogy and their willingness to innovate and grow. It was an exhilarating and fascinating time in my professional life, but it was also incredibly exhausting and oddly addictive. When my term ended, I knew that spending a year or so in a different role in education outside of the school might be a good idea—for me and for the incoming union president. Little did I know at the time that, while I would make democratic education my life's calling, I would not return to high school teaching.

I considered two positions for what I thought was going to be a one-year leave: one was becoming a lobbyist for the state teacher union, and another was joining a very small staff at a civic education organization that was running programs for young people and teachers in Chicago and across the nation as part of a federally funded program to promote "law-related education." The latter was, in essence, a form of civic education that focused explicitly on using highly interactive teaching methods to help young people learn about constitutional and legal issues. This organization, the Constitutional Rights Foundation Chicago (CRFC), still exists, and I am now on its Board. In 1987, when I left teaching to go to work for CRFC, the organization and other national organizations that were part of this law-related education movement slowly began expanding to become more full-service civic education shops, and also began working outside the United States.

While at CRFC, I developed programs for teachers and students, wrote curriculum and, most importantly, designed and led professional development programs in issues-based civics all over the country. Initially, I was assigned to work with teachers in two states, Arkansas and Mississippi. Even though I had done some work in the Chicago Public Schools, a district whose level of funding was far lower than the one in which I had taught, I was both shocked by how poorly funded schools were in Mississippi and Arkansas—and inspired by many of the teachers with whom I worked in these states, in part because the conditions in which they taught struck me as challenging and the needs of their students so immense. I remember thinking that many of the complaints that my high school teaching colleagues and I so often voiced were almost laughable in comparison. Looking back now, twenty-five years after I began working for CRFC, I realize how incredibly naïve and privileged I had been as a high school teacher and how my conceptions of the way schools should function and what teachers should do both in and out of the classroom were profoundly shaped by my early teaching experiences. I realize now that starting my teaching career in a school with a bevy of resources, well prepared teachers who were expected to work hard and were treated as professionals, and in a community in which there was virtually no poverty, so that most children came to school with their basic needs met—conditions in which all schools should operate—was simultaneously beneficial and problematic. It was beneficial because it profoundly shaped my understanding of why resources are critically important to providing a high-quality education and what could happen in a school with strong *career* teachers who were in the profession for enough time to develop craft knowledge. It was problematic because, as I would come to learn, teaching high-quality social studies was much easier in this school than it was for teachers in many other schools. In my school, there was no significant pressure to track the social studies curriculum; there was support from the administration to engage students in issues-rich curriculum and interactive pedagogy; and even though the community was politically conservative overall and the curriculum was, for its time, progressive and fairly edgy, I recall very few instances in which parents complained that their children were being indoctrinated into holding particular political beliefs (which I don't think they were).

In 1995, I left CRFC to study at the University of Washington in Seattle with Professor Walter Parker, considered then (and now) the nation's foremost expert in deliberation as a form of social studies instruction. Because of my experiences as a schoolteacher, I was interested in studying the practice of secondary social studies teachers who are unusually effective at engaging their students in discussions of issues—specifically, of political, legal, and constitutional issues. The first study I conducted did precisely that, using a "models of wisdom" approach that sought to investigate whether there were common conceptions and practices among such teachers, or whether their teaching was so idiosyncratic that the best we could do was see them as interesting, albeit unusual, examples of strong educators (Hess, 2002). I learned that the former was the more warrantable claim. While there were certainly many differences among the teachers, there were common elements in how they thought about what they were doing, which was teaching to improve democracy, and common ways in which they were doing it, most notably by creating a remarkably open classroom climate, teaching "with" and "for" discussion, and going to great lengths to ensure that their students had to grapple both with forming their own views on hot-button issues and engaging thoughtfully with views that were different from their own. Upon completion of my degree, I accepted a position at the University of Wisconsin-Madison, which felt like completing a circle of sorts because some of my strongest mentors had graduated from the very program that I would now teach in as an assistant professor.

My new colleagues at the UW-Madison provided a stimulating, intellectually diverse, and supportive environment for the teaching, research, and work with educators that I set to undertake. During my first year there, I had the distinct privilege of auditing an incredibly high-quality course that Fred Newmann taught on authentic assessment; it had a profound and lasting impact on how I think about the crucial role that assessment plays in both teaching and learning. Conversations with Alan Lockwood, Gloria Ladson-Billings, Michael Apple, Jim Gee, and Simone Schweber taught me about questions I had not even thought to ask and broadened my understanding of the relationship between the political environment in which schools are housed and the opportunities and challenges facing young people and their teachers at these institutions.

Madison turned out to be a very good place for me to continue learning. It provided a rich context in which to focus my research not just on what teachers do with respect to issues-teaching, but on how students experience and learn from this unusually demanding form of pedagogy. The first study I did in my new role as an assistant professor was an inquiry into a required high school course that had as its main learning outcome improving the ability of 10th graders to engage in discussing what I came to call "controversial political issues." In *Controversy in the Classroom: The Democratic Power of Discussion* (Hess, 2009) I defined these as questions of public policy that spark significant disagreement:

> These are authentic questions about the kinds of public policies that should be adopted to address public problems—they are not hypothetical. Such issues require deliberation among a "we" to determine which policy is the best response to a particular problem. These are the public's problems, and as such, they both deserve and require the public's input in some cases (such as what policy a school board or other legislature should adopt) and the public's actual decision in others (often voiced through a ballot initiative or other "direct democracy" process). Controversial political issues are open questions, meaning there are multiple and often strikingly different answers that are legitimate—even though people frequently have strongly held and well-reasoned options about which answer they prefer.
>
> *p. 38*

From this second study, I broadened and deepened my understanding of what constitutes high-quality issues teaching, in large part because one of the teachers whose practice I observed was an extraordinary educator in the last year of a three-decade teaching career. But I learned more from the students, including what it takes to incorporate civility and skill in their discussions of challenging issues; how race and social class profoundly influence classroom experiences; and how and why so many students find it both difficult and exhilarating to be in a course in which student talk (and not teacher talk) is the most valued element in the classroom. I became curious about what impact such a course has on students after they leave high school, This curiosity motivated me to mount a longitudinal study that was markedly more ambitious, challenging, and fruitful than that which I had done to date. Two research questions guided the work:

1.  How do high school students experience and learn from participating in social studies courses that emphasize the discussion of controversial international and/or domestic issues?
2.  Do such discussions influence students' political and civic participation after they leave high school? If so, what are the pathways to participation?

Data collection began in the spring of 2005 and was completed in the spring of 2009. The sample included 1,001 students in 35 classes in 21 schools in three states (Illinois, Indiana, and Wisconsin). I administered pre- and post-course questionnaires to participating students and their teachers. The bulk of other data came from observing classes and students at issues fora, interviewing teachers about their educational philosophies, and interviewing a large sub-sample of hundreds of students during the last two weeks of the courses I was studying. I contracted with the UW Survey Center to conduct two rounds of follow-up telephone interviews. The first was completed in 2007 with 402 participants; the second was completed in 2009 with 369 participants. During these interviews, respondents were asked, among other things, about their political and civic engagement and memories from the class.

In analyzing this data, it became clear that teachers face ethical issues when they choose to incorporate controversy in the curriculum, and that teachers are making a variety of decisions about these pedagogical issues. When Paula McAvoy, a former high school teacher and educational philosopher, joined the study team, she shaped my belief that addressing ethics would be important if we wanted to produce findings that would be valuable to practitioners. To that end, we used the data to identify questions that emerged across multiple contexts, and then used a small grant from the Spencer Foundation's philosophy initiative to invite philosophers, political scientists, and researchers in education to discuss empirically-driven case studies around these questions. Each "cross-disciplinary deliberation" addressed one of the following questions:

1)  Should teachers disclose their views about the political issues they discuss in class?
2)  How should teachers address sensitive political issues, such as same-sex marriage and affirmative action, which are potentially more personally difficult for some students than others? And what should count as a legitimate political controversy?
3)  What should be the aims of discussions of politically controversial issues?[1]

Given the scope and scale of the longitudinal study, it is perhaps not surprising that it profoundly influenced my thinking about how to teach and about what students learn from discussion of controversial political issues. Moreover, throughout all three studies, I had numerous opportunities to share findings with undergraduate and graduate students, practicing teachers, and staff from civic education organizations, and their reactions kept me grounded and pushed my understanding and beliefs in numerous ways. While I continue to have enormous enthusiasm for the role of discussions of controversial political issues in school-based democratic education programs, and incredible respect for the many teachers who are engaging their students in such discussions, I have been sobered by the reality that such teaching is still too rare, exceedingly difficult (although clearly not impossible), not bolstered or supported by many of the dominant trends in education, and challenged by a political climate outside of school that is antithetical and even hostile to some of the most basic tenets of a well-functioning democracy. Thus, I describe the following elements of my pedagogical creed as it relates to the teaching and learning of controversial political issues in a particular time—now—when I fear that this kind of teaching is most likely more difficult to pull off than it may have been at any time in my 30-plus years as an educator.

## Elements of my Pedagogic Creed: What Matters Most?

Both the length of time for which I have focused on the role of controversial political issues in democratic education and the various roles I have played have helped me develop a number of beliefs that form the basis of my pedagogic creed. Here I seek to explain the most significant beliefs—with "significance" defined as what matters most if the goal is providing support for an approach to democratic education that I continue to believe has value in a time when its value is under assault and its implementation is at risk. I will delineate these beliefs by answering three questions, drawing liberally on what I have written in the past. The questions are: Why should young people learn how to discuss controversial political issues? Why should at least a major portion of this learning take place in schools? And what threats does this form of education currently face?

### *Why should Young People Learn how to Discuss Controversial Political Issues? Rationales*

While I support the inclusion of controversial political issues discussions in schools for multiple reasons, none is more important than the reality that an intrinsic connection exists between a healthy and well-functioning democracy and the ability of people to engage with one another productively in deliberations about what "we" should do in response to important public problems. Discussion is a proxy for democracy itself. Put another way, a democracy cannot function without discussion. Why? As I argued in *Controversy in the Classroom*:

> Discussions in democratic societies, especially if characterized by inclusion and widespread participation, are markers of what Robert Dahl (1998) calls "intrinsic equality"—the foundational assumption that the good of every human being is intrinsically equal to that of any other (p. 65). The ideal of discussion supports the validity of intrinsic equality by implying, at least symbolically, that all members of a community are political equals and are therefore equally qualified to participate in discussion and decision making. The listening and talking that constitute discussion physically represent a core goal of democracy: self-governance among equals (Gastile & Levine, 2005).
>
> *Hess, 2009*

Moreover, there are salutary effects of such discussions on the knowledge, beliefs about others, and skills that accrue to those who participate in them. Evidence suggests that such discussions, especially if they occur among people with disparate views, can enhance political tolerance and build knowledge about important public problems and various proposals about what could or should be done to mitigate their most damaging effects. Most importantly, discussions of controversial political issues can lead to qualitatively *better* decisions than those that would be made in their absence.

Notwithstanding this, both theoretical and empirical arguments that support the crucial role that public discussion of controversial political issues plays in a democracy say that participating in such discussions is not an innate skill or disposition. The ability to do so effectively in almost all cases needs to be learned. Moreover, one of the deficits in contemporary democracy in the United States (and many other nations, I would argue) is that relatively few people have either the skill or the desire to engage in such discussions. Even though I am typically circumspect about the ability of schools to "transform" society, and think all of us should be cautious about what expectations we lay on schools, there are good reasons why schools should be the *primary* place in which we attempt to teach the young how to do something better than that which their elders currently demonstrate.

## Why should Schools Teach how to Engage in Discussions of Controversial Political Issues?

Schools reflect and embody the larger political and social contexts in which they are housed, and much of what is happening in many communities is antithetical to the creation of high-quality political talk. That being said, in virtually all schools there are deliberative assets that either are or could be taken advantage of if the goal is to afford young people the opportunities and instruction to learn how to talk wisely and well about controversial political issues. These deliberative assets include curricular opportunities, high-quality educational resources, instructors who either already know or could learn how to teach about issues, and a degree of ideological diversity that is most likely greater than that which young people encounter in the other venues in which they spend significant amounts of time.

Even though there is evidence that students (especially in elementary and middle schools) are not being provided with adequate opportunities to engage in rich social studies instruction, in many schools there are required and elective courses that are or could be excellent venues for the discussion of controversial political issues. For example, virtually all high school students are required to take at least one history course, and the vast majority of students take a civics or government course, as well. Moreover, there is a strong fit between the goals of other subject-area courses (especially in literature and science) and controversial political issues, so the potential to expand opportunities for students to learn and talk about issues exists. In most cases it is not necessary to create new courses if we want students to learn about controversial political issues, but it is essential that we take advantage of the courses students already take by creating a curriculum that is issues-rich. One way to do this is to make use of the existing high-quality curricula on issues that have been developed by many non-profit democracy education organizations and make sure those organizations are supported to continue this important curriculum development work.

Given that students have to be taught how to engage in issues discussions, it is not surprising that the most powerful deliberative assets in schools are teachers who already know how to execute this kind of exceptionally demanding pedagogy, or could be taught with the right professional development.

Finally, a plethora of research indicates that in order for issues discussions to be most effective, it is important to capitalize on the ideological diversity that exists within a community. As I will explain below, this is challenging because as communities become more politically homogeneous, so do the schools within them. That being said, the studies I have done show that even in schools with an unusually high degree of political like-mindedness, enough ideological differences exist among students to create an environment in which they will be exposed to views that are different to their own. Even in schools that are exceptionally and, I would argue, dangerously homogeneous, teachers can insert multiple and competing views by carefully selecting the right kind of curriculum resources, taking advantage of cross-school programs if they are available, and inviting guest speakers who can share opinions that differ from those to which students are typically exposed. Taken together, schools' deliberative assets make them the most promising and logical venue in which all young people are taught how to talk about controversial political issues. Put even more strongly, schools have a responsibility to do this work, and if they do not, they are shirking a core tenet of what we should demand their mission to be.

## *What are the Current Threats to Controversial Political Issues Teaching?*

While there was never a "golden age" of widespread support for focusing students' attention on controversial political issues as part of a democratic education program, the barriers to doing so are especially numerous and challenging now. These barriers include political polarization, which is both the cause and result of the growing tendency of people to live in ideologically homogenous communities; a shrinking conception of what the "public" mission of education should be; and a number of trends in schools, including re-segregation and tracking, that make it less likely that young people will attend naturally occurring heterogeneous schools and classes.

Addressing each of these barriers in turn, Paula McAvoy and I argued recently that the dramatic rise in political polarization harms political talk:

> Political polarization refers to moments in time when political discourse and action bifurcates toward ideological extremes. This causes a crowding out of voices in the middle, leaving little room for political compromise. Polarization has occurred at various times in the United States (such as during the period leading up to the Civil War) and in other modern democracies, and it is a feature of democracy that likely will ebb and flow with the times (McCarty, Nolan, Poole, & Rosenthal, 2006). Scholars are suggesting that the United States is currently polarizing once more, causing a reevaluation of fundamental principles, especially with respect to the role of the government in individuals' lives (Bishop, 2008; Gutmann & Thompson, 2012; McCarty et al., 2006). In addition to the crowding-out problem, another consequence of polarization is the way in which it threatens the likelihood that people will engage in high-quality political discourse. Sadly, at just the moment when we most need productive and public political talk, the political climate of polarization is making it extremely difficult.
>
> *McAvoy and Hess, 2013*

If the climate for healthy political talk is threatened in the world outside school, it is likely that the appetite for this kind of talk within schools will be diminished. Moreover, polarization causes distrust, and the one thing that teachers most need to engage their students in high-quality issues discussions is trust. Parents and community members need to trust that teachers are playing fair and not trying to indoctrinate students into holding particular political beliefs, but, in a climate of ugly and angry political talk in which difference is demonized, some of this trust seems to be evaporating. Moreover, the public needs to believe that schools have an important public mission to prepare young people to participate politically and civically; and, while there is a lot of lip service and nodding about the civic and political mission of schools, education is increasingly being presented and interpreted as a private good, for private gain. I believe this accounts in part for why there is relatively little concern about ensuring that schools are inclusive and that students have multiple and long-lasting opportunities to work with people who are different to themselves in a number of ways that matter, such as race, sexual orientation, socioeconomic status, religion, and political ideology.

If our goal is to prepare young people to participate in an increasingly diverse and divided democracy, then sorting students into schools and classes in which they are surrounded by other students who are very much like them is highly problematic. But, while there is a lot of emphasis on improving the quality of education that young people are receiving (with "improvement" defined very narrowly, I would argue), there is virtually no pressure to ensure that all students are receiving high-quality democratic education in a diverse environment in which they can learn how to engage effectively with others about the pressing public problems facing the society that they will be asked to lead and contribute to in the not-too-distant future. This is why I believe that racial and economic segregation of entire schools, and various forms of tracking within schools, are especially dangerous for democracy. We should be especially concerned that many charter schools are being created using narrow definitions of inclusion; as a result, these schools are extremely segregated. The opening of new schools should be an occasion to create a student body in which all manner of diversity is represented and valued. To do the opposite is to forfeit an important opportunity.

## Conclusion

I was recently talking with some friends who are high school teachers about why I think this is such a perilous time for democracy, democratic education writ large, and, more specifically, the teaching of controversial political issues. They were struck by my gloominess. "Given your concerns," one asked, "do you think we should give up on controversial political issues teaching and try something else?" Could it be the case, another argued, that sometimes the wisest course is one that seeks a different approach, and, given that advocacy for controversial issues teaching goes back many decades, perhaps this is one of those ideas whose time has passed? I have spent several weeks pondering those questions.

But, as I write this, I note an e-mail that just arrived from Senator Dick Durbin announcing that a lunch speech I was scheduled to attend has been canceled because he is heading back to Washington to participate in the debate about whether the United States should bomb Syria. I think about another e-mail I received a few days ago from Walter Parker (our mentors are mentors for life) urging me to watch a video of a ten-minute conversation about Syria that was broadcast on *PBS NewsHour*. After viewing the segment, I was struck by how it exemplifies an argument social studies expert Tom Kelly made to educators back in 1986: aim for a "best case, fair hearing of competing points of view." I was reminded once again that it is critical to cultivate an appetite among students for hearing diverse views about the most important issues facing us. A few days later, I participated in a conversation about Syria with a small group of friends who had very different views about what role the United States should play. Given that I am trying to make up my mind about what I think, it was incredibly helpful not just to listen to others, but to listen to what others thought about my initial and recently formed opinions. This give-and-take, talking and listening, engaging and reflecting, is at the heart of democratic participation. While I believe that significant and powerful challenges face those who seek to teach young people how to talk about controversial political issues, I also believe we would be making a grave mistake to give up on the enterprise now, because the challenges are the very problems that we should be seeking to mitigate. Instead, my recommendation is, quite literally, to double down. That is, our advocacy for the role of schools as key venues for preparing young people for meaningful participation in democratic life is needed now even more than it was in the past. It is critical that we not shy away from making this case clearly and forcefully to the public, to parents, and to school leaders. Given teachers' absolutely vital role, we must stand by the educators who are already engaging their students in discussions of controversial political issues, and encourage those who are not to do so. In the face of intense political polarization, growing inequality, and a narrowing conception of the purposes of schools, we must recognize that abandoning the teaching and discussion of controversial issues is a misguided and destructive option. The stakes, after all, are extraordinarily high: giving citizens the tools to participate actively—and coexist peacefully—in a democracy brimming with competing views.

## Note

1   I am writing a book about the study with Paula McAvoy: Hess D., and McAvoy, P. (forthcoming) *The Political Classroom*. New York: Routledge.

## References

Bishop, Bill. (2008). *The Big Sort: Why the Clustering of Like-minded America Is Tearing Us Apart*. New York, NY: Houghton Mifflin.

Dahl, Robert A. (1988). *On Democracy*. New Haven, CT: Yale University Press.

Gastile, John, and Levine, Peter. (2005). *The Deliberative Democracy Handbook: Strategies for Effective Civic Engagement in the 21st Century*. San Francisco: Jossey-Bass.

Gutmann, Amy, and Thompson, Dennis. (2012). *The Spirit of Compromise: Why Governing Demands It and Campaigning Undermines It*. Princeton, NJ: Princeton University Press.

Hess, Diana E. (2009). *Controversy in the Classroom: The Democratic Power of Discussion*. New York, NY: Routledge.

Hess, Diana E. (2002). "Discussing Controversial Public Issues in Secondary Social Studies Classrooms: Learning from Skilled Teachers." 30 *Theory and Research in Social Education*, pp. 10–41.

Hess, Diana E., and McAvoy, Paula. (forthcoming). *The Political Classroom*. New York, NY: Routledge.

Lortie, Dan C. (1975/2001). *Schoolteacher: A Sociological Study*. Chicago, IL: University of Chicago Press.

McAvoy, Paula, and Hess, Diana E. (2013). "Classroom Deliberation in an Era of Political Polarization." 43(1) *Curriculum Inquiry*, pp. 14–47.

McCarty, Nolan, Poole, Keith T., and Rosenthal, Howard. (2006). *Polarized America: The Dance of Ideology and Unequal Riches*. Cambridge, MA: MIT Press.

# 9

# IMAGINING AND CONSTRUCTING SOCIAL DEMOCRACY

## An Educator's Creed

*William R. Fernekes*

ADJUNCT PROFESSOR, HUMAN RIGHTS EDUCATION, GLOBAL EDUCATION AND
SOCIAL STUDIES EDUCATION, RUTGERS UNIVERSITY

Prior to entering Rutgers College in 1970, I was raised in a lower middle class household in suburban Monmouth County, New Jersey, where discussion of social issues was not common. My mother was largely apolitical, while my father was a staunch conservative Republican who became more rigid in his views as he aged, notably during the civil rights movement of the late 1960s and early 1970s. He embraced his German-American ethnic background in ways that my mother had never seen before, and I later came to understand this development as his reaction to the demands of minorities of color, women, and others who had been denied equal opportunity and their full human dignity in the United States.

During one of our annual summer vacation road trips, I recall my father speaking to a neighbor on the phone about the racial unrest in Asbury Park, New Jersey, a shore town five miles from our home, and expressing his anger at the African-Americans who had rioted, claiming that they had "gotten enough" and should be stopped. He also frequently proclaimed how surprised he was to see pictures of Dr. Martin Luther King, Jr. in homes he visited of African-Americans when he investigated insurance claims as an employee of the Allstate Insurance Co. He felt King was nothing more than an agitator, and that African-Americans were misguided in viewing him as a strong, effective leader.

Without question, my experience at Rutgers University constituted my "awakening" to the importance of social issues, while simultaneously widening the gulf between my worldview and that of my father. My undergraduate education in history at Rutgers College (1970–1974) was a major influence on how I viewed social problems. The books I read and the professors I encountered, including scholars such as Traian Stoianovich (European History), Samuel Baily (Latin American history), Warren Susman (U. S. History) and Michael Adas (History of Western Imperialism), introduced me to alternative sources and perspectives on social change that forced me to look beyond the nationalistic boundaries of my upbringing and embrace a more global vision of how social experience could be analyzed and understood. A sterling example was Sam Baily's course on Revolution in Latin America, where case studies of Cuba, Bolivia, and Mexico challenged mainstream narratives about Latin American society, and introduced me to perspectives on regional and global issues that were not taught in pre-collegiate classrooms.

On a different but related note, with the Vietnam War raging and the Nixon administration exploiting racial divisions in the country, Rutgers was a hotbed of political activity and social activism. I saw firsthand the political commitments and activities of groups such as Students for a Democratic Society (SDS), chapters of the peace movement, and the women's movement, which raised my consciousness concerning the oppression experienced by minorities in the U.S. The Rutgers *Daily Targum* chronicled campus activities comprehensively, and my coursework in the history department and other fields provided me with opportunities to explore texts as diverse as photographic essays from the Farm Security Administration documenting the Great Depression, literary classics such as Dante's *Inferno* and Mariano Azuela's *Los De Abajo* (*The Underdogs*), oral histories such as Studs Terkel's *Hard Times*, and incisive analyses of social change, such as John Womack's *Zapata and the Mexican Revolution* and Jose Ortega y Gasset's *The Revolt of the Masses*. Among the issues we examined were revolutionary movements in Latin America, the challenges facing ordinary Americans during the Great Depression, and comparative studies of slavery in the U.S. and Latin America, all topics that had been "invisible" during my upbringing and pre-collegiate education.

I can vividly remember attending a "teach-in" at the Rutgers College Avenue gymnasium following the revelations about the secret U.S. bombing of Cambodia, and watching one of my professors speaking out against U.S. policy on stage while holding the hand of his young son, arguing that this was not the type of society he wanted his son to grow up in and that the Vietnam War had to end now.

During my junior year, I decided to pursue my teacher certification in social studies, and began taking professional education courses, such as Materials and Methods in Social Studies. I was fortunate to encounter teachers who supported risk-taking and innovation, and I began incorporating the study of contemporary issues in my junior practicum program and my student teaching internship at Madison Township (N.J.) High School. The positive response of students to my use of issues-based approaches encouraged my further exploration of how the "underside" of U.S. history could become more prominent in my own teaching, and it was heartening to also have the support of my subject field professors in the history department, who, as I previously mentioned, had opened my eyes to a much broader range of perspectives on social change. In particular, I was inspired by how Professor Warren Susman approached the study of 20th century U.S. history, in which he incorporated photo albums from the WPA, films of the 1920s and 1930s, literature of the period and oral histories (Studs Terkel's *Hard Times*) as sources for our work, and invited us, his students, to explore historical change in a multi-sensory manner.

There was little doubt that by the time of the Nixon-McGovern election in November 1972, my political views had diverged markedly from those I held when I entered Rutgers in 1970, and it was clear that my father and I would not agree on many critical issues of the day. I always felt bad for my mother, who was a kind and loving woman but who was increasingly alienated by my father's insistence that his views dominate conversations at home and in social settings. By the time I graduated from Rutgers in May 1974, I was already committed to a pedagogical platform that placed issues-focused approaches at the center of my work. As I continued to advance my understanding of those approaches in my graduate study, I know my mother, and to some extent my father, were proud of the fact that I had forged my own path as a professional social studies educator, despite the conflicts that had emerged along the way.

During my master's degree program in Latin American history at the Rutgers-New Brunswick Graduate School (1975–1978), and my subsequent doctoral work in social studies education at the Rutgers Graduate School of Education (1979–1985), my rationale for teaching social studies became progressively more issues-centered, with much credit due to Jack L. Nelson, my dissertation advisor at Rutgers. Jack's willingness to challenge orthodoxy in the social studies field by promoting debate between adherents of a history-centric approach and scholars who advocated social studies as social criticism led me to design a dissertation in which I examined alternative models of curriculum design (aesthetic and radical left) and their compatibility with existing rationales and practices in the teaching of U.S. history.

As I developed my dissertation proposal and embarked on writing it, my pedagogical efforts at Hunterdon Central Regional High School (September 1974–December 2010) involved a move toward a more prominent focus on the study of controversial issues, using student-centered instructional strategies modeled after those developed by Hunt and Metcalf, Engle and Ochoa, and others (Hunt and Metcalf, 1955/1968; Engle and Ochoa, 1988). Their emphases on the critical analysis of social problems and the development of reflective thought, tied to the development of students as effective decision-makers in a democracy, appealed strongly to me, as did their detailed discussions of how to stimulate and nurture critical skepticism about social experience. Students responded well to issues-centered approaches in both U.S. history and classes focused on the social sciences and public policy analysis, notably in topics ranging from how the U.S. should address nuclear proliferation, to debates on capital punishment, and controversies regarding government's responsibility to care for the poor and most vulnerable in society.

Through my work in Holocaust and genocide education in New Jersey, I became deeply interested in the study of international human rights, a development spurred by a special issue of *Social Education* on human rights edited by Samuel Totten (Totten, 1985). Inspired by the contents of that journal issue, I contacted Amnesty International USA and, with the support of a few of my most dedicated students, we initiated a student chapter of Amnesty International at Hunterdon Central Regional HS in Flemington, NJ. For the next 25 years, I served as the sole advisor or co-advisor to this student chapter, which became a model for how young people could not only study pervasive social problems, but learn tools for social activism. Soon after the creation of our school's Amnesty International chapter, I became more deeply engaged in the study of the Holocaust and genocides through my work as a consultant to the education department of the new United States Holocaust Memorial Museum in Washington, D.C. By incorporating comprehensive units on the Holocaust and genocides in my own teaching, as well as through my work as a curriculum developer and supervisor at Hunterdon Central, it became apparent to me that a more effective approach would integrate the study of the Holocaust and genocides within a thematic curriculum design focused on the study of international human rights. For much of the period 1988–2010, my scholarship and daily work as a teacher and supervisor of a regional high school social studies program emphasized how engaging social issues using a human rights lens improved student understanding of issues-centered content and facilitated their active participation as citizens to address social problems.

In 1897, John Dewey stated that "education is the fundamental method of social progress and reform" (Dewey, 1897, p. 80). This view has deeply influenced my personal journey as an educator, as well as the development of my own pedagogical creed.

Believing, as I do, that improving the quality of life in a democracy requires an informed and reflective citizenry, Dewey's claim makes eminent sense, particularly as I examined the ways in which the detailed consideration of social issues engaged students of all backgrounds and abilities, while helping them construct knowledge and develop the skills and dispositions needed to shape and implement public policy changes.

## What Education Is

I believe that for any society to make progress in developing human potential and engendering the common good, education using both formal and informal means is essential. "Formal" education refers to institutionalized structures such as schools and workplaces in which systematic processes are used to facilitate learning directed towards positive social outcomes.

"Informal" education refers to processes of social interaction in both public and private settings in which learning is directed towards positive social outcomes, such as in families, through the mass media, and through self-directed efforts such as personalized reading and research, online study, and tutoring or mentoring processes. Without a strong commitment to education as a core priority, societies are severely hampered in addressing both historic and emergent social issues because the population is neither well-informed nor well-skilled in how to identify, study, and develop solutions to social problems.

I believe that education, by definition, is different from learning and is directed towards a positive social good. Any education seeking to maximize human potential and support the common good must emphasize the empowerment of humans to improve the quality of life in communities and enable people to understand and safeguard their fundamental human rights. In doing so, the content of education must directly engage issues that emphasize the dynamic relationship between sustaining individual freedoms and liberties and supporting the common good, such as when freedom of expression poses challenges to physical or national security. For a vibrant democracy to be sustained, an informed citizenry must be able to interpret and analyze clashing perspectives and make thoughtful decisions on what courses of action are appropriate, along with considering the short and long-term consequences of those decisions. If students are not educated effectively to develop and apply such learning to influence public policy at all levels of governance, then the pathway to tyranny and the end of democracy will be likely outcomes.

I believe that education must be free to all residents in a political unit, universally accessible to students of all ages and cultural backgrounds and that its content and processes should be unrestrained by censorship. Removing the financial barriers to educational opportunities is essential if a society wants to unleash the human potential of its population and enhance opportunities for social mobility. Eliminating requirements based on age and/or cultural characteristics for entrance, advancement, and exit from educational programs enhances the ability of the learner to make progress at their own pace, and supports efforts to meet individual needs of students with specialized characteristics, such as persons with disabilities, individuals who do not speak dominant languages, or students who have faced historic and/or contemporary patterns of discrimination or unequal treatment in society. Implementing guidelines to support and preserve principles of academic freedom, as well as embodying the values in practice which are central to the development of democracy, must be core commitments in any educational setting if the free exchange of ideas is to flourish. There can be no sustained social progress in a society in which education is characterized by authoritarian control and limits on intellectual freedom. No serious examination of social issues can occur in either formal or informal educational settings where the free exchange of ideas is restricted and ideological purity is an overriding priority. As Jack L. Nelson (2012) notes, "Authoritarian, non-democratic governments need not provide academic freedom; indeed they have good reason to fear it. Similarly, authoritarian leaders in communities and schools do not think they need it, and have reason to fear and to react with threats" (p. 509).

I believe that education directed towards achieving social justice and supporting the values stated in the Charter of the United Nations is essential in an increasingly interconnected global society where social issues in one country or political entity impact the lives of residents in other areas of a region or across the globe. Whether the social issue is air quality, access to fresh water, the transfer of arms or narcotics across borders, or one of many others, students must be engaged in investigating it, so they can encounter multiple perspectives on the problem, develop well-informed positions that are open to future revision, propose solutions for public discussion, and develop the skills that will enable them to take action and remedy the problem.[2]

## What the School Does

I believe that the idea of the school is being transformed through the use of digital technology, which has become a very important means for not only making the content of education accessible to global audiences, but also for facilitating dialogue and discussion about the content of education that is not bound by traditional constraints of time and space. What has not changed, however, is the fundamental set of relationships between subject matter, the teacher, and the learner, which requires the teacher to continually reflect on how best to motivate and inspire the learner to inquire about social issues incorporated in the curriculum. How the teacher poses questions, responds to learner inquiries and interests, organizes subject matter (content) for study by the learner, implements pedagogy that stimulates reflection, and develops relevant and meaningful assessments of student understanding remain core aspects of schooling, whether conducted in traditional settings (physical buildings or comparable locations) or in digital environments, such as online classrooms. Thus, the school remains a fundamental location for the development of intellectual activity and growth, a setting in which inquiry into social issues can take place systematically while simultaneously promoting reflection on how to develop solutions to historic and contemporary social problems.

I believe the school must serve as a counter-socializing force to limit the influence of excessive nationalism, the relentless pursuit of greed and self-interest, the destructive impact of bias, prejudice, and hate, and the power of interest groups based in the broader society or within the state itself that seek to advance their political goals while limiting popular involvement in democratic governance (Allen, 1996, pp. 52–53; Freire, 1992).

I believe that placing the study of social issues at the center of the school's curriculum is an essential first step in challenging dominant patterns of power and privilege in the broader society, since students should be taught how to design questions that probe the relationships between democratic ideals and social conditions, and then pursue investigations that reveal the gaps between the ideal and the real. Sans the active engagement of students in pursuing such investigations and in proposing solutions to social problems, the primary purpose of schools is limited to transferring cultural capital from one generation to the next, with little or no commitment to improving the quality of life in society through the reflective consideration of social issues and problems.[3]

I believe that the school must serve as a laboratory of democratic practice if students are to become effective participants in a society that upholds democratic ideals as the foundation of civic life. Too often, schools are governed autocratically, with little or no commitment to democratic practices, and the contradictions between civic ideals and the reality of civic life in schools are endemic. Schools can change this pattern by placing social issues at the center of the curriculum, particularly in social studies, and using the school itself as the focus of issues-based study. Students can be *encouraged* to challenge their exclusion from governance, to study how resources are distributed and employed within schools to advance specific interests or goals, and to investigate how the overt and hidden curricula are designed and delivered, along with their impact on student access to higher education and related societal resources. In doing so, young people can be taught the skills of political engagement, and then develop strategies and campaigns to make schools more democratic and responsive to their needs.[4]

## The Subject Matter of Education

I believe that how we live our lives, and the influences of human activity and natural forces on patterns of social interaction are the legitimate subject matter of education. Because knowledge and human behavior are constantly changing, the subject matter of education must be adjusted and reshaped to address not only historic developments and understandings across subject fields, but the contemporary and emerging social issues encountered by human communities at the local, national, regional, and global levels. By placing issues at the center of curriculum design, educators can pose questions that by their very nature require the use of knowledge and processes drawn from a broad range of subject fields. For example, were a school to engage the theme of human rights as a key organizing principle for curricula, here are three questions that could be posed:

(1)  Are there universal human rights, and if so, how did those ideas develop over time?
(2)  How are the norms set forth in international human rights treaties, declarations and covenants being addressed by world states in the contemporary world, notably in cases where conflict is underway?
(3)  Were international human rights guarantees to be implemented and enforced in the United States, what would be the impact of these changes on daily life?

In addressing these issues-based questions, educators and students would need to examine content drawn from the humanities for question one (examples include history, law, literature, philosophy, political science, and other subjects), from the humanities and sciences for question two (examples include international relations, law, environmental studies, health and medicine, sociology, and other subjects), and the humanities and sciences for question three, with a decided emphasis on content about the United States (U.S. History and government, law, education, environmental studies, health and medicine, and other subjects). This issues-based curriculum would, of necessity, require the study of reflective thought processes so both educators and students could pursue investigations of the core questions using whatever content is appropriate to the problem being studied. Additionally, the school would become a center of knowledge creation, since the study of social issues and problems presumes that developing solutions to social problems would be a logical outcome of inquiry. In this regard, the "subject matter" of education is continually transformed as participants in issues-based instruction develop linkages between subject fields through investigations of social problems, and disciplinary boundaries that in the past constituted obstacles to inquiry are eroded.[5] With access to digital content available on demand and the use of digital media for communication, collaborative endeavors connecting schools and individuals across the globe would facilitate the sharing of ideas drawn from diverse perspectives, which would further enhance the capacity of students to develop insights from a broad range of subject fields and encounter ideas that challenge their understanding of relevant and/or appropriate content.

I believe that too often we neglect the lived reality of students as the subject matter of education, and that an issues-based curriculum can redress that imbalance. Students bring perceptions, understandings, attitudes and knowledge to the classroom at all levels of education. Educators should provide frequent opportunities for students to reveal what they know, believe, perceive, and understand about issues in the curriculum, because, in doing so, meaningful connections can be forged between content from established subject fields and student life experiences. In this way, students have the opportunity to construct meaning and take ownership of the subject matter of education, which enhances their potential to develop solutions to social problems during their formal schooling experience or in other settings.[6]

## The Nature of Method

I believe that active, student-centered pedagogy is integral to any issues-centered curriculum. Educators must model how to critically define issues, pose investigative questions, identify and assess relevant sources of information, interpret and analyze findings, develop tentative conclusions, and continually reassess their findings and conclusions in light of new evidence. As students are taught these skills in the context of real-life problems requiring solutions, an issues-centered curriculum is brought to life. In practice, therefore, no separation exists between the content of the curriculum and instructional methods, since much of the content in any issues-centered curriculum consists of the methods used by scholars in the humanities and social sciences to inquire about social experience.

The process outlined above, however, lacks one critical component—the commitment to directly engage students in the community in political action strategies regarding social problems. Whether that community is defined as the school itself, or, in expanding terms, from the local to the global arena, students require direct engagement with decision-making and problem-solving to test the effectiveness of their ideas. The use of digital media has made communication across time and space far easier than in the past, permitting educators and students to share their ideas and potential solutions with much broader audiences, and in the process develop insights informed by a richer variety of perspectives. Simultaneously, access to a much greater number and range of potential sources heightens the importance of critical media literacy, notably educating students how to effectively assess the credibility and reliability of sources they may use as evidence in their investigations. The temptation to rapidly locate and use information bereft of critical assessment of its merits and drawbacks must be called into question by educators, and students need to question and critique all sources of information thoroughly in order to base their findings, conclusions and action strategies on reliable and accurate evidence.[7]

As students move beyond the classroom and test their ideas to solve social problems in the community, educators must remain engaged and monitor the challenges their students encounter, and provide thoughtful guidance on how to overcome obstacles (for example, recalcitrant bureaucrats or elected officials), develop effective communication strategies for intended audiences, learn how to compromise and negotiate solutions with allies and opponents, and evaluate the results of their efforts, all the while attending to the achievements and excitement, as well as the frustration and disappointments, that transpire.[8] As Henry Giroux argued in 1985:

> Making the political more pedagogical means utilizing forms of pedagogy that embody political interests that are emancipatory in nature; that is, using forms of pedagogy that treat students as critical agents; make knowledge problematic; utilize critical and affirming dialogue; and make the case for struggling for a qualitatively better world for all people.
>
> *p. 379*

Only when ideas learned in the issues-centered classroom are put to the test in the daily practice of civic life, can we determine whether the potential of a truly social education focused on civic competence can be realized.

## Conclusion

The complexity of social experience presents a daunting challenge for the most talented educators as they contemplate the design of curricula, instructional methods, and assessments of student performance. As I reflect on my personal educational journey, the influences of John Dewey and later scholars who elaborated a Progressive vision of the social studies as a laboratory for the development of active, reflective citizens remains paramount in my teaching, research, and writing. Combined with my commitment to making human rights education a central focus of the daily practice of schools, I continue to develop opportunities for educators and students to use issues-centered approaches as the primary means for improving the quality of life in our world.[9]

## Notes

1    See the following articles by the author: William R. Fernekes (1988) "Why Use the UDHR in the Classroom?" 1(1) *The Fourth R*, p. 6; William R. Fernekes (1988) "A Comparison of the UDHR and the United States Constitution: An Activity for Grades 7–12," 1(1) *The Fourth R*, p. 7; William R. Fernekes (1989) "Sample Course Outlines," in William S. Parsons, *Study Guide for "Everyone's Not Here: Families of the Armenian Genocide,"* Washington, D.C.: Armenian Assembly of America; William R. Fernekes (1992) "Children's Rights in the Social Studies Curriculum: A Critical Imperative," 56(4) *Social Education*, pp. 203–204; William R. Fernekes (1992) "Investigating the Rights of Indigenous Peoples," 3(2) *The 4th R*, pp. 9–10; and Beverly C. Edmonds and William R. Fernekes (1996) *Children's Rights: A Reference Handbook.* Santa Barbara, CA: ABC-CLIO Press.

2    See Ronald W. Evans and David Warren Saxe (eds.) (1996) *Handbook on Teaching Social Issues*, Washington, D.C.: National Council for the Social Studies; William Gaudelli and Scott Wylie (2012) "Global Education and Issue-Centered Education," in Samuel Totten and Jon E. Pedersen (eds.), *Educating about Social Issues in the 20th and 21st Century: A Critical Annotated Bibliography, Volume I* (pp. 293–320), Charlotte, NC: Information Age Publishing; and, United Nations, Office of the High Commissioner for Human Rights (2012) "World Programme for Human Rights Education." Third Phase. October. Accessible at http://www.ohchr.org/EN/Issues/Education/Training/Pages/Programme.aspx

3    These ideas were most succinctly presented in the work of Alan F. Griffin and his doctoral student Lawrence Metcalf. See William R. Fernekes (2007) "Alan F. Griffin: Role Model For the Reflective Study of Modern Problems," in Samuel Totten and Jon E. Pedersen (eds.) *Addressing Social Issues across the Curriculum: The Pedagogical Efforts of Pioneers in the Field* (pp. 135–158), Greenwich, CT: Information Age Publishing; and William R. Fernekes (2012) "The Hunt and Metcalf Model of Reflective Study of Social Problems" in Samuel Totten and Jon E. Pedersen (eds.) *Educating about Social Issues in the 20th and 21st Century: A Critical Annotated Bibliography, Volume I* (pp. 115–134), Charlotte, NC: Information Age Publishing.

4    See these sources on how to develop a human rights culture within schools that emphasizes democratic practices and governance: Nancy Flowers, et al (2000) *The Human Rights Education Handbook.* Minneapolis, MN: Human Rights Resource Center of the University of Minnesota; and Audrey Osler and Hugh Starkey (2010) *Teachers and Human Rights Education.* Stoke on Trent, UK: Trentham Books.

5    Two major theorists whose works have influenced my views on this topic are Alan F. Griffin and James Beane. See William R. Fernekes (2007) "Alan F. Griffin: Role Model for the Reflective Study of Modern Problems," in Samuel Totten and Jon E. Pedersen (eds.), *Addressing Social Issues Across the Curriculum: The Pedagogical Efforts of Pioneers in the Field* (pp. 135–158), Greenwich, CT: Information Age Publishing; and Jon E. Pedersen (2012) "James Beane's Integrative Curriculum Approach to Engaging Students in a Study of Social Issues and Community Service," in Samuel Totten and Jon E. Pedersen (eds.) *Educating About Social Issues in the 20th and 21st Centuries:*

*A Critical Annotated Bibliography, Volume I* (pp.351–368), Charlotte, NC: Information Age Publishing.

6   Building upon the work of Alan F. Griffin, Hunt and Metcalf's book *Teaching High School Social Studies* provides a strong argument supporting the centrality of student life experiences as important content sources in an issues-centered curriculum. See William R. Fernekes (2012) "The Hunt and Metcalf Model of Reflective Study of Social Problems," in Samuel Totten and Jon E. Pedersen (eds.) *Educating about Social Issues in the 20th and 21st Century: A Critical Annotated Bibliography, Volume I* (pp. 115–134), Charlotte, NC: Information Age Publishing. Additionally, two chapters in the Evans and Saxe (1996) *Handbook on Teaching Social Issues* (Washington DC: NCSS) provide sample scope and sequence frameworks in which student life experiences and subject field content are combined within an issues-centered curriculum: Ronald W. Evans and Jerry Brodkey (1996) "An Issues-Centered Curriculum for High School Social Studies," pp. 243–264; and, William G. Wraga (1996) "Teaching Societal Issues across the Secondary Curriculum," pp. 265–275.

7   Two very useful sources regarding the critical evaluation and use of digital media content are Nicholas Carr (2010) *The Shallows: What the Internet Is Doing to Our Brains*, New York, NY: W.W. Norton and Co., and the Media Literacy Clearinghouse, accessed at http://www.frankwbaker.com/home1.htm.

8   See Fred Newmann (1975) *Education for Citizen Action: Challenge for Secondary Curriculum* (Richmond, CA: McCutchan Publishing) for an in-depth presentation of a curriculum designed to actively engage students in social change processes, and the work of non-governmental organizations such as Amnesty International on how students can learn the skills to promote social change in schools and communities, accessible at www.amnestyusa.org/resources/students-and-youth.

9   See Valerie Ooka Pang, Jack L. Nelson, and William R. Fernekes (eds.) (2012) *The Human Impact of Natural Disasters: Issues for the Inquiry-Based Classroom*, Silver Spring, MD: National Council for the Social Studies; and Human Rights Educators-USA, a national network of human rights educators launched in December 2012. The network can be accessed at www.hreusa.net.

# References

Allen, Rodney F. (1996). "The Engle-Ochoa Decision Making Model for Citizenship Education." In Ronald W. Evans and David Warren Saxe (eds.). *Handbook on Teaching Social Issues* (pp. 51–58). Washington, D.C.: National Council for the Social Studies.

Dewey, John. (1897). "My Pedagogic Creed." 54 (January) *School Journal*, pp. 77–80.

Engle, Shirley H., and Ochoa, Anna. (1988). *Education for Democratic Citizenship*. New York, NY: Teachers College Press.

Freire, Paolo (1992). *Pedagogy of the Oppressed*. New York, NY: Continuum.

Giroux, Henry A. (1985). "Teachers as Transformative Intellectuals." 49(5) *Social Education*, pp. 376–379.

Hunt, Maurice, and Metcalf, Lawrence. (1955/1968). *Teaching High School Social Studies: Problems in Reflective Thinking and Social Understanding*. New York, NY: Harper and Row.

Nelson, Jack L. (2012). "Issues of Academic Freedom." In Samuel Totten and Jon E. Pedersen, eds., *Educating about Social Issues in the 20th and 21st Centuries: A Critical Annotated Bibliography, Volume 1* (pp. 509–532). Charlotte, NC: Information Age Publishing.

Totten, Samuel (ed.). (1985). "Special Issue on International Human Rights," 49(6) *Social Education*.

# 10

# PREPARING EFFECTIVE CITIZENS VIA AN ISSUES-CENTERED APPROACH

*Mark A. Previte*

ASSOCIATE PROFESSOR, SECONDARY EDUCATION,
UNIVERSITY OF PITTSBURGH AT JOHNSTOWN

Currently, I am an Associate Professor of Secondary Education at the University of Pittsburgh at Johnstown, coordinating the secondary social studies program. From 1976 to 2004 I was a secondary social studies teacher and department chair at Northern Cambria High School in Pennsylvania, where I taught courses including American Cultures, Sociology, Contemporary Affairs, and Psychology. In 1988, I began my doctoral program in Curriculum and Instruction at the Pennsylvania State University under the mentorship of Murry Nelson. Nelson's mentor at Stanford University was Richard Gross, a past president of the National Council for the Social Studies and a pioneer of the issues-centered movement. My dissertation was entitled "Shirley H. Engle: Decision Making in Social Studies Education." I am currently serving as program chair of the National Council for the Social Studies Issues Centered Education Community, with which I have been affiliated for over 20 years.

My family business has been anchored in the field of education. The strongest influence in my development emanated from my father. From the late 1950s to the late 1980s, he fulfilled several roles in two rural school districts in west central Pennsylvania, including secondary social studies teacher and high school principal. My younger brother and I remember watching him correct papers, record grades, and compose lesson plans. We also remember him providing us with a daily situational report on his day's comings and goings. Some our family vacations turned into social studies field trips—walking about the deck of the USS Niagara anchored on the shores of Lake Erie trying to imagine Oliver Perry's strategy during the War of 1812, and inspecting the battlefields at Gettysburg and conjuring up images of brothers fighting against brothers in that bloody conflagration.

During my high school years, I remember many conversations about politics and the news at the supper table, the front porch, and the golf course. It was not surprising that, when I made my decision to attend Slippery Rock State College in the fall of 1971, my chosen path would be to graduate with a degree in secondary social studies with an emphasis in political science. My undergraduate course work provided a solid foundation in the social sciences and pedagogy from a citizenship transmission approach.

Looming over all-male college freshmen at that time was the 1971 draft lottery during the Vietnam War. The war was a hot button issue in many communities in west central Pennsylvania and ours was no different. I knew families who had sons fighting; one of our closest neighbors lost their eldest son in 1966. I still remember a car pulling up to the house and two military officers walking up to the front porch. I watched enough news at that time to have convinced me that my friend had been killed. I have vague recollections of my parents discussing the possible ramifications of my being selected in the lottery. My lottery number was 63, so my first semester of college also included a trip to Pittsburgh for a physical examination, which was mandatory for those who were facing the military draft. Fortunately, or unfortunately, the doctors discovered I had a heart murmur, and thus the doctors designated me as 4F, so it was back to campus to continue my studies.

My high school teaching career transitioned through the three competing traditions espoused in the National Council for the Social Studies publication, "Defining the Social Studies" (Barr, Barth, and Shermis, 1977). My first few years of teaching could be described as being isolated on an island without much support from veteran colleagues. I was encouraged by the school administration and one of my social studies department members to use the textbook as *the* primary source vis-à-vis the curriculum. As I looked through the book cabinet in my classroom I discovered that there were few, if any other, curriculum materials.

During the summer after my first year of teaching, I started to comb through social studies publication catalogues to begin building my classroom resource library. During my third year of teaching I began a master's program at the Indiana University of Pennsylvania, at which time I was introduced to Edwin Fenton and the New Social Studies. Embarking on the inquiry path dovetailed nicely with my initiation of a long and fruitful relationship with the National History Day program involving my 10th grade American Cultures students.

It was not until I began my doctoral research in 1988 that I became immersed in the literature of the issues-centered education movement in the United States. Beginning at that time, I transitioned to an issues-centered philosophy, where my classrooms became democratic sites of deliberation in which I challenged students to questions their most basic thoughts and values about perennial and contemporary issues.

Moving from a citizenship transmission (Barr, Barth, and Shermis, 1977)/ banking method of teaching (Freire, 1970) to an inquiry philosophy and then on to an issues-centered philosophy was exhilarating—but also fraught with conflict and resistance from my high school and university students who were accustomed to a citizenship transmission methodology (whereby students are inculcated in coming to appreciate a traditional, though unreflective, understanding of U.S. history and so-called American values with the hope that such traditional beliefs will be internalized and passed onto future generations without any critical thought or judgment). First, the students at both the secondary and university levels were apprehensive about the open-ended questioning that forced them to defend their positions with factual information versus their providing a brief (and often perfunctory) response or nothing at all. Second, moving from objective to subjective assessments and projects that required them to think critically and reflectively placed greater demands on their time; this conflicted with after-school jobs and their taking part in extracurricular activities. Indeed, many of these were long-term assignments that required many hours of after school time. Third, it also reduced the guessing that is inherent in certain forms of objective exams. Now they were being encouraged to provide evidential information and extended explanation in their written exams, position papers, and projects. Fourth, departing from the textbook and introducing other source materials that provided conflicting evidence and interpretation moved them away from the "Jeopardy"/"Trivial Pursuit" mode of learning. As the academic year progressed, I noticed that some pockets of resistance disappeared; indeed, many students adjusted and eventually became advocates of the open-ended atmosphere. They were beginning to understand that becoming effective citizens was more than memorizing and regurgitating the factual information they had learned during lectures and their readings. These experiences as an issues-centered educator have shaped my pedagogical approach and publication agenda by deepening my appreciation as to how an issues-centered curriculum can be successfully applied in a standards-based environment.

## Education

I believe that education should assist students in their development as current and future citizens. They will face many issues as their life roles develop and change. The prime directive for educators is to create a classroom environment in which student-citizens practice the art of effective citizenship within an issues-centered philosophy of curriculum and instruction that: (a) promotes the study of open ended questions, past and present; (b) focuses on topics that may be controversial, and encourages reflective thinking; and (c) leads to position-taking through the analysis of large quantities of data (Engle and Ochoa, 1988, pp. 515–516). Here, the investigation of issues relevant to the lives of students and our democratic way of life should be the prime directive. Evidence gathered from the study of these issues will enrich their critical thinking and decision-making skills, affording students the ability to examine bodies of evidence and to come to their own conclusions. The objective is to assist students in digging deeper into a study of issues, to conduct a deep analysis of the issues under study, with the goal that students can then justify their decisions to effect social progress.

I believe that education should involve a pedagogical process that focuses on the hypothetical mode, where change, critical thinking, and open-mindedness are the norm (Engle and Ochoa, 1988). Students should be provided opportunities to examine and question the origins of issues, the values that support various vantage points vis-à-vis those issues, alternative solutions, and the consequences of those alternatives. Without engaging in such a critique, the student is less likely to truly understand the issue, less likely to have constructed his/her own response to the issue, and less likely to be able to provide a rationale for his/her position in regard to the issue. Maintaining the status quo, i.e., the expository method, renders the student effectively brainwashed and incapable of critical thought.

I believe that "student as critic" should be a principal characteristic in an issues-centered classroom. Teachers should nurture in their students an open mind in questioning society's values system (Hunt and Metcalf, 1968). Since values are the cement that holds the issues-centered structure together, it becomes necessary to compare and contrast those beliefs that are at the core of our very being (Engle, 1947). If students are to take their rightful place as effective citizens, to be able to address the continuous stream of events and experiences that life will present to them, and make decisions that will help them—and their city, state and nation—to survive and prosper, values must be questioned and dissected without fear of scorn or reprisal (Nelson and Stanley, 1985). The purpose of the issues-centered approach is to openly discuss and question the values of individuals, using factual information as evidence, to promote a democratic environment similar to the real world (Griffin, 1942).

## Aspirations

I believe that teachers are the "guardians of democracy" (Gould, 2003), and schools should be places in which students are regularly engaged in democratic behavior. Unfortunately, Dewey's dream of schools as democratic institutions has fallen short. Students, of course, do learn about "democracy," but the concepts are generally not practiced in schools and that is due to the fact that most school administrators and teachers, oddly, see such as a challenge to their place in the system. In this situation and milieu, controlling student behavior by limiting the type of knowledge that will reduce student cynicism and create a more manageable classroom environment (Leming, 1989) is seemingly of utmost concern, almost to the point at which a calm classroom is more greatly desired than true student learning. Until those inside and outside the educational arena mobilize to propel school reform toward the establishment and implementation of a true democratic model for schools, we will continue to pay lip service to the latter through our rhetoric and contrived actions (Beane and Apple, 1995, pp. 1–25).

The goal of social studies arises out of the need to help young people to integrate human experience and human knowledge. Given an issues-centered model, young people should, ideally, come to understand and apply the approach when being confronted with life's problems. According to Engle (1982):

> The primary role of the school in a democracy is to help children to gain some distance from their society. It is to help children to gain the capacity for objectivity concerning the beliefs and institutions otherwise imposed upon them by the status quo. It is to help them gain the capacity to participate in the continual reconstruction and improvement of society. . . . Participation implies the right to reflect on one's own beliefs and those of others, the right to harbor doubt about beliefs, and full access to information whereby beliefs may be studied and validated. Education, if it is to serve the purposes of democracy, should reflect these rights at every turn and should help citizens to build the skills and the kind of ordered knowledge required for the exercise of these rights. . . .
>
> *p. 49*

I believe that the school should become a forum for investigation of the human condition, in which young people identify society's issues, gather evidence, and offer solutions. Participation in the classroom should be a prerequisite for participation in life in order for the student to "acquire a social sense of their own powers and of the materials and appliances used" (Dewey, 1916, p. 40). Schools should provide an access for students to study issues and to choose a course of action (Previte, 2002). As Dewey (1916) asserted:

> Action with a purpose is deliberate; it involves a consciously foreseen end and a mental weighing of considerations pro and con. It also involves a conscious state of longing or desire for the end. The deliberate choice of an aim and of a settled disposition of desire takes time. During this time complete overt action is suspended. A person who does not have his mind made up, does not know what to do. Consequently he postpones definite action so far as possible.
>
> *p. 347*

## Subject Matter

I believe that it is the responsibility of the teacher to evaluate the applicability of the subject matter to be presented in relation to the pupil's life experiences. For too many years, the social studies educator has maintained the status quo by implementing a standard operating procedure in the classroom dominated by 1) the textbook as the single, "encyclopedic" source, rather than recognizing what it truly is: just another source with its own particular biases, vantage points, and interpretations; and 2) employing the lecture method to continue the tradition of purportedly exposing students to information that will transform them into effective citizens. It is no wonder that students have been anesthetized by these practices; they believe that playing "Jeopardy" or "Trivial Pursuit" is *the sin qua non* of the social studies classroom. As a result, they never become fully cognizant of the relevance of the curriculum to their own life experiences and the experiences of those beyond their own culture.

The overall attitude that was pounded in to me as I began my teaching career was to maintain the status quo: adopting a "sage on the stage" mentality utilizing the banking method of education whereby factual information would be deposited for future use (Freire, 1970). My classroom was a traditional social studies classroom. This included the employment of the textbook as the chief—and sometimes exclusive—source of information. Another component of this pedagogy was the lecture method, which assumed that continued talk about this and that fact would eventually transform the student into an effective citizen. Unfortunately, my students became anesthetized by my pedagogy; the quizzical looks on their faces was a constant reminder that they did not see the connection of the day's lesson to their lived lives. Essentially, my version of social studies education involved transmitting to, and inculcating basic American values into, the younger generation in the hope that a host of traditional beliefs would be internalized and passed on to future generations (Giroux, 1988).

I believe that social studies educators must periodically critique their curriculum and pedagogy in order to maintain a strong connection to the students' understanding of human behavior. Engle (1982) feared that the citizenship transmission mode "trivializes education and robs learning of any potential for developing citizens of substance, capable of participating in deciding the important questions that face society" (p. 50). If the educational process is to succeed then it is the teacher's job to construct a classroom environment that stimulates and challenges students to think about past and present issues. Dewey (1933) and Griffin (1942) advocated the use of "evidential information" to ground a belief. Employing evidence as part of the classroom procedure ensures that students, through the use of higher order thinking skills (interpretation, analysis, synthesis, and evaluation), will assist students to become critical thinkers and, as a result, hopefully, critically thinking citizens.

## Method

I believe that classrooms should be viewed as sites of deliberation in which the practice of democratic citizenship skills is paramount. Greater voice and control should be placed in the hands of the students, especially in the areas of curriculum selection, which, hopefully, will help them to see and make relevant connections between their school work and their lived lives (VanSickle, 1990). Students have been anesthetized by traditional social studies practices, and, more often than not, they do not perceive the relevance of what they are studying. Hence, it is the responsibility of the teacher to evaluate the applicability of the subject matter to be presented in relation to the life experiences of the pupil.

The tradition of socializing students with this nation's time honored traditions and values has been persistent, and rightly so as it serves a vital function within our school system, and that is to teach students the political, economic, social, and religious tenets that have withstood the test of time in our turbulent history. But that only constitutes half the job; teachers must also incorporate the process referred to as "countersocialization—the process of expanding the individual's ability to be a rational, thoughtful, and independent citizen of a democracy" (Engle and Ochoa, 1988, p. 29).

I believe that an open classroom environment affords students the comfort to voice their positions, concerns, and queries about subject matter, including, of course, controversial and other types of social issues. In turn, I believe that this will lead to better decision-making by them as they mature into adults.

I believe that if teachers adhere to the philosophy that a major goal of social studies education is to help young people become effective decision makers, then teachers may have to revamp their thinking about their role in the classroom. Moving from a traditional to an issues-centered educational philosophy entails a great deal of work and reflection on the part of the teacher. This necessitates a philosophical change of direction, which means that instead of using the language of the status quo (transmission, imposition, exposition, and silence), teachers need to use the language of reflection, possibility, and critique (change, hypothetical, creativity, social, and active) (Dewey, 1938; Evans, 2001; and Oldendorf, 1989). Giroux (1981) emphatically reminds us that "critical reasoning becomes an empty exercise if students do not learn how to both reflect on, as well as transform, the nature and meaning of their own lived-worlds" (p. 124).

## Social Progress

If education is to be a reflection of life, I believe social studies teachers must prepare their students to be able to solve those issues that students will face in their life experiences. In this regard, social studies educators must seriously consider the value of developing and implementing an issues-centered class-room environment. Issues-Centered Social Studies Education is an approach to teaching history, government, geography, economics and other social studies courses through a focus on persistent social problems. It focuses on problematic questions that require thoughtful consideration, deliberation, and resolution, at least provisionally, in order to construct a path to social progress. Problematic questions may address problems of the past, present, or future; they may involve disagreement over facts, definitions, values, and beliefs; they may arise in the study of any of the social studies disciplines, or other aspects of human behavior. Humans are inexorably tied to their world and thinking is the mental process that binds them together.[1]

In conclusion, I believe that the following words and sentiments of John Dewey (1936) still ring true today, in the 21st century: "Today, freedom of teaching and learning on the part of instructors and students is imperatively necessary for that kind of intelligent citizenship that is genuinely free to take part in the social reconstruction without which democracy will die" (pp. 165–166).

## Note

1   This, of course, does not mean that the issues-centered approach is the end to all social studies education. A dogmatic perspective would be unbefitting an open-minded, reflective educator.

## References

Barr, Robert, D., Barth, James. L., and Shermis, Samuel S. (1977). *Defining the Social Studies* (Vol. 51). Arlington, VA: National Council for the Social Studies.

Beane, James A., and Apple, Michael W. (1995). "The Case for Democratic Schools". In Michael Apple and James A. Beane, eds., *Democratic Schools* (pp. 1–25). Alexandria, VA: Association for Supervision and Curriculum Development.

Dewey, John. (1916). *Democracy and Education.* New York, NY: The Macmillan Company.

Dewey, John. (1933). *How We Think.* Lexington, MA: Heath and Company.

Dewey, John. (1936). "The Social Significance of Academic Freedom," 2(6) *The Social Frontier*, pp. 165–166.

Dewey, John. (1938). *Experience and Education.* New York, NY: Macmillan.

Engle, Shirley H. (1947). "Factors in the Teaching of our Persistent Modern Problems," 11(4) *Social Education*, pp. 167–169.

Engle, Shirley H. (1982). "Alan Griffin, 1907–1964." 17(3) *Journal of Thought*, pp. 45–54.

Engle, Shirley H., and Ochoa, Anna S. (1988). *Education for Democratic Citizenship: Decision Making in the Social Studies.* New York, NY: Teachers College Press.

Evans, Ronald W. (2001). "Thoughts on Redirecting a Runaway Train: A Critique of the Standards Movement," 29(2) *Theory and Research in Social Education*, pp. 330–339.

Friere, P. (1970). *Pedagogy of the Oppressed.* New York: Continuum.

Giroux, Henry A. (1981). *Ideology, Culture, and the Process of Schooling.* Philadelphia, PA: Temple University Press.

Giroux, Henry A. (1988). *Teachers as Intellectuals: Toward a Critical Pedagogy of Learning.* Granby, MA: Bergin & Garvey.

Gould, J. (ed.). (2003). *Guardian of Democracy: The Civic Mission of Schools.* Philadelphia, PA: Leonore Anenberg Institute for Civics of the Annenberg Public Policy Center.

Griffin, Alan F. (1942). *A Philosophical Approach to the Subject-Matter Preparation of Teachers of History.* Ph. D., The Ohio State University.

Hunt, Maurice, and Metcalf, Lawrence E. (1968). *Teaching High School Social Studies* (2nd edn.). New York, NY: Harper & Row Publishers.

Leming, James S. (1989). "The Two Cultures of Social Studies Education," 53(6) *Social Education*, pp. 404–408.

Nelson, James L., and Stanley, William B. (1985). "Academic Freedom: 50 Years Standing Still," 49(8) *Social Education*, pp. 662–664, 666.

Oldendorf, Saundra B. (1989). "Vocabularies, Knowledge and Social Action in Citizenship Education: The Highlander Example," 17(2) *Theory and Research in Social Education*, pp. 107–120.

Previte, Mark A. (2002). "Seeing the Whole Board: An Exercise in Presidential Decision Making." 38(1) *OCSS Review*, pp. 25–30.

VanSickle, Ronald L. (1990). "The Personal Relevance of the Social Studies," 54(1) *Social Education*, pp. 23–27, 59.

# 11

# FROM CONTROVERSY TO DECISION-MAKING

## The Heart of Social Issues Instruction

*William B. Russell III*

ASSOCIATE PROFESSOR, SOCIAL SCIENCE EDUCATION,
UNIVERSITY OF CENTRAL FLORIDA

## My Background

I was born in Ohio, and I moved to Florida when I was a young child. When I was in 5th grade, I got a new Nike hat—the very kind that just about every kid in the school wanted. I wanted to wear that hat all day, every day. Every time I was told to remove my cap, it was like pulling out my heart. One particular day, I was sitting on the floor in a resource room at my elementary school wearing my hat when Mr. Penn, the P.E. teacher, came in and snatched it off my head as he walked by, yelling at me, "No hats in the building." I did not complain to Mr. Penn, because I knew the rule. However, I took note that Mr. Penn said nothing to a girl named Rosa who was also wearing a hat. I went home and told my mother what happened and asked, "How is this fair?" My mother said life is not always fair and encouraged me to ask for an explanation. The next day I wore my hat to school, and, once again, Mr. Penn snatched it off my head but said nothing to Rosa for wearing a hat. I politely asked why Rosalind was allowed to wear her hat in the building and I was not. Mr. Penn responded by saying, "A gentlemen does not wear a hat in the building, because it is not proper etiquette." He also said, "A girl can wear a hat in the building because it is part of her outfit." I told Mr. Penn that my hat was part of my outfit. He said, "Boys don't have outfits," and dismissed me from his presence.

Then, when I was in sixth grade, I was sent to the principal's office for whistling. My teacher, Mrs. Beans, explained to the principal that I was whistling throughout the class and would not stop after she repeatedly asked me to do so. I told the principal that I did not whistle. Mrs. Beans asserted that I was lying and that she saw and heard me with her own eyes and ears. I told her and the principal that Mrs. Bean was wrong and that she was lying, because there was no way she saw and/or heard me whistle, because I cannot whistle. Actually, at no point in my life have I been able to whistle. The principal suspended me. My mother arrived and expressed her disappointment and substantiated the fact that I cannot whistle. I enjoyed my long weekend by playing video games, skateboarding, and surfing.

For the record, I was not always innocent. Indeed, I was involved in my fair share of escapades. The point is, I am not trying to paint myself as a saint. However, these examples, although they may sound trivial to some, were shattering to me as a young person. The impact of these events, along with numerous others, heightened my awareness of the various issues people face. I was angry, baffled, nervous, and a little fearful from those experiences.

Tellingly, I actually, in some odd way, attribute my interest in education and social issues in part to the numerous negative experiences I had as I made my way through school. I guess, my desire is to eliminate and eradicate these types of circumstances for future generations. Many teachers often forget what it is like to be a kid/teenager. We forget what they find important, the issues they face (whether local or global), and how hard being a kid/teenager can be for elementary, middle, and high school students.

I attended and graduated from St. Augustine High School and during the latter part of high school (and, actually, throughout college) my best friend was an African American. My school did not have big race issues per se, but there really had not been a friendship of this caliber in the school (at least in the four years I attended). Wallace and I got a lot of flack from various social groups for being friends. Nothing major, really; it was more like a teen movie in which the nerds, the jocks, the preps, etc., were unsure how to handle our friendship. Essentially, we made waves in the social balance of high school and college. However, it struck us as strange that our friendship was an issue then, and it is something that still perplexes us to this day.

I attended college to be a social studies teacher, and after four years I graduated from the University of North Florida with a degree in Social Science Education. In school I took a class called "Historical Jesus." I consider this class to be one of the most eye-opening courses of my entire education. The course examined Jesus Christ as a man, not the Son of God. For those of the Christian faith this course was extremely difficult to wrap one's mind around, but it forced me to truly open my eyes and "see the other side." This course cemented by interest in social issues, in that it provided me with the opportunity to see and understand perspective.

While teaching high school at First Coast Technical High School in St. Augustine, Florida, I started working on a Master's degree in Instructional/Educational Leadership at the University of North Florida. After finishing my Master's degree, I moved to Tallahassee, and started working on my Ph.D., in Social Science Education, at Florida State University. I am now an Associate Professor of Social Science Education at the University of Central Florida.

Throughout my life and studies, I was always interested in touchy subjects. Any topic that was controversial and taboo sparked my interest. However, once I began reading social studies education literature in college, I realized my interest was related to "teaching social/controversial issues." My true interest was in the process as much, if not more, than the topic itself. I started to explore the seminal works on Engle (1960), Massialas and Cox (1966), Oliver and Shaver (1966), and Hunt and Metcalf (1968), and the topics related to social issues curriculum such as "decision-making," "inquiry," and "issue-centered learning." As I continued to develop, other works by Rath, Harmon, and Simon (1966), Engle and Ochoa (1988), Evans and Saxe (1996), Kohlberg (1966), and many others had an impact on my personal pedagogical creed as well.

## My Works

Over the years I have published a number of works (books, chapters, and articles) that relate to teaching and learning about social issues. The two books are entitled *Teaching Social Issues with Film* (Information Age Publishing, 2009) and *Reel Character Education* (with Stewart Waters, Information Age Publishing, 2010); they combine teaching social issues and related topics with the teaching of film. *Essentials of Elementary Social Studies* and *Essentials of Middle and Secondary Social Studies* (with S. Waters and T. Turner, 2013) are methods textbooks which have a central focuses on decision-making. I have also published peer-reviewed articles related to teaching and studying social issues. These articles have appeared in *Social Education, The Social Studies, The Clearing House, The Journal of Social Studies Research, Action in Teacher Education, The History Teacher,* etc. Additionally, I have authored book chapters, and I have presented at an array of professional conferences on topics related to teaching and study social issues.

## My Pedagogical Creed for Teaching and Learning Social Issues

I believe that there are five pedagogical requirements/conditions for teaching and learning social issues. These five requirements/conditions are:

1) Understanding What Constitutes a Social Issue
2) Understanding the Role of the Teacher
3) Understanding the Role of the Student
4) Understanding the Environment
5) Understanding the Purpose.

### Understanding what Constitutes a Social Issue

I believe a social issue is any topic that relates to people and their beliefs within society. Social issues are topics related to politics, religion, character, values, morals, and beliefs. Social issues are controversial in nature; indeed they are often synonymous with controversy. They are everywhere in society, and are abundant within the social studies curriculum. "They involve multiple points of view, with ideas and insights, from many fields of study, including humanities as well as the social sciences" (Ochoa-Becker, 1996).

This belief is based on the melding of concepts or lines of thinking. It blends the traditional political "hot button" topics (such as abortion or the death penalty) with character, morals, and values teaching; these latter aspects are included in my definition of social issues, because I think nothing is more of an issue in society than one's personal belief, attitude, value, and/or moral code. Additionally, how an individual's beliefs and actions align with the social climate and what is considered to be socially acceptable is what forms the foundation of a social issue.

## Understanding the Role of the Teacher

I believe that a teacher should not be judgmental when teaching and learning social issues. A teacher should focus on the process that social issues invite and not on the outcome. A teacher should not attempt to indoctrinate students or sway their personal beliefs to align with his/her own regarding an issue. A teacher should welcome controversial topics into the classroom. A teacher should foster an environment that allows for thoughtful deliberation. Social issues and topics that are controversial

> must be studied in the classroom without the assumption that they are settled in advance or there is only one right answer in matters of dispute. The social studies teacher must approach such issues in a spirit of critical inquiry, exposing the students to a variety of ideas, even if they are different from their own.
>
> *NCSS, 2007*

This belief was formulated from firsthand experience as a secondary student and teacher, and sprinkled with theory for support. When I was student, I had teachers that attempted to indoctrinate me and my classmates. I remember feeling, as many of my peers did, that I could not form or share my own opinions without fear of persecution. I carried this line of thinking into my own classroom when I started teaching. I attempted to be cognizant of my role in educating young minds.

## Understanding the Classroom Environment

I believe that, for social issues to be meaningful and powerful, then, before any quality instruction can take place, the classroom environment must be welcoming, encouraging, safe, managed, and controlled. A well-managed and controlled classroom, free from disciplinary, disruptive, and/or disrespectful problems, is the only truly effective environment for social issues. The importance of this is often underrated and forgotten, and this is the downfall of many social issue lessons.

As with the previous requirement/condition, this belief was spawned from experience more than anything else. I remember counseling and consoling peer teachers who had attempted to implement a social issues curriculum but had no classroom management skills. The utter failures my peer teachers encountered were mainly due to their lack of classroom control. Therefore, I encourage teachers to control their classroom, *prior* to implementing social issues curriculum. I do not mean to imply that there must be regimented, drone-like control.

## Understanding the Role of the Student/s

I believe students need to be taught how to think about social issues, and their role in a social issues activity. Not WHAT to think, but, HOW! The first time you teach a social issue related lesson, the students need to be taught the process and what is expected. The students need to motivated and encouraged by the teacher to be open minded. The students need to focus on the thinking and decision-making process of the lesson, formulate ideas and opinions, and understand the need to respect others' beliefs and viewpoints—to learn to think and learn to accept varying perspectives. When students play an active role in the learning process, they are more likely to retain content information and make learning meaningful (Driscoll, 2009). Social issues curricula allow

> students [to] investigate, [and] probe their fellow learners as well as the teacher, and [they] are encouraged in the rigorous study of social issues, which involves intellectual analysis, decision making, and social action.
>
> *Engle and Ochoa, 1988, p.13*

This belief was mostly developed through experience. However, at its core, it aligns with basic concepts of communication, educational psychology, and assessment. A teacher must effectively communicate his/her expectations to students. In addition, training students in the process, and modeling the process, is much more impactful than not doing so. Telling (and, in some cases, yelling) is not teaching.

## Understanding the Purpose

I believe the purpose of teaching social issues is to allow students the opportunity to become effective decision-makers. "Decision-making is the heart of social studies" (Engle, 1960). Furthermore, it is the heart of teaching and learning social

issues. Social issues curricula encourage discussion, analysis, synthesis, and evaluation; all are necessary decision-making skills. The National Council for the Social
Studies explains that the study of social issues and controversial topics can help
develop the following skills and attitudes:

1.   The ability to study relevant social problems of the past or present and make
     informed decisions or conclusions;
2.   The ability to use critical reasoning and evidence-based evaluation in the
     study and analysis of significant issues and ideas; this includes development of
     skills of critical analysis and evaluation in considering ideas, opinions, infor-
     mation, and sources of information;
3.   The recognition that differing viewpoints are valuable and normal as a part of
     social discourse;
4.   The recognition that reasonable compromise is often an important part of the
     democratic decision-making process.

*NCSS, 2007*

The teaching and learning of social issues is an open ended process. The social
issues curriculum

> does not measure success by the degree to which students can regurgi-
> tate the so-called facts presented in textbooks and teacher lectures. Rather
> it measures success by the degree to which student performance reflects
> an intellectual capacity to address public issues. Rather than stressing the
> recall of information, the issue-centered curriculum encourages students to
> actively participate in the improvement of society.
>
> *Ochoa-Becker, 1996*

This belief was clearly influenced by Shirley Engle. Decision-making is key,
and when a student is equipped and armed with decision-making skills, then
learning, knowledge, citizenship, and their role in society are clearer and more
important.

## Conclusion

When the five pedagogical requirements/conditions are adhered to, the teaching and learning of social issues curricula will be more powerful and meaningful. Teaching and learning social issues transcends content area and grade level,
because it focuses on instilling an intrinsic desire to learn. Teaching social issues is
focused on the process in which one builds and constructs knowledge and skills.
Social issues curricula should be taught without a focus on an end product or a
correct answer. Rather, teaching social issues is about engaging students with the
decision-making process to practice developing higher-order thinking skills in

analyzing information for the purpose of formulating rational and justifiable solutions to the problems at hand.

With social issues curricula, teachers need to play a supportive role and realize that the focus is on the students and the decision-making process. Teachers should also remind students that there are often multiple solutions to problems, and justification of the decision made is the key to helping others understand perspective.

Teachers should maintain a positive environment that fosters learning. They, along with students, should keep in mind the purpose of teaching and learning social issues and the array of benefits that the social issues curriculum provides.

## References

Driscoll, M.P. (2009). *Psychology of Learning for Instruction* (4th edn.). Boston, MA: Pearson.

Engle, S.H. (1960). "Decision-Making: The Heart of Social Studies Instruction," 27(4) *Social Education*, pp. 301–304.

Engle, S.H., and Ochoa, A.S. (1988). *Education for Democratic Citizenship: Decision-Making in the Social Studies*. New York, NY: Teachers College Press.

Evans, R.W., and Saxe, D.W. (1996). *Handbook on Teaching Social Issues*. Washington, D.C.: The National Council for the Social Studies.

Hunt, M.P., and Metcalf, L.E. (1968). *Teaching High School Social Studies: Problems in Reflective Thinking and Social Understanding.* (2nd edn.). New York, NY: Harper and Row.

Kohlberg, L. (1966). "Moral Education in the School," 74(1) *School Review*, pp. 1–30.

Massialas, B., and Cox, C. (1966). *Inquiry in the Social Studies*. New York, NY: McGraw-Hill.

National Council for the Social Studies. (2007). *Academic Freedom and the Social Studies Teacher*. Retrieved online at http://www.socialstudies.org/positions/freedom/

Ochoa-Becker, A. (1996). "Definition and Rationale: Introduction." In R. Evans and D.W. Saxe, eds., *Handbook on Teaching Social Issues* (p. 1). Washington, D.C.: National Council for the Social Studies.

Oliver, D., and Shaver, J.P. (1966). *Teaching Public Issues in High School*. Boston, MA: Houghton Mifflin.

Raths, L., Harmin, M., and, Simon, S. (1966). *Values and Teaching: Working with Values in the Classroom*. Columbus, OH: Charles E. Merrill.

Russell, W. (2009). *Teaching Social Issues with Film*. Charlotte, NC: Information Age Publishing.

Russell, W., and Waters, S. (2010). *Reel Character Education: A Cinematic Approach to Character Development*. Charlotte, NC: Information Age Publishing.

Russell, W., Waters, S., and Turner, T. (2013). *Essentials of Elementary Social Studies*. New York, NY: Routledge.

Russell, W., Waters, S., and Turner, T. (2013). *Essentials of Middle and Secondary Social Studies*. New York, NY: Routledge.

**PART III**
# Critical Studies

# 12

# "PREPARE TO BE ON CENTER STAGE"

## A Critical, Issues-Centered Approach to Teaching for Social Understanding

*Ronald W. Evans*

PROFESSOR, SCHOOL OF TEACHER EDUCATION, SAN DIEGO STATE UNIVERSITY

Social studies teaching and learning tends to be dominated by teacher talk, textbook, drill, and memorization. Advocates of meaningful learning in social studies face resistance from institutional mandates, pressure for coverage over depth, pressure to stick to the textbook, and mandates for students to perform well on standardized measures of their learning. Given the dilemmas of the field and the profound barriers to widespread realization of engaging and meaningful social studies instruction in schools, what might lead a person to choose to become a social studies scholar?

In my own case, it was naïveté combined with the drive for success. My career is a story of youthful idealism tempered by the realities of life in a mass, bureaucratized, capitalist society in which schools are dominated by a process of cultural transmission, a place focused on "drilling children in cultural orientations" in which subject matter becomes "the instrument for instilling them" (Henry, 1963, p. 283). My life as a social studies scholar developed out of a number of influences both within and outside formal education. Multiple influences as a child instilled in me an interest in social studies and a predisposition to focus on social issues. Family, church, school, and the culture of the 1950s and 1960s were all important influences on my thinking and orientation to teaching. I grew up in the south, in Georgia, Florida, Alabama, and Oklahoma. I witnessed the contradictions of Jim Crow segregation first hand, and benefited from the advantages of being white and middle class.

My father, raised in the north and a social liberal, was broadly interested in issues of the day and spent many hours reading the newspaper, watching news programming on TV, and engaging our family in dinner table conversations about important issues and topics. He had grown up in a large family in which discussion and argument frequently focused on social issues and competing ideas of the 1920s and 1930s. In part, this came from the social gospel of the Methodist church and from my grandfather, who spent a few years as a Methodist minister. I, too, was raised in the Methodist church and got a strong dose of its social gospel and a missionary zeal to save the world.

Gradually, I developed an interest in history, biography, and current events. I remember enjoying the *Weekly Reader, Junior Scholastic, Current Biography*, TV programming such as "Biography," historical documentaries, war movies, and westerns, and devouring books in the "Biography," "Landmark," and "We Were There" series during the upper elementary grades.

I never really liked school all that much, and hated it at times. Nonetheless, a few teachers spiked my interest in social studies and contributed to my development. Mr. John Amick was an excellent sixth grade teacher who brought in biographies, important social studies topics, and regular discussions of current events and social issues. By my high school years in the late 1960s, the national consensus was exploding—civil rights, the Vietnam War, the sexual revolution. We were innocents in the throes of the 1960s "revolutions."

During my early years in college at the University of Oklahoma and at Oklahoma State University, I protested the war, listened to Bob Dylan, and experimented with the things for which my generation is infamous. I remember seeing books like the Leinwand series, *Problems in American Life* (1968–1969), Postman and Weingartner's *Teaching as a Subversive Activity* (1968), and Illich's *DeSchooling Society* (1971). I chose not to apply for a student deferment, got a high number in the draft lottery, and slacked my way through school.

During my freshman year at the University of Oklahoma, I took a U.S. History survey course, a large lecture section combined with once-a-week discussion. It was the first time I'd had a history class in which alternative ideas and interpretations were presented and discussed. The professor was a leftist historian and my graduate assistant instructor disagreed with many of his interpretations. The dissonance created depth and a new understanding that the background to the explosive issues of the 1960s was contested, just as then-current issues were, and I found that interesting. I ended up majoring in history.

After college, I became a VISTA volunteer because of my deep concern over social injustice, and was assigned to a community re-development project in Kansas City, Missouri, led by former Black Panthers. It was an eye-opening experience. We learned that freeways were officially "National Defense Highways," with many exit ramps but very few on-ramps, so that the militia could occupy the neighborhood on a moment's notice. Large swathes of housing in the area had been removed as part of a freeway development plan that was later halted by community pressure. Housing in the area was in poor condition, and there was a general feeling of hopelessness.

That experience taught me that the problems and issues of our society were deeply entrenched. I was quite naïve about social realities and the impediments to change. I had been a history major, but hadn't learned much about the historical rootedness of social institutions and behaviors. My VISTA experience taught me how difficult and profoundly ingrained the problems of poverty were, that there was a human face behind every statistic, that issues of social class were intractable, and that I had to find a point of leverage, an institutional niche, where I could translate my idealism into action. Why not go through schools? I knew I could do a better job than most of my social studies teachers had.

Resistant at first, because I didn't really like the idea of becoming an authority figure, I fell into teaching. Back to school I went to earn a teaching certificate and to study social studies methods under Daniel Selakovich at Oklahoma State. He introduced me to the inquiry methods of the new and newer social studies, and shared with us many innovative teaching materials. Though I struggled, as a beginning teacher, with those aspects of the job that beginners often find difficult, I learned that issues and problems of the past and present struck a nerve with students, just as they had with me, and helped make history and the social sciences come alive. Many of our class discussions and debates were highly energized. Though I failed in many ways that first year, my failures only increased my determination to succeed.

Following several months of drifting, and a lengthy hitchhiking trip to the east coast, I returned to Oklahoma State University to work toward a master's degree in Curriculum and Instruction and was fortunate to be offered a teaching assistantship. It was a rich and rewarding growth experience. I put long hours and a great deal of thought into planning for my discussion sections of "Schools and American Society." Students responded very positively. Following that, I taught for three years in culturally diverse urban middle and high schools in Portland, Oregon. My commitment to a critical, issues-oriented approach gradually evolved through the crucible of first-hand experience in a social studies classroom.

Graduate school at Oklahoma State, and later at Stanford, confirmed my critical, issues-centered orientation and assisted in my growth as a teacher/scholar. Additional inspiration stemmed from a fundamental problem I had personally experienced in school, which was the general failure of my teachers to make history interesting; to relate or connect it to present day realities. Much of what I experienced was conditioned by the standard grammar of schooling, a rather lifeless and traditional approach, despite the fact that the society outside the school seemed to be exploding.

There were specific issues that inspired my interest, including racial injustice and the civil rights movement, social class, the war in Vietnam, and the counterculture. The fundamental divisions in our society and our world, between rich and poor, black and white, oppressor and oppressed, created specific issues that combined with my early experiences as a teacher and seemed to prove the resonance and power of social issues with students. As Harold Rugg (1941) once wrote, "To keep issues out of the school . . . is to keep thought out of it; it is to keep life out of it" (pp. xv–xvi).

In the context of a troubled society, one that is classist, racist, and sexist, I came to believe that attention to social issues in schools is an imperative. Of course, my understanding of reflective teaching and the issues-centered approach was rooted in the works of many other scholars who were seminal thinkers in the social studies field, including Shirley Engle and Anna Ochoa, Donald Oliver and James Shaver, Fred Newmann, and others. As a young scholar advocating an issues-centered approach, many of these icons of social studies became informal mentors and friends, and strongly influenced my thinking.[1]

## Pedagogic Creed

My pedagogic creed is essentially built around my critical, issues-centered approach. It is, I believe, a workable "progressive" approach to teaching that I have evolved over the years. I agree with John Dewey's (1897) statement that "Education is the fundamental lever of social progress and reform" (p. 437). This is a basic truism. But, I am also aware, drawing on much of the work from a critical perspective, that schools do not always contribute to social progress, and, indeed, often stand in its way, serving to obstruct change and perpetuate or reproduce social inequalities. This fact complicates any statement of a pedagogic creed.

In terms of teaching methodology and approach, I believe that we must focus much of our attention on the needs and interests of the child. For too long, and in far too many classrooms, the focus has been on the subject, the textbook, or the teacher, and becomes an imposition of materials, of fragmented facts, topics, and concepts, accompanied by underlying beliefs and assumptions. Students are often asked to memorize these materials and recite them in class and on tests; to accept with little or no questioning. In contrast, using whatever creativity he or she possesses, the teacher's role is to design and implement a process by which students will inquire into the topic or subject matter, into problems and questions posed by students and teacher, in an interactive, reflective, and stimulating process, and in as much depth as is reasonably possible given the constraints of schooling (schedules, curriculum guides, standards, testing, etc.).

The latter is best conceived as a shared process that involves a sort of dance among teacher and students in which the teacher and students construct a shared experience of inquiry and investigation, a search for truth, in which evidence, alternative choices, potential consequences, and consideration of values are all involved. At its best, this is an iterative, open-ended, and inherently interdisciplinary and extra-disciplinary process in which schools at all levels serve as a church of reason (Pirsig, 1974). It is a process in which students are asked to make decisions, to grapple with the most difficult questions raised in life and in each subject area, and to develop their own perspectives.

Unfortunately, this kind of open-ended investigation, and the in-depth deliberation and search for truth and knowledge that it implies, is often in tension with a culture and context that uses schools as a tool for imposition of certain values, knowledge, and skills; that sorts students into multiple pipelines for developing workers/citizens with an emphasis on current and projected demands for labor; and that seems bent, in the current era of business domination, on schooling for development of human capital. Though the context of corporate domination has long been a strong presence in schools, in recent years, especially since the late 1970s and early 1980s, it has moved to center stage.

## *On Process: The Nature of Method*

I believe that teachers should foster critical inquiry, interaction for deliberation, and depth over coverage. Pedagogy is a process. The question before us is what processes shall we prioritize and enact in our classrooms. The forms of pedagogy I believe we should strive to implement are aimed at deep reflection, a process of critical questioning, and counter-socialization. Pedagogy should be interactive and inquiry-oriented, employing a variety of formats. Students and teachers should pose problems, make decisions, develop projects, and make tentative judgments on a host of topics and subjects that are in the curriculum, and some that are not (LGBT, social class, wealth and power). Teachers should respect childhood, the child's needs and interests, and use students' interests as a hook, linking student interests to topics, problems, and issues in the curriculum through use of an introductory grabber and continuous probing of issues and questions. Many, if not most, of the most important questions have no "right" answer. In every lesson and unit of study, students need to be engaged in an interactive process that capitalizes on student interests and connects the topic of study to important and persistent issues and dilemmas. This should include a judicious mix of child and adult issues, with a multitude of personal, public, and private components.

I believe that open forum discussion, employing a variety of large and small group formats, should be a mainstay of the social studies classroom. Students should arrive at our doorstep with the expectation that they will be asked to read, write, interpret, and think about important questions, and to communicate in a variety of modes, but especially, and most importantly, in face-to-face discussions with other students and their teacher. In order for discussions to work effectively, students need something meaningful to discuss, and a proper forum that will facilitate in-depth and meaningful reflection. They should be asked to make decisions on important questions and issues related to and drawn from the subject matter under study. In social studies classrooms in particular, they should examine richly detailed primary source material, conflicting secondary interpretations, essays, research, and position papers, and be asked to interrogate sources and develop their own interpretations and tentative conclusions. I believe that a variety of other formats, methods, and activities will also prove helpful to the thoughtful and creative teacher in constructing a classroom experience that prizes diverse and conflicting viewpoints.

I believe that the most meaningful discussions will occur only when students feel that they have an open and supportive classroom climate, one in which alternative perspectives are prized, in which every voice is valued. This is a classroom in which honest and open sharing can occur, in which students' knowledge and views are highly prized (Engle and Ochoa, 1988).

I believe that students should be put on center stage in a manner that will motivate them to study and prepare to play a leadership role. This can be accomplished via a variety of formats, including panel discussions, Socratic seminars, mock trials, simulations, town meetings and councils, and other interactive formats (Passe and Evans, 2007; Garland, 1933).

## On Content: The Subject Matter of the School

I believe that the curriculum should build from the disciplines and go beyond to transcendent issues and values. Though much of school content is defined by university-based disciplines, those disciplines themselves are constantly shifting and changing by the winds of educational politics, by fashion, and by shifts in our society and the world. Therefore, I believe that it is helpful to go beyond the disciplines in schools. Too often, schooling is limited by what educational psychologist William G. Spady (2007) has called "educentrism," by curricular "boxes" and other structures that often serve to limit inquiry rather than fuel it. For example, in the field of social studies, over the past 30 years we have moved increasingly toward disciplinary boxes, most often rooted in history and a few other social sciences, and away from interdisciplinary, critical, and issues-centered work. The boundaries between disciplines are socially constructed, and largely fictional. Too often they are reified in school subjects and courses, bordered by impenetrable walls, focusing study on topics in the textbook and curricular standards, and on content as fodder for memorization or material to cover, thus limiting deep inquiry, reflection, and exploration across or beyond the disciplines.

On the other hand, the disciplines provide powerful lenses for critical inquiry, along with concepts and richly detailed materials for students to explore. Judicious use of inquiry activities exploring topics and materials from the disciplines can help students gain an understanding of the key ideas and/or the fundamental structure underlying social realities (Bruner, 1960; Evans, 2011a). Experimentation, research, and curriculum development during the era of the new social studies, as well as in more recent years, illustrate that students can learn exciting, significant, and thought-provoking concepts from discipline-based inquiry in history and the social sciences; they can learn to think like a historian or anthropologist; and they can grow depth of skill in analysis and interpretation. However, the synthesis required for thoughtful citizenship necessitates going beyond the disciplines and applying those skills, concepts, and knowledge to new situations that demand creative ways of thinking and that insist on making decisions or choices among alternatives.

I believe that persistent societal issues and questions should serve as themes around which student work can revolve, as a framework for the curriculum, linking study of school subjects and topics to real world issues and problems. Persistent issues and questions can spiral through the curriculum to great advantage. Though subjects organized by university-based disciplines as they appear in schools are a social construction, they have and will likely continue to frame, shape, and dominate the way we define subject matter in schools. Changing this, going beyond the disciplines to a more holistic approach to learning, is possible, and occurs with regularity in some classrooms and in some experimental schools (i.e., witness problem-based learning at High Tech High in San Diego). However, a wholesale change to an interdisciplinary and extra-disciplinary approach is unlikely to happen on any large-scale basis in the near future. A workable alternative, recommended by most advocates of issues-centered social studies during the past century, involves the infusion of reflective, issues-centered approaches in a discipline-based curriculum.

## On a Framework for the Curriculum

I believe that thoughtful planning is essential for a strong curriculum, but that planning must be balanced with openness and flexibility. On the one hand, frameworks too often constrain learning, serving as a curricular "box." On the other hand, some framework or curricular sequence is necessary as an organizational tool, whether chronological, topical, or thematic. I believe that a topical or thematic sequence is most appropriate because it allows for depth and coverage. However, it needs to be held together by a larger framework that makes sense. Moreover, if the framework is too closely linked to the disciplines, it can lose its connection to children and citizens. Therefore, I believe that it is helpful for teachers and others to develop reflective, issues-centered frameworks that can be used to facilitate the relation of disciplinary content to broad and persistent societal issues. In teaching history, for example, the question of governmental power is a persistent theme. An issues-centered framework can assist teachers in highlighting key aspects of the theme, as well as relevant questions. Borrowing an example from the Public Issues Series pamphlet *American Revolution*, key questions could include:

> What is a proper government and where does its power originate? When should governmental power be challenged? In what ways should people—as groups or individuals—be able to express themselves to constituted authority? Is violence ever the "right" course? . . . Should the colonists have protested British actions with violent demonstrations? Was violence a major or effective part of the protests?
>
> *Giese and Glade, 1988, pp. 3–4*

Some questions would be specific to the time period and historical episode under study, while others would be important to consider in other times and in our nation today. A thoughtful teacher and group of students would explore discipline-based questions, wearing the historian's hat, and learning to think like a historian. However, they would also be asked to think like a citizen, exploring persistent issues, analogous cases and historical episodes, and current manifestations of key issues and questions.

A second example, focused on the proper role of government, from another Public Issues Series pamphlet, *The New Deal*, may prove helpful. The authors pose three central questions in the introduction to the unit, questions that were raised during the New Deal era, and that persist and "remain with us today." They include:

> How responsible should the government be for the economic well-being of citizens? To what extent should this responsibility outweigh traditional ideas of property rights? What are the alternatives to the market system as a means of determining prices and wages? What advantages and disadvantages arise from centralized economic planning? How can we assure all Americans a fair share in the fruits of the economic system?
>
> *Quoted in Singleton, 1990, p. 4*

Unfortunately, many such questions are seldom, if ever, asked in discipline-based approaches to the teaching of history and the social sciences, even though they are central persistent issues of American life, and of life on the planet.

I believe that an issues-centered framework can serve as a useful overlay and source of deeper, persistent systemic issues that should be explored as the central recurring focus in social studies courses, regardless of the specific subject area. An issues-centered framework can be used alongside a disciplinary one, and can help a teacher focus on important issues that may otherwise be lost in a rush to cover content. A thoughtful course of study should include episodes of discipline-based inquiry focused on important concepts from the disciplines and related fields of study, involving a wide range of interactive learning formats and activities, accompanied by richly detailed source materials. A thoughtful course of study should also include critical inquiry on selected topics, studied in depth, and focused on persistent issues relating to social justice, racial and gender inequality, and the struggles of the oppressed for freedom and full share participation in life. It should include an understanding of power relations, of the narrative of history, and a wide range of alternative and critical views. It should also include global study in world history and geography strongly linked to issues of development, progress, nationalism, conflict, and sustainability.

Thankfully, several scholars in social studies have developed thoughtful frameworks that can be very helpful to teachers and scholars seeking guidance in constructing both an inquiry-oriented approach to disciplinary knowledge, and an issues-centered framework that can help teachers make linkages to persistent issues. To cite one example, in the 1950s, Maurice Hunt and Lawrence Metcalf developed what they described as "Problematic Areas of Culture" and discussed dilemmas and questions related to each. They focused, in particular, on "closed areas" of culture and proposed that "problems, units, and blocks of work" should focus on these areas without "major disruption of present curriculum patterns," arguing that teachers could apply their "problem-centered approach" by conceiving of social studies more broadly, by focusing on key persistent issues, and by including data and materials from sociology, anthropology, and other disciplines and areas of study. Their "problematic areas" included: power and the law; economics; nationalism, patriotism, and foreign affairs; social class; religion and morality; race and minority group relations; and, sex, courtship, and marriage. (Hunt and Metcalf, 1968; Evans and Brodkey, 2007). Donald Oliver and James Shaver (1966) proposed several "general problem areas" including racial and ethnic conflict; religious and ideological conflict; security of the individual; conflict among economic groups; health, education, and welfare; and security of the nation. Other scholars have developed similar alternative frameworks or conceptualizations that may prove helpful to the creative teacher (Evans and Brodkey, 2007).

## On Developing a Rationale

I believe that every teacher should be asked, even required, to develop his or her own pedagogic creed and rationale for teaching, and strive to enact that creed in classroom practice. This should be part of the professional growth and tenure process for teachers in our schools, much as it is for university professors. Unfortunately, many teachers fail to do this, falling into a rationale and practice by mere happenstance, by the influence of a particular mentor, or by distant memories of their own school experience. The great progressive educator Harold O. Rugg (1923) once wrote that the rationale behind most teachers' work was all but non-existent, that courses focused on "reading (in textbooks) and answering teachers' questions about the reading" (p. 22), stressing mere acquisition of information. He went on:

> The school is following the easiest way, the path of least resistance . . . What theories is this practice based upon? No theories at all, I fear. The present practice wasn't born—it just grew. The practice implicitly assumes, however, that clear thinking and right conduct will issue from the mere acquiring of information.
>
> *Rugg, 1923a, pp. 22–24*

While one might hope that during the intervening century since Rugg drafted this statement we would have made great progress in the development of teacher rationales and thoughtful implementations, recent evidence on classroom practices suggests that we have not.

In his statement of rationale, Rugg (1923b) argued that social studies should prepare students to participate in life activities and equip them to be constructively critical of contemporary society. He posited that development of a curriculum for a "troubled society" required confronting young people with "the most critical problems of that society" (Rugg, 1923b pp. 261–262). He held that social studies subjects in schools existed in the context of a "troubled society," and that, by becoming aware of the "insistent and permanent" problems, students would develop a commitment to active citizenship aimed at social improvement (Rugg, 1923b, pp. 261–262). Thus, in selecting episodes, topics, and issues for inclusion in the curriculum, social value would be the litmus test, and social improvement would be the teleological goal. Rugg's approach, similar to other more recent issues-centered theorists, emphasized the importance of active learning and student participation, meaning that rather than just a reading curriculum, the course would involve a stream of activities and a wide range of learning and discussion formats, including student research in books, magazines, and newspapers, discussion through open forum and debate, engagement with primary sources, and first-hand experiences outside school. Topics would be studied in depth and arranged in "thought provoking form" in which the student would not only gather and "absorb facts," but would be provided with constant practice in "making decisions with facts" (Rugg, 1929, p. 5). The teacher and textual materials would play a key role in developing student interest, and focusing student attention on one topic and one particular task at a time.

More recent issues-centered theorists have also developed rationales, sometimes with a slightly different twist, but with similar underlying assumptions. Shirley Engle and Anna Ochoa (1988), for example, developed what has been called the "counter-socialization" theory of social education, positing that while traditional forms of schooling emphasized socialization and acculturation, a reflective, issues-centered approach would balance that with a much stronger emphasis on counter-socialization focused upon multiple curriculum strands, such as environmental studies; institutional studies on the "origins and present circumstances" of social institutions, including the political, economic, social, and cultural; as well as several additional strands (p. 134). Evans and Brodkey (2007) developed a proposal for a series of themes that could be used as a source for issues, topics, or themes to be infused into a discipline-based course sequence, or stand alone as one-semester courses. Their framework includes:

- Introduction to Problems and Issues
- Race and Ethnicity in American Life
- Social Class, Stratification, and Social Responsibility
- Gender and Sexuality in Social Life and Culture
- Ideology and Economic Life

- Power in America
- Nationalism, Patriotism, and American Foreign Policy
- Philosophy and Life

*Evans and Brodkey, 2007*

In agreement with Rugg, Engle and Ochoa, and Evans and Brodkey, I believe that, in an avowedly democratic society, and in order to encourage thoughtful citizen participation, we need a social studies curriculum focused on active inquiry, rational discourse, and persistent and "troubling" issues.

Critical theorists have made important contributions to my beliefs, to my pedagogic creed, and to my rationale for an issues-centered approach to teaching and learning, contributions that help us all better understand the nature of human society in the modern and postmodern eras.[2] Critical theorists in a variety of fields have contributed enlightening frameworks, perspectives, concepts, and analyses that provide key insights without which our knowledge of the current state of our society and its origins through the vagaries of capitalism, militarism, neo-colonialism, racism, sexism, ageism, and other forms of difference would not be so clear or unvarnished (Totten and Pedersen, 2015). Without critical theory we might not be as aware of the domination of the common people by an elite; of the historic and continuing oppression of persons of color, women, and of those with alternative sexual identities or lifestyles. We might accept the 1950s stereotypical social life portrayed in the sitcom world of "Leave it to Beaver," "Father Knows Best," or a host of more recent entries, as the norm. We might not question the hegemony of dominant interests over economic structures and other issues and concerns that matter in determining the context in which we live.

Without critical theorists in education, we might not understand the ways that schools function to reproduce oppression through tracking, the savage inequalities of school funding, and the pigeonholing of student performance via so-called "standards," the textbook regime, and the testing machine. Furthermore, we might not understand the ideological implications of pedagogical choices; that is, how we teach can liberate or oppress. We might not comprehend the ways that mainstream ideologies are transmitted through our socializing institutions, customs, and culture. We might not fully grasp the fact that we are living in the heart of a vast military and economic empire, and that we too often view other nations through a distorted lens. We might be deluded into believing that the wonderful world of consumer and entertainment culture is, for most of us, little more than a temporary palliative to help us escape the harsh realities of human society.

I believe that a critical perspective is warranted. The evidence and the literature supporting a critical perspective are well established (Domhoff, 2013; Freire, 1970). Its contours are broad and deep, rooted in concepts of injustice, exploitation, and oppression. These are not just empty concepts, but are a reflection of the social realities faced by a majority of humans on the planet. Critical theorists have added a conceptual richness to our language that has, sometimes, moved outside the realm of the academy. Empowerment, oppression, marginalization, resistance, hegemony, agency, praxis, and possibility are all useful concepts that have—to varying degrees—seeped into common parlance. Driven, for some, by Utopian visions, by deep dreams of social justice and fair play, or by a general commitment to social melioration, I believe that critical theorists have made important contributions to both the rhetoric and realities of our world. As Harold Rugg once wrote, "The world is on fire, and the youth of the world must be equipped to combat the conflagration" (Rugg, 1932, p. 11).

## Challenges or Opportunities?

My creed is a restatement and reconceptualization of the critical, issues-centered position that has developed over the past century. However, as part of a larger critical project aimed at improving the teaching in our schools, at making our social world more humane and compassionate, it has made only a little progress. I believe that advocates and practitioners of critical, issues-centered education face several important challenges and constraints. For my creed, for any creed to matter in the larger universe of schooling in American society, I believe that it must account for context. The ongoing struggle among competing interest groups to define and enact the curriculum in U.S. schools means that critical, issues-centered theory is not without opposition. Critical perspectives are frequently challenged as politically biased, Marxist, socialist, or extremist. For example, during the heyday of social reconstructionism, a forerunner of more recent theory, school administrators complained about its limited prospects for success, or charged that it was a visionary romanticism that "wouldn't work" (Krug, 1972, pp. 238–239). One superintendent reportedly said that the Teachers College, Columbia University oligarchy "should be put in rear seats and muzzled" (Krug, 1972, p. 251). Over the past century or so, competing interest groups have struggled over the direction of schools and the content of the curriculum, projecting differing visions of the future and of the core purposes of the American school. Such struggles among competing interest groups reflect the broader ideological struggles among political parties over the future of U.S. society and the globe. Essentially, they reflect differing beliefs and value orientations.

Within this context, I believe that the critical, issues-centered project in education faces several difficulties or obstacles that have served to limit its influence and impact. Among these are: conceptual density and perceptions of irrelevance; limited influence in schools due, in part, to the persistence of recitation-style teaching; the difficulties inherent in translating critical pedagogy into thoughtful classroom practice; and the inevitable controversies that arise when pedagogy stems from a particular ideological base rooted in critique. In what follows I shall briefly address each of these concerns.

First, critical theory, which forms a rationale base for many issues-centered educators and the substantive basis for my personal creed, is rooted in the rhetoric and language of the academy. I believe that critical theory includes many difficult and slippery terms. How many teachers or teacher educators have taken the time and energy needed to understand them? Take for example the terms postmodernism, post-structuralism, deconstructionism, and neo-liberalism—each of these concepts can be difficult to understand and most teachers, indeed most teacher educators, have a limited grasp of them, if they are even familiar with them at all. We have had some work on helping with this from such educators as Joan Wink, Antonia Darder, Bill Bigelow, and others at Rethinking Schools—but its impact has been, seemingly, minimal.

Second, based upon my reading of the evidence, and as I said above, I believe that critical, issues-centered theory has had only limited influence on schools and classrooms. I believe that this reality provides an important contextual insight for my creed and the creeds of other issues-centered educators. Classroom practice is dominated by the persistence of the recitation and the grammar of schooling, which frequently constrains teacher choices and leads to pedantic approaches focused on textbooks, workbooks, test prep, and other low-level strategies aimed at "drilling children in a cultural orientation" (Henry, 1963, p. 283). Frank Ryan's 1970s description of students sitting in rows, responding to low-level teacher questions focused on textbook content still rings true (Ryan, 1971; Tyack and Cuban, 1995; Evans, 2011b). Of course, we must accept the fact that a significant number of teachers will not be ideologically supportive of a critical perspective, or will choose another curricular path.

Moreover, I believe that the present climate in educational policy is not particularly supportive of the critical, issues-centered project. In fact, for most of the recent past, educational policy has been explicitly anti-progressive in orientation. The current school reform movement is rooted in corporate values and culture, and is reconstructing schools as training grounds for worker-citizens, with the emphasis on worker productivity. The Business Roundtable, the most active group initiating a business-driven approach to school reform, was created in the early 1970s largely as an answer to a memo from Lewis Powell Jr., then a corporate lawyer and later a Supreme Court justice, in which he called for business to fight for greater control in American politics and institutional life. Powell's 1971 memo, which was entitled, "Attack on American Free Enterprise System," outlined a broad approach by which corporate America could organize for greater policy influence, touching a variety of institutions (Powell, 1971; Hacker and Pierson, 2011). The resulting impact on schools has been devastating, and explicitly anti-progressive in orientation. It has, for the most part, led to teaching to the test, policies that reinforce low-level approaches to learning, and restrictions on the teacher and student freedom necessary for critical inquiry to blossom. In the schools I visit, I see a focus on recitation, almost without interruption. As I help my children with their homework, I witness nearly continual use of textbook-focused worksheets. In recent years, critical, issues-centered pedagogy has lost ground in the struggle over school curricula. It is no coincidence that policy moves favoring corporate influence over education and a host of other institutions parallel a striking rise in the micromanagement of workers to raise productivity (Semuels, 2013), an alarming rise in measures of social isolation (Mohan, 2013; Putnam, 1995), and the burgeoning threat of environmental catastrophe in a society built largely on the foundation of rugged individualism, greed, and ambition.

Third, critical teaching, my own teaching practice in schools and universities—and perhaps all of teaching, for that matter—is subject to difficult conundrums in regard to questions of theory into practice, some of which center on the question, "What is the role of a teacher's beliefs in her or his teaching?" I believe that critical, issues-centered pedagogy is especially prone to the danger of the dogmatic teacher clumsily imposing his or her beliefs on unsuspecting or resistant students. How do those of us whose creeds embody critical, issues-centered perspectives introduce our perspectives to others? We are in agreement that students must confront the critical issues, be challenged with "critical perspectives," and engage persistent issues. But at least two major dangers crop up, inherent with this project: (1) the teacher who lectures students providing only his or her preferred critical interpretation with little time devoted to discussion of alternatives, student beliefs, or competing views; and, (2) the teacher who raises critical issues, questions, and topics, but then provides a biased set of materials for students to read or view, omitting the rich balance of resources, competing viewpoints, and dissonant primary sources that can inspire deep student inquiry, investigation, and reflection.

Over many years of teaching, I have learned that for an effective critical, issues-centered dialogue to occur, students and their teachers must confront crucial issues within the framework of an open and supportive classroom climate guided by compassion and the unrelenting search for truth, driven by a steely determination to get to the bottom of the matter, to consider evidence, alternatives, value implications, and consequences (Engle and Ochoa, 1988; Evans and Saxe, 2007). I believe that this implies putting students on center stage as much as possible, with teacher guidance, and encouraging them to find their own answers to some of the most persistent and troubling questions faced by human societies. There is a fine line that teachers must be careful not to cross, lest it lead to students feeling that the teacher is trying to impose her or his perspective on them. With few exceptions, I believe that the teacher's point of view, my point of view, should be minimized, or withheld, except, perhaps, as an example tracing how the teacher arrived at her or his beliefs. As Michael Harrington (1980) once confided to me, "I tell students what I think, but I bend over backward to include other perspectives" (Personal communication, 1980).

Fourth, controversies spawned by teaching innovations and ideas, especially when rooted in a critical or issues-centered framework, illustrate another constraint on teaching for social justice and can lead to imposition of sanctions, or self-censorship. I believe that such controversies constrain and limit the potential for critical, issues-centered teaching. Let us consider a few examples. In January, 2012, the Tucson, Arizona, school board voted to suspend its Mexican American studies program to avoid losing $14 million in state funds—this was in response to a state law that banned classes primarily designed for a particular ethnic group or that "promote resentment toward a race or class of people" (Cesar, 2012, p. 1). The incident followed a long and highly politicized period of controversy over the program, which corresponded with a move to limit immigrant rights.

The more distant past is littered with controversies spawned by attempts at innovative and critical teaching, such as the early 1940s controversy over the innovative Rugg social science textbooks, leading to the removal of his books from the schools; the 1970s turmoil over MACOS (*Man: A Course of Study*); and the broad reaction against new wave humanist and progressive school reforms and materials. Among the local controversies of the 1970s, a seedtime for the conservative restoration and accountability reform efforts, were: the textbook war in Kanawha County, West Virginia; the burning of Values Clarification materials in Warsaw, Indiana; and, the controversy over MACOS in multiple cities and towns across the nation (Dow, 1991; Evans, 2011[P1]). In each case, these controversies garnered national attention and led to reversals for critical teaching. The list could go on and on. To one degree or another, teaching innovations that were perceived as challenging mainstream values and traditional approaches to teaching stirred opposition and censure. In more than a few cases, teachers were literally put on trial. In a similar vein, my own teaching has led to controversy among students and parents on a few occasions. Advocacy can be difficult. It can lead to hurt feelings, and can stir opposition or resistance from students. In my own teaching experience, I have sometimes found such reactions counter-productive or detrimental to establishing and maintaining the open and supportive classroom climate necessary for free inquiry to occur.

## On Possibility

Though the obstacles to a critical, issues-centered approach to teaching are very real, I believe that we nonetheless have the opportunity to make a difference. Teachers and teacher educators should continue to pursue a vision of the teacher as a transformative intellectual and creative designer of curricula, rather than simply a gatekeeper, or worse, a script reader. Though increasingly threatened by de-professionalization, our aim should be to help each teacher develop and learn to thoughtfully enact a purposeful pedagogic creed. Many of our brightest and most committed teachers and student teachers will pursue a critical, issues-centered approach or implement their own versions of teaching for social justice. We can support robust pedagogical choices for K-12 teachers. Though in many states it is a struggle to implement any thoughtful or in-depth approach to learning in the current test-driven framework, I believe that we should support teachers in the effort to become thoughtful practitioners who will create an open and supportive classroom environment and facilitate critical thought and consideration of alternative perspectives within a framework of open inquiry.

If we are to make progress, I believe that we must maintain eternal vigilance in the fight for academic freedom. Basic intellectual freedom, the freedom for teachers to teach and students to learn, is threatened by the current regime of corporate influence over schools; by the standards, textbook, and testing regime; and by privatization. It is threatened by the commodification of curriculum materials, by which student learning is packaged, sanitized, and controlled from above, then imposed on teachers and students. As seen from a distance, current school reform is a case of education for social efficiency taken to a new and dangerous extreme. For critical, issues-centered perspectives to flourish in this context, academic freedom is a prerequisite.

Despite the dangers and constraints I have discussed, the future offers possibility. I believe that we must continue the effort to educate teachers, introducing them to critical, issues-centered approaches to teaching and its many useful variations. This is important work and it can and has made a difference. One teacher who thoughtfully implements a critical, issues-centered perspective in the classroom can touch thousands of lives, and that should be all the motivation we need.

## Notes

1   A different version of this segment, concerning my personal background, served as a preface to *Educating about Social Issues in the 20th and 21st Centuries: Critical Theory and Critical Theorists: An Annotated Bibliography*, edited by Samuel Totten and Jon E. Pedersen.

2   A different version of this segment of my essay appeared as a preface to *Educating about Social Issues in the 20th and 21st Centuries: Critical Theory and Critical Theorists: An Annotated Bibliography*, edited by Samuel Totten and Jon E. Pedersen.

## References

Bruner, J.S. (1960). *The Process of Education*. Cambridge: Harvard University Press.

Cesar, S. (2012). "Tucson Students Confront Loss of their Chicano Studies Class." *Los Angeles Times*, January 11, 2012. (Accessed April 10, 2013 at http://articles.latimes.com/2012/jan/11/nation/la-na-ethnic-studies-20120112).

Dewey, J. (1897). "My pedagogic creed." In Reginald D. Archambault. ed. (1964*). John Dewey on Education* (pp. 427–439). New York, NY: Random House.

Domhoff, G.W. (2013). *Wealth, Income, and Power*. (Accessed April 10, 2013 at http://www2.ucsc.edu/whorulesamerica/power/wealth.html).

Dow, Peter F. (1991). *Schoolhouse Politics: Lessons from the Sputnik Era*. Cambridge, MA: Harvard University Press.

Engle, Shirley H., and Ochoa, Anna S. (1988). *Teaching for Democratic Citizenship: Decision Making in the Social Studies*. New York, NY: Teachers College Press.

Evans, R.W. (2004). *The Social Studies Wars: What Should We Teach the Children?* New York, NY: Teachers College Press.

Evans, R.W. (2007). *This Happened in America: Harold Rugg and the Censure of Social Studies.* Charlotte, NC: Information Age.

Evans, R.W. (2011a). *The Hope for American School Reform: The Cold War Pursuit of Inquiry Learning in Social Studies.* New York, NY: Palgrave Macmillan.

Evans, R.W. (2011b). *The Tragedy of American School Reform: How Curriculum Politics and Entrenched Dilemmas Have Diverted us from Democracy.* New York, NY: Palgrave Macmillan.

Evans, R.W., and Brodkey, J. (2007). "An Issues-centered Curriculum for High School Social Studies," in R.W. Evans, and D.W. Saxe, eds., *Handbook on Teaching Social Issues.* Charlotte, NC: Information Age (Originally published in 1996 by National Council for the Social Studies).

Evans, R.W., and Saxe, D.W. (eds.). (1996). *Handbook on Teaching Social Issues.* Washington, D.C.: National Council for the Social Studies.

Freire, P. (1970). *Pedagogy of the Oppressed.* New York, NY: Continuum.

Garland, J.V. (1951). *Discussion Methods Explained and Illustrated.* New York, NY: Wilson.

Giese, J.R., and Glade, M.E. (1988). *American Revolution: Crisis of Law and Change.* Boulder, CO: Social Science Education Consortium.

Hacker, J.S., and Pierson, P. (2011). *Winner-Take-All-Politics: How Washington Made the Rich Richer and Turned its Back on the Rest of Us.* New York, NY: Simon and Schuster.

Henry, J. (1963). *Culture Against Man.* New York, NY: Vintage Press.

Hunt M.P., and Metcalf, L. (1968). *Teaching High School Social Studies: Problems in Reflective Thinking and Social Understanding.* New York, NY: Harper & Brothers.

Illich, I. (1971). *Deschooling Society.* New York, NY: Harper and Row.

Krug, (1972). *The Shaping of the American High School, 1920–1941.* Madison, WI: University of Wisconsin Press.

Leinwand, G. (ed.). (1968–1969). *Problems of American Society* [series]. New York, NY: Washington Square Press.

Mohan, G., (2013). "Social Isolation Increases Risk of Early Death, Study Finds." *Los Angeles Times.* March 26, 2013, p. A9.

Oliver, D.W. and Shaver, J.P. (1966). *Teaching Public Issues in the High School.* Boston, MA: Houghton Mifflin.

Passe, J., and Evans, R.W. (2007). "Discussion Methods in an Issues-centered Curriculum." In R.W. Evans, and D.W. Saxe, eds., *Handbook on Teaching Social Issues.* Charlotte, NC: Information Age (Originally published in 1996 by the National Council for the Social Studies.)

Pirsig, R.M. (1974). *Zen and the Art of Motorcycle Maintenance: An Inquiry into Values.* New York, NY: Morrow.

Postman, N., and Weingartner, C. (1969). *Teaching as a Subversive Activity.* New York, NY: Delacorte.

Powell, L.F. (1971). Lewis F. Powell to Eugene B. Snydor, "Confidential Memorandum: Attack on American Free Enterprise System." August 23, 1971. (Accessed April 10, 2013 at http://billmoyers.com/content/the-powell-memo-a-call-to-arms-for-corporations/2/).

Putnam, R. (1995). "Bowling Alone: America's Declining Social Capital." 6(1) *Journal of Democracy*, pp. 65–78.

Rugg, H.O. (1923a). "Do the Social Studies Prepare Pupils Adequately for Life Activities?" In H.O. Rugg, ed., *The Social Studies in the Elementary and Secondary School.* National Society for the Study of Education, Twenty-Second Yearbook, Part II (pp. 1–27). Bloomington, IL: Public School.

Rugg, H. O. (1923b). "Problems of contemporary life as the basis for curriculum making in the social studies." In Harold O. Rugg, ed., *The Social Studies in the Elementary and Secondary School*. National Society for the Study of Education, Twenty-Second Yearbook, Part II (pp. 260–273). Bloomington, IL: Public School.

Rugg, H.O. (1929). *Teachers' Guide to Accompany "A History of Western Civilization."* Boston, MA: Ginn.

Rugg, H.O. (1932). "Social Reconstruction through Education." 9(8) *Progressive Education*, pp. 11–18.

Ryan, F. (1973). "Implementing the Hidden Curriculum of the Social Studies." 37(7) *Social Education*, pp. 679–680.

Singelton, L. (1990). *The New Deal: Government and the Economy*. Boulder, CO: Social Science Education Consortium.

Semuels, A. (2013). "How the Relationship between Employers and Workers Changed." *Los Angeles Times*, April 7, 2013, p. A1.

Spady, W.G. (2007). "The Paradigm Trap." *Education Week*. http://www.edweek.org/ew/articles/2007/01/10/18spady.h26.html

Totten, S., and Pedersen, J. (2015). *Educating about Social Issues in the 20th and 21st Centuries: Critical Theory and Critical Theorists: An Annotated Bibliography*. Charlotte, NC: Information Age.

Tyack, D., and Cuban, L. (1995). *Tinkering toward Utopia: A Century of Public School Reform*. Cambridge, MA: Harvard University Press.

# 13

# THE ART OF TEACHING[1]

*Carlos Alberto Torres*

PROFESSOR, SOCIAL SCIENCES AND COMPARATIVE EDUCATION,
UNIVERSITY OF CALIFORNIA, LOS ANGELES

## If You Scratch a Theory You Would Find a Biography

Sometimes in the evening a face looks at us from the bottom of a mirror;
art should be like that mirror that reveals our own face to us.

*Jorge Luis Borges*[2]

My memories of childhood and youth now seem to me both current and distant. I think we live by memory. But there are moments when memory lives within us, almost independent of our desires despite the fact that it is constructed from them. This is also clearly the result of the deconstructionist storm unloosed by Derrida and his collaborators. There are no innocent texts.

I was a typical son of a working class family in the middle of the past century in Buenos Aires, Argentina. A family in which my mother worked in a factory making rubber sandals and my father lugged beer barrels as a peon in a brewery. A working class family that later became a middle class family. They told me that when I was less than two years old, my unemployed father went looking for work in the Abasto market in the center of the city. The Abasto market was the central wholesale market. An Italian immigrant told him, "Kid, there's no work here." When my father answered that he had to feed his family, the Italian said to him: "Take a box of peaches. They're worth this much. Go sell them at some street corner. Ask this much. Then you pay me and keep the difference."

My father took the box and soon came back for another. He had sold all the peaches. He had created income for his family. He paid his bill. This Italian, in the style of the era, had opened a running retail account (practically without knowing my father) and he began to work as a fruit-seller. Together with my mother, he set up a fruit stand at an outdoor market but the economic crisis of 1952 ruined them. My mother opened a leather-sewing workshop in our house, where she worked for more than 20 years and my father looked for work as a prison guard in the nascent Federal Penitentiary Service, where he wound up as a high-ranking officer by the end of his career.

After living in the province of Buenos Aires, very close to a shanty town, they moved with me from one rented apartment to another until finally, when I was six, they rented a dilapidated house in the Flores neighborhood with an enormous yard, a house which we shared with two other tenants, a brother and sister. As a historical curiosity, Pope Francis grew up in the same neighborhood; his family's house was two blocks from mine.

I was raised in that big house in Flores, next to one of the glories of the tango, Señor Razzano, an early partner of Carlos Gardel in the duet Gardel and Razzano until he lost his voice. I attended an elementary and secondary parochial school administered by the LaSalle brothers four blocks from my house.

My childhood memories are fragmented. I am very sure that I had to wear short pants until I was more than twelve years old simply because my mother did not have the money to buy me long ones—the sign, in that era, that one had reached puberty. This was a kind of mark of poverty that I will never forget.

I remember, too, that my family, in the midst of its interminable contradictions, was always seeking a sense of unity in diversity. For example, whenever we had a family party, almost always a barbecue, there were apocalyptic arguments between the socialist uncles and the uncles who backed Perón.[3] But, when it came time for dessert, someone with good common sense would switch the conversation to less controversial subjects than Argentine politics.

I also remember how difficult it is to be the eldest brother and the eldest cousin. Deep down, since I am five years older than my next brother and twelve years older than the youngest, I feel like I was raised an only child. Sometimes, when these family get-togethers became nostalgic for an endless past in a country always in construction, my paternal uncle would get out his *bandoneón*[4] and play tangos. All my uncles and grandparents and my parents would dance, the little boys would play, and I would feel sad and alone as if the spectacle I was watching did not include me as a participant.

Finally, and not to tire the reader with these childhood memories, if there is someone I am never going to forget it is my father, an imposing and intelligent man who lived a very difficult life, always ready to explode, agonizing every day with a life that consumed the best of his spirit.

My mother was the backbone of the family, managing to get additional income in the workshop we had at home (and in which all of us worked at different periods in our life) while simultaneously taking care of the children and the house. Her sense and sensibilities helped to soothe the broken spirit of my father when things got very bad.

My father needed restful moments in his struggles to survive and to keep our family afloat, paying the innumerable bills beyond our modest living budget. He would sit with me on peaceful weekend afternoons or amid the oppressive heat of a Buenos Aires summer when I was only eight or nine years old and we would read, side by side, examples of the poorest literature. The title of the series said it all: *Hazañas Bélicas (Exploits of War)*. Books of Second World War stories were the beginning and end of my introduction to reading. I must have read hundreds of those little books. Those moments in my father's company turned me into an aficionado of reading. It is worth noting clearly that my recognition of my father's pedagogical diligence—deliberate or not—came from many conversations with my psychoanalyst, and is in no way a folkloric observation of the era. Very often, as I say in one of my books, paraphrasing the poet T.S. Eliot, we have the experience but we miss the meaning—and getting closer to the meaning restores the experience.

From the *Hazañas Bélicas* I went on, in the fifth grade, to read the work of Emilio Salgari, particularly his two books about Sandokán, and the Malaysian Tiger Pirates. In retrospect, these books were very important for me and a whole generation of Latin Americans because Emilio Salgari—an Italian author who ended up a suicide when he found he was being used by a publisher who paid him a pittance without offering him a percentage of his enormously lucrative bestsellers—was an anti-colonialist and anti-imperialist thinker, a critic of the British Empire.

I say this because, at ten or eleven, to travel in my imagination from a modest Buenos Aires neighborhood to the jungles of Borneo, Java, or Indonesia, and to think about a daring pirate like Sandokán or his friend Yañez, the Portuguese adventurer, and their constant battles with the British imperialists, forged almost without my knowing it an anti-colonial perspective that I was able to recuperate more consciously when I began my university studies. Today I call my black German shepherd "Sandokán." Perhaps, like most of us, I am still trying to come to terms with my past.

I want to say some words about the political period in which I was raised. I was in primary school between 1956 and 1962. In other words, between the military coup that toppled Perón and the military riot of the blues and reds that set the table for the future government of Onganía,[5] one of the military juntas that governed during most of my secondary studies. I was the educational product of a generation obliged to ignore the name of Perón, which was in the mouths and hearts of the country's popular majorities but remained unpronounceable in the schools and state institutions that euphemistically christened him the "fugitive tyrant."

I am part of a generation that was forcefully politicized by the "*Cordobazos*," the "*viborazo*" in Rosario, the taking of the city of Garín by the *Montoneros*.[6] This is a generation that turned to politics during the night of the long sticks in 1966, that culminated with the occupation of the faculties of the University of Buenos Aires and the end of university autonomy; henceforth, the University was under the police control of a dictatorship incomparable in its violence with the one which followed it after 1976.

In my case, starting at about seventeen, I began to participate in Catholic youth groups, which soon became the first groups of Liberation Theology in the country and in base communities as well. My real politicization was due to two simultaneous processes. First, I joined a group of radicalized Christians who decided to offer a new perspective on politics and religion, and who went to live in communities where popular politics and religiosity was practiced in unison with a commitment to the people. Second, as a university student, I read Hegel, Marx, Marcuse, and the social scientists of the Third World, particularly Paulo Freire, Camilo Torres, and Frantz Fanon. The mystic poet and Nicaraguan monk Ernesto Cardenal deeply influenced my own generation, especially through his book, *Ernesto Cardenal En Cuba*.

I got married the day before the general elections of 1973 that marked the nation's return to suffrage (for the first time since 1966) and the massive triumph of Perónism, a government coalition led by Dr. Hector J. Cámpora, personal representative of Juan Domingo Perón. I finished my studies in 1974, graduating with a license and professorship in sociology. I also became Secretary General of ECLA (*Estudio de la Ciencia en América Latina*), an important social science research institute.

In 1975, following a crisis in the Christian based community where we were living, made worse by the psychotic conditions of Argentine political life, I decided to launch a totally Utopian project and try to establish a Freire-style rural "freedom" school in Patagonia. This was a total failure or, to borrow a phrase from García Márquez,[7] "the chronicle of an announced death."

I left Argentina for a very simple reason: the choking-off of all freedoms of expression by the military junta, which took control in March, 1976 and eliminated all civil rights.[8]

One anecdote will serve to illustrate the drama of a situation of which, at that moment, only a few people were aware. I finished my first book, *Lectura Crítica de Paulo Freire*, in Patagonia. It ended up being published in Spanish in Mexico in 1978 as a part of a trilogy which was translated into Portuguese for publication in Brazil in 1980.

I traveled from Esquel to Buenos Aires to take the manuscript to Julio Barreiro, the director of Editorial Tierra Nueva, and the publisher of Paulo Freire before he signed over his Spanish language rights to Siglo XXI publishers in Mexico. I was happy to be handing the book to Barreiro, a Uruguayan, who was also a Protestant minister and a philosopher and a mentor to me.

Our meeting took place a few days after the military coup of 24 March, 1976. Julio welcomed me with great cordiality. He took the manuscript and told me he would go over it with an editor's eye. Then we sat down to talk. The first thing he told me was that he might not be able to publish the book in Argentina because the recently installed military dictators had made the situation very difficult. He suggested that perhaps it could be published in Italy.

Then he asked me what I was doing in Patagonia. I told him that I was working in the recently created Patagonia National University as an assistant professor, and that I was also teaching a night school course in adult education at the Costa Rica Superior Normal School, in Esquel, as well as working as a medical sociologist in a hospital there.

He looked at me with a worried expression and asked me what I was teaching in my classes. I told him that the authors were Freire, Marx, Piaget . . . He stopped me right there: "Carlos, you must return immediately, ask for your course outlines and bibliographies and destroy them. Then replace them with functionalist sociological and conductive materials in a new study guide. Piaget, Marx, Freire, and countless other intellectuals were prohibited by the new military junta. They have been blacklisted."

In real innocence, I asked him why. Few people at that time foresaw the imminent national tragedy, but Julio, who had gone through something similar in Uruguay, was very clear about it. His answer was to open a widely-read, middle-class Argentinean magazine to a two-page article entitled "Our Children's Marxist Education." I remember very well reading it and being surprised that they had lifted whole paragraphs from two of Freire's books, *Education for Critical Consciousness*[9] and *Pedagogy of the Oppressed*. The article concluded with a laconic sentence I will never forget. The text said something like: "The revolutionary process of the Argentinean military junta is waged against such education."

"This is propaganda, nothing more," Julio said. "But you must get your course outlines back and exchange them for others. SIDE, the acronym for the State's information and espionage system, has been investigating people who use books that they consider leftist, anti-Christian, etc. There may be very serious consequences for those teachers."

I left Julio Barreiro's office crushed, totally disheartened. I had gone to take my first book to my editor and I left convinced that I was in real danger. I connected it to a letter that my friend Dr. Emilio Mignone sent me. He had been the Director of ECLA, where I used to work, and now he was working at FLACSO, Argentina. In this letter, sent at the end of October, 1975, he was talking about the disappearance of his daughter Mónica, who was kidnapped from her family's apartment on Santa Fé, Barrio Norte, by a group which said they were members of the Argentinean Armed Forces. Mónica, together with close friends María Marta and César Lugones, was part of the community that I was trying to recreate in Esquel. César Lugones was an agronomist, while María Marta, his wife, and Mónica Mignone, were both psychologists—all three were militants in the Perónist Youth and worked as literacy tutors in a shantytown. In October, 1975, Mónica, María Marta, and César were among the first *desaparecidos*[10] to be detained by one of the ominous task forces of the Argentinean army and police. Mignone also wrote in this letter that he was searching for them because they had literally disappeared, as if the earth had swallowed them. I did not yet understand that the suffering of the Mignones would be reproduced in thousands of families or that, a little later, the Mothers and then the Grandmothers of Plaza de Mayo[11] would be born, searching for their sons and daughters, grandsons and granddaughters.

I went back to Patagonia very depressed. I told my wife that we had to leave the country, that the conditions were impossible: I didn't know what to teach if everything I knew and believed in was banned.

My wife was pregnant with our third child, Laura Silvina. I began to send letters. I believe I typed and sent two hundred letters to embassies and graduate programs around the world, applying for scholarships and work outside of Argentina.

I received only two positive responses. One was from the El Colegio de México, telling me that the Master's program in Social Sciences had already closed but, as I had good qualifications, I could apply again for the new program that would begin in October, 1976, at the Facultad Latinoamericana de Ciencias Sociales, FLACSO, in Mexico City.

The second one was from the Algerian embassy inviting me to interview to work as a sociologist in a health post in the Algerian desert; naturally the job would entail my speaking French.

I immediately began the application to FLACSO and got a scholarship to travel to Mexico City. I left at the end of September. My then wife and three children joined me in December. I had no idea then that I would not return to Argentina until the end of the dictatorship in 1984 and that I would be an immigrant for the rest of my life. Nor did I find out until many years later that this decision to leave the country due to the violence of the dictatorship had saved my life.

I lived in Mexico from 1976 to 1980, where I got a Master's degree in Political Science and worked in government education agencies and various universities; and then in the United States from 1980 to 1983, where I got a Master's and a Doctorate in International Education and Development at Stanford University. In 1983, I returned to Mexico to work as a professor at FLACSO-Mexico and remained there until 1986 when I went back to the U.S. as a Fulbright Fellow to work in a now defunct private liberal arts college, World College West, in Petaluma, California. I then went to Edmonton, Alberta, Canada, to do a post-Doctorate in Educational Foundations, becoming a professor at the University of Alberta where I remained until I got a contract from UCLA in 1990.

To be an immigrant is to live astride two worlds. Perhaps I ought to say "without giving into nostalgia," since we immigrants long for what we have left and, when we return (even temporarily) to our place of origin, we may feel we belong somewhere else. This sense of bifurcated belonging seems to be one of the keys to immigrant identity. It is also true that when we emigrate, we adopt, albeit grudgingly, the new country and the new language. But we are also marked by the old class, gender, and racial stereotypes that are so pronounced in a social formation like the United States.

In more than one of my books, I describe scenes where I personally experienced subtle verbal or non-verbal micro-aggressions, usually made automatically or unconsciously, to which all immigrants and people of color are exposed.[12]

Certainly such micro-aggressions are magnified or minimized by class dynam-ics. They are tempered but never eliminated when the immigrants are middle or upper class, like a university professor in the U.S., but we are never exempt from discrimination. Racial and ethnic dynamics play a prominent role in determin-ing the routines, practices, and (especially) the cultures of institutions of higher education.

What has been eminently positive in my integration into the North American academy is to have one job that supports my life—for Argentinean professors, this is Utopian. Being at an excellent research and teaching university like UCLA has provided me unequalled opportunities for professional and intellectual develop-ment. There is still another advantage. It is difficult to manage to buy the character and the narrative of a *tenured* university professor (one with academic stability) and a good salary yet still criticize international organizations such as the World Bank and International Monetary Fund, promoters of neo-liberal politics, without hav-ing to eat from their harvest. It is also interesting to watch how such organizations silence their critics by buying them. Soon after I came to UCLA, in 1991, people from the World Bank called to ask if I were interested in the position of director of one of their research institutions. I was so surprised by the call that I asked if they read what I wrote. The answer was yes, and that is why they wanted to inter-est me in such a position. I decided not even to apply in spite of the fact that the salary was much higher than that of an assistant professor at UCLA.

It is also certain that my inclusion in North American academia has allowed me to have an international presence, working in Europe and Asia as well as undertaking constant peregrinations around Latin America, from which I have learned so much.

We must never forget that the Greeks defined philosophy as traveling among people and things. In other words, the philosopher is an itinerant traveler. It is incredible what you can learn by traveling—not as a tourist, but as a politically and socially involved intellectual—discussing and dialoguing with colleagues and friends or social movements in different parts of the world and, naturally, trying to create a sphere of public deliberation where university autonomy is fundamental.

## Teaching to Change the World: Building Community (in and through) your Teaching, Research, and Writing

> I don't believe that we can change moral intuitions except as educators—that is, not as theoreticians and not as writers.
>
> *Jürgen Habermas*[13]

We are all traveling scholars. We travel through cultural and social constructions, through theoretical and meta-theoretical constructions, and through empirical analyses. I do not believe that any Critical Theorist can reach the best of his or her contribution without serious empirical analysis. At the same time, I am cognizant of the fact that some technocrats, who call themselves scholars, compile, analyze, even "torture" data until it tells them exactly what they want to hear or expect to get.

We travel but we do so framed by the politics of location and the politics of identity. This positionality should lead us to understand not only our sources of wisdom but, for any Critical Theory-oriented traveling scholar, should also let us locate our own positionality and politics of identity against the proverbial racism, sexism, religious absolutism, homophobia, or classism of our societies. Therefore, to separate analysis from advocacy is a very difficult process.

The best way of rationalizing teaching as a philosophy is to establish your own philosophy of teaching. Herein, I draw from my own experience and the influence of Freire and the pedagogues of liberation to outline key objectives in my teaching:

- To engage students in rigorous consideration of the key intellectual questions discussed in the course;
- To challenge them to consider the substantive—i.e., theoretical, normative, and ethical issues involved in education, both at the level of theory and methods of inquiry;
- To challenge graduate students in education to take advantage of the classic texts of philosophy, as they have informed the work of Freire, and the variety of social sciences available to them—particularly history, political science, sociology, political economy, and anthropology—in order to develop an intellectual framework that is broadly interdisciplinary and comparative;
- To involve students in independent analysis and writing;
- And, finally, to allow them to experiment with the techniques proposed by Paulo Freire, Orlando Falls Borda and the founders of Participatory Action Research (PAR), and the contributions of feminist pedagogy to radically change classrooms, bringing the promises of democracy from the ideal to a true reality in the lives of their students.

Michele Fine (2008) has presented a sharp description of what PAR entails: "PAR stands on the epistemological grounds that persons who have historically been marginalized or silenced carry substantial knowledge about the architecture of injustice, in their minds, bodies, and souls; in ways that are conscious and floating; individual and collective" (p. 223).

Without attempting to provide an exhaustive list, I would like to identify nine components that I believe are essential in thinking about rigor and excellence, and that will help the pedagogical task in the classroom:

1) Respect for students' knowledge and experiences. From a Freirean perspective, this is the starting point of any serious academic engagement and community building.

2) Respect for the classics properly deconstructed. If teaching and research is a never-ending process of deliberation and analysis, the classics of social theory and pedagogy cannot be ignored or brushed aside. They are central to our teaching and research endeavors. The dictum of C. Wright Mills is very appropriate, and I would like to quote him at length. Speaking about the classics of sociology, he stated that:

> The important thing about the classic sociologists is that even when they have turned out to be quite wrong, and inadequate . . . even then, by their work and by the way in which they did it, they reveal much about the nature of society, and their ideas remain directly relevant to our work today . . . In general, our immediate generation of social scientists are living off their ideas.
>
> *Mills, 1960, pp. 3–4*

3) Data emphasis. Without creating a fetish out of using data to document any and every aspect of our teaching and research, and knowledge content, the proper utilization of data is important in our teaching. Likewise, without falling into the epistemological trap that by resorting to methods we will achieve scientificity, it is imperative that we address data as much as we can in dealing with epistemology, methods, meta-theories, and theories in the classroom.

4) Sound methods of inquiry. Classroom activity should be based on a multitude of strategies linking sound methods of inquiry with a healthy dose of analytical skepticism. Defining precisely what sound methods of inquiry mean, how we integrate them into our practice, and avoiding relying too heavily on certain methods to the exclusion of others is part of the art of teaching.

5) Relational analysis. Perhaps it is my own obsession, but when one begins to analyze a specific problem and places specific focus on the different dimensions of the problem, it is imperative to do so relationally, relating that analysis to the other dimensions that we typically deal with in education. To be brief, I would argue that we are constantly relating the economic, political, and cultural domains or spheres of praxis and knowledge with questions connected with ethnicity, race, gender, sexuality, class, and many other "variables" of the analysis. Thus, adopting a relational analysis is fundamental to teaching.[14]

6) The distinction between what is normative and what is analytical should be preserved in our teaching. I have already stated that Critical Theorists teach to change the world, not to simply reproduce it.

7) Respect for contradictions and tensions. For a long time, one of the key axes of distinction in sociology was considered the distinction between a sociology of conflict and a sociology of consensus. However, both conflict and consensus take place constantly in our classrooms. We should pay attention

to and respect the degree of contradictions and the tensions that all of us, teachers and students together, experience in a given class.

8) Our teaching should also address the connections between theory, praxis, and transformation. This is part of the moral commitment of teaching. With the pervasive presence of a "value-free science" approach in universities, the question of moral commitment in our teaching becomes a lynchpin in linking the normative and the analytical moments of scientific work. Alvin Gouldner, in his Presidential Address at the annual meeting of the Society for the Study of Social Problems on August 28, 1961, said it very well, and I would like to quote him extensively, making his observations my own:

> If today we concern ourselves exclusively with the technical proficiency of our students and reject all responsibility for their moral sense, or lack of it, then we may someday be compelled to accept responsibility for having trained a generation willing to serve in a future Auschwitz. Granted that science always has inherent in it both constructive and destructive potentialities, it does not follow that we should encourage our students to be oblivious to the difference. Nor does this in any degree detract from the indispensable norms of scientific objectivity; it merely insists that these differ radically from moral indifference.
>
> *Quoted in Gouldner, 1964, p. 216*

9) Finally, in the long classical tradition of academic engagement, it is imperative to promote critique, criticism, and dissatisfaction in the treatment of the material and classroom analysis.

The advocacy role inherent in good teaching and scholarship is ever present in the scholarship and pedagogy of feminism. In a fascinating presentation at a 2007 workshop organized by the Paulo Freire Institute at UCLA discussing Freire's contributions to Feminist pedagogy, and a critique of his limitations, anthropologist and women's studies professor Sondra Hale highlighted a series of themes that I deem extremely important in regard to linking the Feminist Classroom with the tradition of Liberatory pedagogy à la Freire (Freire, 1971). The first premise of Hale's analysis is the following:

> As we know, liberatory pedagogy has been associated with Paulo Freire, and is one of the inspirations behind some ethnic studies classrooms. However, Freire's neglect of gender and sexuality marginalizes women, lesbians, and gays as a categories of people to be empowered, and has made him less attractive to Women's Studies. Feminists have, however, borrowed heavily from him and from others before him—sometimes without acknowledgement.
>
> *Hale, 2007, p. 4*

A second premise is that there are shared pedagogical qualities of Feminist and Ethnic Studies and that they also overlap with the traditional Liberatory Pedagogy. However, these conditions have not been fully operationalized into a truly emancipatory agenda, though sharing a similar "*raisons d'etre* (to examine the 'intersections' of oppressions)" (Hale, 2007, p. 4). In this regard, Hale has asked: "Why has feminist studies remained more focused on gender and sexuality, and ethnic studies on race and ethnicity? Besides, class, as a variable, is increasingly falling between the cracks" (Hale, 2007, p. 4).

Defining basic principles of Feminist pedagogy, Professor Hale suggested that the central concern is process rather than product. Analytically and normatively, the Feminist Classroom shares much in common with a Pedagogy of the Oppressed classroom. Professor Hale's list of these commonalities is illuminating:

(1) Generating the student as subject; knowledge emanating from her/him;
(2) Using self-disclosure as a way of using self as subject—now often referred to as "situating," "positioning," or "locating" ourselves; I sometimes think of it as modeling;
(3) Teaching and/or facilitating through questioning: the self as inquirer;
(4) Interjecting the experiential into theory and practice;
(5) Challenging a singular/essentialized "voice," and recognizing the dynamism of "otherness" and "alterity;"
(6) Facilitating self-definition (labeling/naming/renaming/reappropriating);
(7) Fusing teaching with consciousness raising, and dialogue with presentation;
(8) Creating space for the traditionally silenced;
(9) Validating everyone's experience;
(10) Positively integrating pain and hostility into the classroom/group/community process;
(11) Building change into the process;
(12) Challenging the claims of neutrality and value-free process in positivism and empiricism, and the resultant abstracting away of the researcher as a discrete unit;
(13) Fusing self-knowledge and social knowledge;
(14) Building on each other's ideas and work in collaboration;
(15) Fusing theory with our everyday lives;
(16) Perhaps more importantly, to quote Freire, "Through dialogue, the teacher-of-the-students and the students-of-the-teacher cease to exist and a new term emerges: teacher-student with students-teachers";[1]
(17) Again, to use Freire, the banking system of education (where the student is a receptacle and knowledge is deposited) is replaced by the partner-teachers or what some feminist educators refer to as "teacher as midwife" (Freire, 1970, p. 67); and
(19) Encouraging students to use their knowledge in everyday life, and I would add, everyday politics; and many others.

*Hale, 2007, pp. 6–7*

For a Feminist Pedagogy and a Pedagogy of the Oppressed, teaching is a form of militancy, one that is at peril in the context of the reorganization of the models of higher education in the United States, and here I would like to make clear that advocacy is an important aspect of the art of teaching.

A good teacher is also a performer. Many good university researchers are perpetually criticized because they cannot teach, have no desire to teach, pay no attention to the students, are authoritarian, or simply do not have a pedagogical gift. Very often their classes are dull, boring, and uninteresting.

This critique acquires more relevance in the context of Schools and Departments of Education. Many professors of education work with students who will be elementary and high school teachers. We should teach them how to become good teachers. Yet, occasionally, but also perhaps all too often, they find their own teachers to be terrible pedagogues.

Of course it helps more than hinders a teacher to be charismatic, or a formidable public speaker, or a good entertainer. There is an element of artistry in teaching as there is an element of craft in research. But neither teaching nor research can be restricted or based solely on artistic entertainment or crafty projects. I should also emphasize that it helps if the teacher has a formidable memory, but it is more important if the teacher speaks from the heart.

In closing, I would like to validate one of the oldest forms of teaching: storytelling. By storytelling I mean telling stories and vignettes of your own life, and of other people's lives. This is one of the oldest pedagogies in the world, practiced by the elders in many communities, and certainly the type of pedagogical love we may have experienced when we were children listening to family stories or world stories from our grandmothers and grandfathers. To bring storytelling into the classroom is to validate the "lived experience" of individuals and communities, another extremely important source of knowledge.

While teaching my annual course as a Visiting Professor at the Universidade Lusófona de Humanidades e Tecnologias in Lisbon a few years ago, in one of my sessions Professor Antonio Teodoro, coordinator of the graduate program in education, argued that teaching is an appetizer to open the palate.

To think of teaching as an appetizer that opens the palate makes a lot of sense. We have all experienced that sensation of arriving at a restaurant for dinner but not having much of an appetite. In the Iberoamerican tradition, the servers will immediately bring some appetizers with the drinks, and *voilà tout*, we are ready to have a wonderful dinner. We are suddenly hungry.

The appetizers open our palate, and we are ready to explore other flavors, colors, smells, and shapes in the iconography of a liturgy of dining. That is in essence the role of teaching: to open the palate, to tease the students, to open new avenues for students to continue their own processes of education through being exposed to readings, themes, questions, experiences, and problems that make sense, excite, preoccupy, or challenge them. Teaching is one of the landmarks, but only one of many in a lifelong learning experience.

# Notes

1 Brief commentary accepting the Distinguished Teaching Award in recognition of Outstanding Dedication in Teaching and Mentoring by the Department of Education, Graduate School of Education and Information Studies, UCLA, Convocation, September 25, 2012.
2 Borges on the Art of Poetry. http://sedulia.blogs.com/sedulias_translations/2006/09/borges_on_the_a.html
3 Juan Domingo Perón (1895–1974), was an Argentine military and political leader; and President from 1946–55 and 1973–74.
4 A large concertina, said to be of German origin, providing the melancholy spirit of the tango.
5 General Juan Carlos Onganía, head of the military junta which took over the government in June 1966.
6 The first two refer to civil disturbances in the industrial cities of Córdoba and Rosario. The Montoneros were a radical and clandestine group of armed guerrilla opposed to the dictatorship.
7 Gabriel García Márquez, the Colombian novelist and short story writer, was born in 1928 and won the Nobel Prize for Literature in 1982. "*Crónica de una muerte anunciada*" is the title of one of his works.
8 A detailed analysis of this period is made in my book *First Freire: Early Writings in Social Justice Education*. New York, NY: Teachers College, in press.
9 This was the English-language title (New York, Continuum, 1973) of *Educação como prática da liberdade*.
10 Literally, "disappeared ones." The so-called "dirty war" in Argentina revolved around the kidnapping, torture, and disappearance of thousands of political progressives. Sometimes, post mortem, their infant children were "adopted" by their torturers.
11 Mothers and grandmothers of those disappeared picketed daily, armed with "Have you seen [Names Inserted]?" signs and photographs of their loved ones in one of Buenos Aires' busiest plazas. Their courageous defiance of curfews and censorship is credited with helping to restore civilian rule.
12 See Carlos Alberto Torres. (1998). *Democracy, Education and Multiculturalis. Dilemmas of Citizenship in a Global World* (pp. 223–225). Lanham, MA: Rowman and Littlefield.
13 Jürgen Habermas. (1992) *Autonomy and Solidarity* (p. 202). London, UK: Verso.
14 Cameron McCarthy and Michael Apple discussed this relational nonsynchronous parallelist perspective in their 1988 essay, "Race, Class and Gender in American Education: Toward a Nonynchronous Parallelist Position" in L. Weiss, ed., *Class, Race, and Gender in American Education* (pp. 9–39). Albany, NY: State University of New York Press.

# References

Fine, Michelle. (2008). "An Epilogue, of Sorts." In Julio Cammarota and Michelle Fine, eds., *Revolutionizing Education?: Youth Participatory Action Research in Motion* (pp. 213–234). New York, NY: Routledge.
Freire, Paulo (1971). *Pedagogy of the Oppressed*. New York: Seaview.
Gouldner, Alvin. (1964) "Anti-Minotaur: The Myth of a Value-Free Sociology." In Irving Louis Horowitz, ed., *The New Sociology: Essays in Social Science and Social Theory in Honor of C. Wright Mills* (pp. 196–217). New York, NY: Oxford University Press.
Habermas, Jürgen. (1992). *Autonomy and Solidarity*. London, UK: Verso.
Hale, Sondra (2007). "Appreciating and Critiquing Freire: The Connections between Education and Power in the Feminist Classroom." Paper presented at "Paulo Freire

at UCLA: A Dialogue on His Contributions 10 years after his Death." Paulo Freire Institute, Graduate School of Education and Information Studies. UCLA, November 6, 2007. Unpublished paper.

McCarthy, Cameron, and Apple, Michael. (1988). "Race, Class and Gender in American Education: Toward a Nonsynchronous Parallelist Position." In Lois Weiss, ed., *Class, Race, and Gender in American Education* (pp. 9–39). Albany, NY: State University of New York Press.

Mills. C. Wright (1960). *Images of Man: The Classical Tradition in Sociological Thinking.* New York, NY: George Braziller.

Torres, Carlos Alberto. (1998). *Democracy, Education and Multiculturalism: Dilemmas of Citizenship in a Global World.* Lanham, MA. Rowman and Littlefield.

Torres, Carlos Alberto. (In press). *First Freire: Early Writings in Social Justice Education.* New York, NY: Teachers College.

# 14

# TEACHING FOR CHANGE

## Social Education and Critical Knowledge of Everyday Life

*E. Wayne Ross*

PROFESSOR, CURRICULUM AND PEDAGOGY, AND CO-DIRECTOR OF THE INSTITUTE
FOR CRITICAL EDUCATION STUDIES, UNIVERSITY OF BRITISH COLUMBIA

## Introduction

One summer in the early 1990s, my partner, Sandra, and I drove from our home in upstate New York to my hometown, Charlotte, North Carolina. Like all new couples, we had spent a lot of time talking about our past lives, our families, and growing up, but this was the first time she was meeting my entire family. After a couple of days in Charlotte, Sandra and I were in the car heading toward I-85 and our next vacation stop, when she not so much asked, but declared, "What the hell happened to you?

Good question and one I, too, have pondered.

How does someone who grew up in 1960s North and South Carolina, the son of a Pentecostal minister, who spent time working in the church as a lay member of the ministerial staff, end up a non-believing anarcho-syndicalist living in Canada? How does anyone become who he or she is?

I grew up in the racially segregated South of the 1960s, in a fundamentalist, Pentecostal family. Trying to make sense of those experiences had a tremendous influence on the way I think and teach about the social world today. Perhaps not technically a total institution in Erving Goffman's sense of the term, our all-white Pentecostal church nonetheless served a similar purpose: it was organized to protect the community against what were felt to be intentional dangers to it and to provide a retreat and training that served to cut off people from the wider community, at least culturally. As a youngster I felt I lived in a doubly segregated world. There was the pathological separation of Whites from Blacks on an everyday basis; and this segregation was intensified by a home life that was nearly inseparable from church life at a time when *de facto* racial segregation extended to churches to such an extent that Dr. Martin Luther King (1968) remarked that

"We must face the sad fact that at eleven o'clock on Sunday morning when we stand to sing 'In Christ there is no East or West,' we stand in the most segregated hour of America."

My life within the church segregated me further from those I considered then to be "normal people." The Church of God (Cleveland, Tennessee) sprang from the holiness movement, which places an emphasis on John Wesley's teaching of "Christian perfection," or the idea that it was possible to live life free of voluntary sin and with a total love of god and others. The Church of God in the 1960s emphasized what they called "Practical Commitments," which were intended to shape the social practices of its members, outwardly separating them from "the world." This was to be achieved by dressing "according to the teachings of the New Testament." The Church demanded modesty, forbade the use of cosmetics and ornamental jewelry, and regulated hair length (no short hair for women or long hair for men). In addition, it was taboo to participate in "mixed swimming," watch movies or television, go to dances, or otherwise participate in "ungodly amusements." My dad was considered a "liberal maverick" among his peers because he sponsored church sports teams and had nothing against judicious viewing of television. As I grew older, I increasingly felt manipulated, controlled, and constrained by the teachings of the church and the not-so-subtle expectation that I serve as a role model for my peers. I also began to face the contradiction of loving my family, whose lives were framed by a total institution I was beginning to call into question and would ultimately reject.

I have continually struggled with authority and hierarchy. At times, I have been earnest in my submission (such as when I left public school teaching to work in the church), but the arc of my life and work has been toward freedom. The oppressive and inequitable consequences of authority and hierarchical organizations in social relations—the church, the state, and capitalism—have motivated me in my journey from conservative to liberal Christian, to Deweyan democrat, and onward to a concern for creating a society characterized by positive liberty. In such a society, individuals have the power and resources to realize and fulfill their own potential, free from the obstacles of classism, racism, sexism, and other inequalities encouraged by educational systems and the influence of state and religious ideologies. It is a society where people have the agency and capacity to make their own free choices and act independently based on reason, not authority, tradition, or dogma.

I begin my pedagogical creed with the statement "education is a process of becoming." In this sense, education is life, but not all experiences in life are educative. Experience is education when it is critically examined in relation to the past, present, and the future, and when external conditions interact with the subjectivities of the person having the experience. An educative experience suggests the past is part of who we are now, and that the present is important as a precondition for resolving major social contradictions in the future. These kinds of experiences help us construct personally meaningful understandings of the world and, in the process, to make change.

Investigating social issues provides an opportunity to examine the history of an issue, its present social context, and what that issue means for us in the future. Studying how people (and things) change is the heart of social understanding. For me, perhaps the most compelling element of social issues education is that active investigation of social issues contributes to change. As Mao Zedong said,

> If you want to know the taste of a pear, you must change the pear by eating it yourself. If you want to know the theory and methods of revolution, you must take part in revolution. All genuine knowledge originates in direct experience.

Mao's position on the role of experience in learning is remarkably similar to those of John Dewey. Both of these philosophers, although poles apart ideologically, share what has been described as an activist conception of human beings; that is, the view that people create themselves on the basis of their own self-interpretations. As Marx points out, however, while people make their own history, they do not make it as they please, but under circumstances existing already, given and transmitted from the past. This activist conception of human beings can be understood as a function of four fundamental dispositions: intelligence, curiosity, reflectiveness, and willfulness. The disposition of intelligence refers to the ability to alter one's beliefs or actions based on new information, and the disposition of curiosity is that which compels us to seek new information for the sake of making better judgments. Reflectiveness is the disposition to evaluate our desires, beliefs, and actions to determine what the proper aim of our life should be. And, willfulness is the disposition to act on one's reflections.

The interesting thing about answering a question like the one Sandra posed to me almost 25 years ago—"What the hell happened to you?"—is that what we understand about ourselves and the world is determined by what the world is, who we are, and how we conduct our inquiries; that is, how we engage those dispositions that make us human. That's why social issues education matters.

## Article One: What Education Should Be For

Education is a process of becoming.

Education is a transformational process that fundamentally alters our understanding of self, others, the world, and our relationship with the environment. Thus, education is a social process that leads to individual and social change.

Education is a lifelong process that takes place in collaboration with others. Only in collaboration with others can individuals fully develop their potential, thus only in community is personal freedom possible.

Education is inclusive of, but transcends, the acquisition of knowledge, skills, and habits that are part of the formal curriculum of schools, universities, and other social institutions.

Education is not a commodity that can be bought or sold. However, the conditions of late capitalism have led to a widespread decline of authentic educative experiences to the point that the recent history of education (or at least schooling) can now be understood as the decline from *being* into *having*, and *having* into *merely appearing to have* an education.

Education that does not offer insights into the liberation of the oppressed should be rejected.

## Article Two: What the School Should Strive For

Schools are sites of an unresolved ambiguity, the source of both alienation and—at least potentially—emancipation. Are public schools the source of hidden riches and starting points for the transformation of society or are they impoverished zones to which the construction of real education can only be opposed? This remains an open question, but just barely. The initial challenge for anyone interested in the creation of schools that serve the public interest is to negate what has become the prevailing image of a successful school and what has come to constitute good learning and teaching.

Accountability—strategies that rely heavily on measuring outcomes, especially student achievement, and attaching consequences, either positive or negative, to various levels of performance—is the prime concept driving education reform in North America. These reform efforts are the ironic product of unaccountable corporate/state power that has made self-interested decisions ostensibly on behalf of the public when, in fact, the public has no meaningful say in what or how decisions are made or what can count as legitimate knowledge for students. Coordinated control of goal setting, curricula, testing, teacher education, and evaluation works to restrict not only what and who can claim the status of real or official knowledge, but also who ultimately has access to it. There can be no freedom apart from activity, and, within accountability-driven education, all activity other than the pursuit of the test score is considered irrelevant.

Where accountability-driven educational reform prevails, teaching and learning are presented as an immense accumulation of test scores. Education that was directly experienced has become mere representation: students and teachers quickly learn that what you know or can do doesn't matter, only the score counts. Even assuming that the demands of these reforms could be met, this kind of education can never offer a qualitatively rich life, because its foundation is quantity, banality, and standardization.

We are now in an age in which all social relations within schools are mediated by test scores. The entirety of social activity is appropriated by the spectacle for its own ends, and, in education, like any other aspect of everyday life, there has been a continual downgrading from being, to having, to appearing. Educational reality has been replaced by image. In the topsy-turvy world of schools, what is true has become a moment of falsehood.

In today's "reformed" schools, every moment of life, every idea, and every gesture achieves meaning only from without. Direct experience and the determination of what is taught and learned by individuals themselves has been replaced by a passive contemplation of the images of good schools, students, and teachers. These images have been chosen by other people and are organized in the interests of only one portion of society—affecting the real social activity of those who contemplate the images.

The real social contradiction is between those who want (or are obliged to maintain) the alienation produced by accountability-driven education and those who would abolish it. What now passes as education reform implies the continual reversing of thing and image; material reality of learning in schools has now achieved its freedom from the idea of learning as a personally meaningful process.

Education, as a whole, really is a critical knowledge of everyday life. In this form, education constitutes the only reality in the face of the unreality produced by accountability-driven schooling (which now seems more real than anything authentically human).

Genuine community and genuine dialogue can exist only when each person has access to a direct experience of reality, when everyone has at his or her disposal the practical and intellectual means needed to solve problems. The question is not to determine what the students *are* at present, but rather what they *can become*, for only thus is it possible to grasp what, in truth, they *already are*.

## Article Three: The Subject Matter of Education

Knowledge is derived from and maintained by social interactions, and developed through language.

Reality is contingent on human practices, constructed by individuals in dialectical interaction with others and with their world (i.e., through experience).

Truths are relative to contexts.

Meaning is constructed internally and socially.

Knowing is an ongoing and dynamic process of interpretation.

Individuals have agency and choice, but are also constrained by recursive interactions between self and the environment/social system.

There should be no restrictions on the subject matter or topics included in the school curriculum.

Worthwhile curriculum knowledge takes the form of personal meanings that express both truth and value (intelligence and a moral stance).

Reduced to its most basic elements, schools should seek to create conditions in which students can develop personally meaningful understandings of the world and recognize they have agency to act on the world, to make change.

Education is not about showing life to people, but bringing them to life. The aim is not getting students to listen to convincing lectures by experts, but getting them to speak for themselves in order to achieve, or at least strive, toward an equal degree of participation and better future.

## Article Four: The Nature of Method

What we understand about the world is determined by what the world is, who we are, and how we conduct our inquiries.

Things change. Everything in the world is changing and interacting. When studying social issues we should begin by challenging the commonsense idea of society or particular social issues as a "thing," and consider the processes and relationships that make up what we think of as society or a social issue, which includes its history and possible futures.

Inquiries into social issues help us understand how things change, and also contribute to change.

In understanding social issues and how things change it helps to "abstract" or start with "concrete reality" and break it down. Abstraction is like using camera lenses with different focal lengths: a zoom lens to bring a distant object into focus (what is the history of this?), and a wide-angle lens to capture more of the scene (what is the social context of the issue now?) This raises important questions: where does one start and what does one look for? The traditional approach to inquiry starts with small parts and attempts to establish connections with other parts, leading to an understanding of the larger whole. Beginning with the whole, the system, or as much as we understand of it, and then inquiring into the part or parts of it to see how it fits and functions, leads to a fuller understanding of the whole.

Analysis of present conditions is necessary, but insufficient. The problem is that reality is more than appearances and focusing on appearances; the face value of evidence from our immediate surroundings, can be misleading.

How do we think adequately about social issues, giving them the attention and weight they deserve, without the distorting them? We can expand our notion of a social issue (or anything for that matter) to include, as aspects of what it is, both the process by which the issue has come to life and the broader interactive context in which it is found. In this way, the study of a social issue involves us in the study of its history (preconditions/connections to the past) and encompassing system.

Remembering that "things change" provokes us to move beyond analyzing current conditions and historicizing social issues, to project probable or possible futures. In other words, our inquiry leads to the creation of visions of possible futures.

This process of inquiry, then, changes the way we think about a social issue in the here and now (change moves in spirals, not circles), in that we can now look for preconditions of a future in the present and use them to develop political strategies (i.e., organize).

## Article Five: The School and Social Progress

Fundamental to human nature is the need for creative work, for creative inquiry, for free creation without the arbitrary limiting effects of coercive institutions.

Schools are continually threatened because they are autocratic, and they are autocratic because they are threatened—from within by students and critical parents and from without by various and disparate social, political, and economic interests. These conditions divide teachers from students and community and shape teachers' attitudes, beliefs, and actions. Teachers, then, are crucial to any effort to improve, reform, or revolutionize curriculum, instruction, or schools. The transformation of schools must begin with the teachers, and no program that does not include the personal/collective rehabilitation of teachers can ever overcome the passive resistance of the old order.

Schools should enable people to analyze and understand social problems, envision a future without those problems, and take action to bring that vision into existence.

Social progress is enhanced when we rewrite the narrative of the triumphant individual working within the system into a story of the creation of self-critical communities of educators (individuals) in schools (society) working collaboratively toward transformative outcomes.

People who talk about transformational learning or educational revolution without referring explicitly to everyday life, without understanding what is subversive about learning, and love, and what is positive in the refusal of constraints, are trapped in a net of received ideas, the common-nonsense and false reality of technocrats (or worse).

Schools are alluring contradictions, harboring possibilities for liberation, emancipation, and social progress, but, as fundamentally authoritarian and hierarchical institutions, they produce myriad oppressive and inequitable by-products. The challenge, perhaps impossibility, is discovering ways in which schools can contribute to positive liberty. That is a society in which individuals have the power and resources to realize and fulfill their own potential, free from the obstacles of classism, racism, sexism, and other inequalities encouraged by educational systems and the influence of the state and religious ideologies. A society in which people have the agency and capacity to make their own free choices and to act independently based on reason, not authority, tradition, or dogma.

*This pedagogical creed reflects my experiences and interactions with many people (and their work), including John Dewey, Karl Marx, Bertell Ollman, Guy Debord, Paulo Freire, Noam Chomsky, Raoul Vaneigem, Willard Waller, Sandra Mathison, Rich Gibson, Kevin D. Vinson, and my own students.*

# 15

# KNOWLEDGE, EDUCATION, AND POWER

## A Social Justice Pedagogical Creed

*Charlene Johnson-Carter*

ASSOCIATE PROFESSOR OF CURRICULUM AND INSTRUCTION,
UNIVERSITY OF ARKANSAS, FAYETTEVILLE

The centerpiece of my pedagogical creed is the power that knowledge gives to individuals and, ultimately, to society. Social justice is an integral component of this maxim and is reflected and implicated in it. I believe a good education, i.e., a store of knowledge, is beneficial to one's self concept and a source of positive self-esteem.

For me, knowledge and education are as integrally linked as a baobab tree and the soil in which is stands. Initially, the soil nourishes the developing plant. At maturity, the tree returns nutrients to the soil. No one questions the right of the baobab to draw strength from its foundation. Likewise, the right of persons of color to build themselves up by using the store of knowledge in society is an unquestionable right and a critical dimension of social justice.

My education was mostly in Catholic schools. From kindergarten to 8th grade, I attended an elementary Catholic school (St. Joseph's) in my low-income neighborhood in Cincinnati, Ohio, whose student population was largely comprised of African American children. In grades 9 to 12, I traveled across town to a Catholic, all-female high school (Marian) in an upper-middle-class neighborhood, with a student body primarily comprised of European Americans. There, I was one of twelve Blacks in a class of 150. Though my ability to perform at a high level was never questioned in elementary school, on several occasions in high school it was made clear I was not expected to do well because of my race and home neighborhood. These situations occurred despite my consistently excellent work in all my classes.

One experience in particular, involving race, was pivotal for my educational perspectives.

One afternoon, my 11th grade English teacher, a short, white man who wanted to be considered "cool" by his students, came into class and asked if we thought it would have been better if the slaves had been freed gradually rather than all at once. I remember looking up from the homework I was completing for the next class and wondering, "How is this a question for an English class?" Then, I wondered, "Why is he asking this question?" During the next 50 minutes of class, the students of African descent were subjected to an onslaught of heinous assertions regarding "our people's" abilities (slow, cognitively limited, and natural athletes), proclivities (lazy, uncivilized, and prone to crime), and achievements (little to none, given slavery saved us from the "dark" continent).

My attempts to address the biases and misperceptions emanating from all around the room were not supported by the teacher. I was left feeling defeated, exhausted, and devastated. It was not the first time I had heard these views, but it was the first time I had heard them from those I considered friends. It was hard to believe they held such ideas regarding people who looked as I do. It was then that two realizations began to emerge: (1) I was among the highest achievers in the class *and* junior class president, but this did not offset my teacher's and peers' negative perceptions of people of color; and, (2) I knew, based on my lived experiences with family and community, that such perceptions were erroneous, but I had little ammunition to "fight" those views because my education was that of a European American in content, with an emphasis on the accomplishments of people of European descent. Such an education provided little to no recognition of the contributions of people of color. Essentially, these two revelations framed (and continue to frame) my evolving perceptions on education, and thus have influenced my pedagogical creed.

My experience in that English class was my impetus to learn as much as I could about my history and the implications of race/ethnicity in society, including in the educational system in the United States—which impacts students of color and their dreams, many of which, as Langston Hughes put it, were and are forcibly deferred.

Although I was not aware of it at the time, this was the beginning of a journey to better understand and accept myself. Gradually, this journey took definitive form through my study of alternative perspectives regarding people of African descent. Critical Race Theory's emphasis on the salience of race vis-à-vis educational systems and practices, and roles and opportunities in society, has been instrumental in this regard.

I have always been fascinated by the power/influence of the mind over what happens in our lives, physically, mentally, and spiritually. This led me to major in Psychology at the University of Cincinnati. The number of courses for my major was matched, if not exceeded, by the courses I took in Afro-American Studies. The latter department was instrumental to me, academically and personally, in attaining a degree and acquiring a greater appreciation of the contributions and culture of people of African descent. Courses such as Black History, Black Literature, Swahili, Black Psychology, and African History introduced and familiarized me with my culture and the multifaceted contributions made by people of

African descent to the world. More importantly, the courses offered an empowered perspective on the culture of people of African descent in contrast to the deficit explanations and paradigms that were (and, sadly, continue to be) prevalent. On a personal level, the Department of Afro-American Studies nurtured my self-concept, much as my elementary school did. It provided a shield from the negative assumptions and misperceptions that surfaced elsewhere on campus. It was a psychological haven for me.

After completing my undergraduate degree in Psychology and Afro-American Studies, I remained at the University of Cincinnati and completed a master's degree in Counselor Education. After graduation, I accepted a position in St. Thomas, Virgin Islands, as a guidance counselor. There, I gained more knowledge about culture and its varied manifestations, particularly among people of African descent. The dualism of Africanisms and Americanisms was clearly elucidated for me. Although our shared African heritage was evident in certain sayings, rituals, and customs, there were others that were uniquely American. Pleasantly surprising was the realization that in the Virgin Islands neither negative nor deficit allusions or innuendos were associated with the practices of either culture.

Another major revelation in the Virgin Islands involved the use of words with sociopolitical meanings; for example, the word "minority." Although the Island's population was 80–90% people of African descent, it was curious to me that we continued to reference ourselves as a "minority." Gradually, I became more cognizant of how power is implicated in one's choice of words. Having become more aware of global realties, I chose to use "people of color" as a more accurate term for depicting our global existence than the term "minorities."

The way culture is embedded in educational practices was another revelation that I had during my time in the Virgin Islands. A major tenet of counseling is reflective listening/responding—as a student talks, the counselor seeks to reflect the emotive quality embodied within the words; however, in St. Thomas, students used few, and sometimes no, verbal responses to questions regarding their feelings on sensitive areas such as family, school, friends, and social activities. Their respectful one-and two-word responses yielded little emotional content upon which to reflect. I recognized their reluctance to discuss feelings as a cultural norm, but also believed in the precept that assisting students with their emotional development hinged on understanding their feelings as they voiced them. Instinctively, I knew that I had to find a less intrusive way to get students to talk about their emotions. Rather than ask questions, I started telling stories and presenting scenarios that I perceived as, at least roughly, mirroring a student's emotions about the issue/concern we were addressing. As I told a story, I'd ask the student if he/she agreed with the characters' words and behaviors in situations and why or why not. I encouraged them to revise the story if they so desired and to indicate whether a situation was true for them or not. In these story sessions, feelings were elicited, and concerns associated with the feelings they were experiencing.

My experiences in the Islands taught me many valuable lessons about the multifaceted nature of culture, its manifestations, and implications for practice. A major lesson was that my culture or world view is not the *only* lens for viewing the world. In order to meet students' needs, I had to become knowledgeable about their worldviews. With the help of various individuals—mostly students—I gained valuable knowledge that supported and informed my work with them.

Further study at Atlanta University, a historically Black university, and at Emory University in Atlanta, Georgia, (where I earned my doctorate), advanced my understanding of culture, its manifestations, and how race affects all aspects of education, including the theories and principles that undergird its practices and interpretations of behavior.

Eventually, it became my quest to provide a more accurate portrayal of our lives, experiences, and significance so that those in education could develop more empowering, equitable practices for students of color—as opposed to those practices steeped in deficit philosophy that undermine their potential. For example, in foundational courses such as classroom learning theory, educational psychology, development, introduction to education, multiculturalism, classroom management, etc., my goal is for preservice educators to extend their thinking regarding the implications of culture and positionality for learning and teaching. Incumbent in this endeavor is the development of critical thinking skills. While a Catholic education certainly engendered and enhanced my critical thinking abilities, it did not equip me with the knowledge to adequately address the biased and narrow perspectives regarding the abilities and contributions of people of African descent, and thus my goal has been to connect the two in order to provide future and current educators with the perspectives and skills to engage in such work.

Numerous experiences within and outside the classroom influenced the development and evolution of my pedagogical creed. Essential in this regard was (and is) the thinking and efforts of such historical giants as Carter G. Woodson (*Miseducation of the Negro*), David Walker (*David Walker's Appeal*) and W.E.B. Dubois (*Souls of Black Folks*)—all of whom have been instrumental in demonstrating the long, arduous struggle of African Americans to have our perspectives, history, and contributions accurately presented. Furthermore, contemporary educators such as Asa Hilliard, John Henrik Clark, Michele Foster, Lisa Delpit, and Joyce King showed me that success in the Academy was not contingent on becoming assimilationist and perpetuating the deficit paradigm regarding people of African descent.

The writings of critical theorist Paulo Freire added new dimensions and insights to my understanding of the potential of education for liberation. Critical race theorists Derrick Bell, Gloria Ladson-Billings, William Tate, Marvin Lynn, and Adrienne Dixson demonstrated that one can successfully challenge prevailing paradigms regarding people of color, and have provided me with arguments that have been instrumental for framing my own discourse on race and education. Toni Morrison, Nobel Prize for Literature and Pulitzer Prize literary genius, has inspired me and helped disentangle messages regarding our people, our community, and our interactions. I would be remiss if I did not include my family: my mother, who worked tirelessly so that her nine children could receive the best education possible, and who instilled confidence in us and helped us to believe that we could accomplish that which we dreamed and never allowed us to accept anything less than what we were capable of; and, my siblings, who provided the initial impetus for the development of my critical thinking skills, because one could not exist in our household without them. My husband, children, and grandchildren ensure that my critical thinking skills remain honed.

## My Creed

- I believe knowledge is power and, likewise, powerful. Knowledge is capital in the sense that the more one has, the more secure one is in his/her views and perspectives, and the higher his/her value to society. The power of knowledge—including facts, ideas, and skills—can be seen in the ways it buoys students. When students seek and find information on a topic, gather data, and, subsequently, support ideas and inferences with key and accurate information and sources, the power of knowledge is underscored. Learning and constructing knowledge becomes an asset, which not only furthers their awareness and understanding of the world but also validates their very existence.

- I believe in the importance of context for knowledge. I believe that when facts and ideas are contextualized and relevant to the lives and interests of students, learning becomes a means of power and meaningfulness. This is especially true for students of color and poverty whose experiences are oftentimes not reflected or associated with the material being covered. The power of knowledge is most felt when it reflects one's realities and is used to address questions about the world and one's place in it. This becomes "knowledge in use" rather than a list of unrelated facts spewing from a textbook or other source. When used to address questions of import to the students, knowledge has purpose. The latter also facilitates the incorporation of new knowledge into a student's schema and psyche. Contextualized knowledge in use is instrumental to addressing key issues in classrooms and to empowering students for their futures as responsible, critically-thinking citizens.

- I believe that knowledge is empowering. As students seek knowledge to address their questions, the answers they are able to find broaden their scope and understanding of the issues that perplex them; and this, in turn, increases their capital. Substantive information regarding the sources and meanings of ideas, concepts, and key social issues helps students frame and conceptualize a sense of purpose. A major constraint for students of color and poverty is the lack of substantive information regarding their existence. If mentioned, the reference to their experiences is mostly deficit in nature regarding their contributions to the world. When students are able to access and use knowledge that substantiates their lived lives (existence), they are more likely to realize their potential and, more importantly, act on it—this is the ultimate quest of empowerment and social justice. Students' capital is also enhanced by the acquisition of additional skills for finding needed information. This bolsters one's self-efficacy, which is also empowering.

- I believe that learning or incorporation of knowledge is a personal experience/journey. It can only be facilitated, not dictated or determined by an instructor. As instructors, we provide the materials and, more importantly, the environment and means for learning, i.e., seeking knowledge, but it is incumbent on the student to make meaning of the information. Experiences are integral to the making of meaning but it is also a by-product of the students themselves. Novelty and uncertainty are two of the beauties of this process.
- I believe knowledge and empowerment is tied to civic duty and requires civic engagement. Knowledge informs our interaction with the world. Education can and should serve societal goals, whether it is to sustain them or revise them to be more inclusive and reflective of the democratic idea we tout in this country. Students must be exposed to the most advanced information available so that they become proficient in the skills needed for success in today's world. This is especially true for students of color and poverty as they are oftentimes provided limited and/or deficient instruction in areas that are crucial for success in contemporary society such as math, science, and technology. With increased proficiency in these areas, they are more able to not only contribute to the larger societal order but also note how instrumental knowledge is to societal functioning. This enhances their capital and involvement as citizens, which is critical to the democracy we tout as our mission in this society.
- I believe in the transformative potential of knowledge. This idea is captured by Paulo Freire's statement, "There is no such thing as a neutral education process." Education either maintains the status quo or becomes an "instrument of freedom." For me, it became an "instrument of freedom"; for others, especially those in power, it becomes a mechanism for ensuring their dominance. Those in power believe they determine what is accepted as "truth" but, historically, knowledge takes on a life of its own and effects change in unexpected ways.
- I believe that teaching is a moral endeavor because of the effects it has on lives and the larger society. As educators, we have a moral duty to approach our duties with high standards and expectations and with an eye to expanding students' knowledge base and abilities, extending them intellectually, and helping them become, fully functioning citizens of the world.
- I believe it is incumbent on the educator to establish an environment in which questions and answers can flourish. Educators effectively guide knowledge

acquisition by being aware of, and capitalizing on, students' experiences and culture for initiating, conducting, and interpreting classroom processes. Educators are a powerful means for students to acquire the knowledge needed to transform themselves.

- I believe learning, teaching, and education are not always comfortable. Discomfort and disequilibrium are incumbent in the transformative process of learning and incorporating new and unfamiliar concepts—especially when culturally different perspectives and realities are involved. Whereas children are instructive in helping educators negotiate this terrain, as evidenced by my experiences counseling students in St. Thomas, this is a personal journey that continually evolves when working with students of color and/or poverty.

- Like Dewey, I believe that educators are invaluable in the knowledge-acquisition process, which is a lifelong endeavor. The results of our efforts are not readily visible but can be realized and developed over the course of students' lives. The ultimate indicator of success is their use of knowledge to ensure a more equitable world. As with the baobab tree, the tree, when mature, returns nutrients to the soil—our society.

# 16

# FROM VOICING TO NAMING TO RE-HUMANIZATION

*Miguel Zavala*

ASSISTANT PROFESSOR, DEPARTMENT OF SECONDARY EDUCATION,
CALIFORNIA STATE UNIVERSITY, FULLERTON

## My Pedagogic Creed: Biographical Interlude

My story of coming to a decolonizing pedagogical framework is deeply rooted in my own personal biography growing up as a Chicano in southeast Los Angeles. Yet, my personal biography is intertwined with the collective experience of my family and the broader Chicano community in the southwest. Both of my parents migrated[1] to the United States from Mexico during the 1960s and joined the ranks of *Mexicano* industrial workers in southeast Los Angeles. Some family members eventually moved to other areas, toiling the fields as migrant farm workers in California and Texas. On both my father's and mother's sides, we trace our histories to the indigenous peoples of central Mexico—a history that has been denied, erased, and eventually forgotten. The exploitation, institutional racism, and marginalization my families have endured are a living memory that greatly impacts my commitment to collective struggle. This struggle continues to this day as *Raza*[2] communities find themselves under attack by draconian and racist policies that have positioned us as "ontological foreigners" (Tejeda, Espinoza, and Gutierrez, 2003). It is this very experience of struggle, of economic survival, and family efforts to learn how to navigate oppressive education, legal, political, and economic systems, that has become the greatest resource for making the study of social issues central to my teaching and organizing.

Yet this history of family struggle has been enriched in ways I could not predict vis-à-vis my own involvement in grassroots organizing. Since 2005, I have been immersed in various grassroots organizations and have assumed an active role in both in their development and the political work that grows out of these. Precisely because grassroots organizing places scholar-activists in the midst of community struggles from below, my own involvement in these organizations has led me to think and operate in ways that prioritize community issues and social problems. Thus, my involvement in the local struggle to transform racist education policies in those schools in which our members teach, the wave of neo-liberal privatization impacting urban communities, the deportation raids against Raza families, etc., has transformed my own pedagogical praxis and has shaped my ideological perspective. More recently, I have written about the possibility of popular, grassroots education and the lessons that can be gleaned from indigenous struggles in Latin America and New Zealand (see Zavala, 2013). Reflecting on grassroots popular education, I have been investigating the processes by which popular education is mediated within grassroots organizations (see Zavala, 2014). As a teacher educator in a major public university (California State University, Fullerton), I continually strive to make social issues central to my teaching. In my literacy work with urban and migrant youth, literacy is infused with historical and sociological analysis. I believe a pedagogy informed by a decolonizing framework is meaningless without making colonized peoples' survival and recovery central to it; this requires a critical re-framing of their lives and an understanding how to transform the neo-colonial situation that limits their development. In sum, a critical study of any subject matter must ultimately address the very social issues that impact the peoples' lives, with the goal to reclaim their cultural histories and thereby lead to community self-determination.

## Decolonizing Pedagogies: Standpoint and Tenets

I cannot separate my own lived experience as a Chicano from my own pedagogical praxis. While I attempt to articulate general principles of a decolonizing *pedagogical* framework, my own political and ideological stance grows out of a collective experience that I shall name a *Chicano standpoint*. Much like feminism as a standpoint (Harding, 2009), a Chicano standpoint represents a collective, political achievement and vision by and for Chicanos. This standpoint is emergent; its internal contradictions are ongoing and to be resolved by Chicanos themselves. The principles articulated here in my pedagogic creed need to be reinvented in the context of working with non-Chicano communities. *I believe that, for Chicanos, the question of colonialism is central to the curriculum and its investigation should emerge as an expression of Chicano communities' self-determination.*

Decolonizing pedagogies (Iseke-Barnes, 2008; Nakata, et al., 2012; Tejeda, Espinoza, and Gutierrez, 2003) represent an expansion and departure from critical pedagogical strands. Decolonizing pedagogies—distinct from critical, feminist, anti-racist, and humanist pedagogies—begin with the assumption that colonialism and imperialism are central to our oppression. Although other pedagogical approaches can be integrated within the broader framework of de-colonization, a distinguishing feature of decolonizing pedagogies is their explicit engagement with the question of colonialism at all levels of education. The extant curriculum that I am talking about here interweaves reading and writing the world (Freire and Macedo, 1987) against neo/colonialism, guided by concepts that assist colonized people in an understanding of how colonizing discourses and practices are lived today. Similar to Red/Indigenous Pedagogies (Grande, 2004), Tejeda, Espinoza, and Gutierrez (2003) have made a call for this general decolonizing strategy, with its emphasis on the study of colonialism:

> We contend that developing a critical consciousness of our internal neo-colonial condition and its possible transformation is fundamental to what teachers and students do in decolonizing pedagogical spaces. This requires explicit attention to the history and contemporary manifestations of internal neocolonialism in a manner that clearly explicates their social origin and rejects their historical consequence. It also introduces students to robust theories and conceptual frameworks that provide them the analytic tools to excavate history and examine the present.
>
> *p. 30*

From the standpoint of the colonized, the goals, processes, and outcomes of decolonizing projects are to be struggled for and placed within the spatial-historical process of *survivance* (Grande, 2004). Colonized peoples and historically dominated groups are caught in the midst of a set of historical contradictions and processes set off by colonialism. Viewed more broadly, decolonizing projects take historical form against the backdrop of colonialism and materialize as part of a broader strategy of community self-determination. Using the metaphor of ocean waves, Maori scholar Linda Tuhiwai Smith (1999) has developed a useful framework for understanding these broader geo-political and historical forces as currents set off by the waves of colonialism. Thus, Chicano communities engaged in the processes of decolonization, healing, mobilization, and transformation must view their struggle both spatially and historically.

*Thus, within a decolonizing framework, questions of "whose interests?" and "towards what ends?" sometimes precede questions of "how?" The context in which decolonizing pedagogies take form, who undertakes this education, and towards what goals are often more significant in the struggle for self-determination than questions of pedagogical mediation and process.*

## Healing as a Decolonizing Pedagogical Strategy: From Voicing to Naming Our Colonized Lives

### Dialogue

> Dialogue is the encounter between [people], mediated by the world, in order to name the world.
>
> *Freire, 1970, p. 88*

> Dialogue is a moment where humans meet to reflect on their reality as they make and remake it.
>
> *Shor, 1992, p. 86*

Dialogue as a pedagogical process is part of a long tradition in Critical Pedagogy. In *Pedagogy of the Oppressed*, Paulo Freire iterates that dialogue is a particular form of human communication that involves critically reflecting upon the world. Thus, not all communication is dialogical. Moreover, the term dialogue conjures the image of people talking, deliberating, and discussing. Although this is part of the process of dialogue, Freire comments that dialogical mediation happens "not just at the intellectual level, but at the level of action," (Freire, 1970, p. 96). From a decolonizing framework, dialogue amongst colonized peoples is not a given but something that must be struggled for. Although language is a tool for social reflection, language and thinking must be interrogated and reclaimed. It is a mistake to assume that dialogue takes place among equals or that it represents a "safe space" where people come together. In practice, dialogue is imbued with both violence and love. *I believe dialogue is integral to education, yet dialogue is not a given and must be struggled for.*

## *Naming*

> To exist, humanly, is to name the world, to change it.
>
> *Freire, 1970 p. 76*

Naming is a process that emerges through dialogue and critical reflection. Given the colonial legacies of violence that encircle the lives of historically dominated communities in the United States, naming involves a complex process of reflection, through the use of historical and sociological concepts, on the ways in which our lives are affected by colonial discourses and practices. In my experience working with migrant and *Raza* students from southeast urban Los Angeles, the process of naming grows out of one's lived experience and is transformed into a collective process whereby students bring their often contradictory experiences together within a broader framework generated from concepts derived from social theory/analysis. Such concepts include Colonialism, Capitalism, Patriarchy, Hegemony, and Eurocentrism.

Naming often involves "naming one's pain" (hooks, 1989). Colonialism, Capitalism, Hegemony, White Supremacy, Eurocentrism, etc., seem like abstract concepts but, when internalized and interwoven with personal experience, are powerful bridges that assist students in naming interpersonal and "horizontal" violence as constituted by macro- and "vertical" forms of State violence. Colonized peoples, precisely because of their subjection and domination, experience violence on so many levels: in family settings, among family members; in the workplace, where *Raza* communities are exploited daily; in schools, when they encounter uncaring school administrators, racist teachers, and schooling as deculturalization; in public spaces, when they are targeted by the police; and in the media, through stereotypical and dehumanizing representations (Acuña, 1988; Spring, 2012; Yosso, 2006). No social space is left untouched by the colonial legacies of violence.

Naming is not merely a cognitive activity. Although students are apprenticed into academic literacies, and although the readings are derived from sociological, anthropological, and political theory, said readings are used as resources for critically reflecting upon and transforming students' understanding of oppression in everyday life, thus equipping them with tools for understanding the way schools and schooling systems operate and shape their lives. *I believe naming or "reading the world," when accompanied by conceptual tools, is integral to a critical understanding of students' lives and the world in which they live.*

## Counter-Storytelling

One of the cultural resources I have borrowed from Black, Chicano, and other historically dominated groups in making sense of our present day realities and the colonial past is counter-storytelling (Delgado and Stefancic, 2001). Counter-storytelling is a medium for challenging the dominant/master narratives we hear in our society. For example, one of the most pervasive dominant/master narratives about the causes of the deplorable "drop-out" rates for Black and Chicano youth in the United States is grounded in a deficit perspective that overtly reduces a complex, historical process into self-blame, lack of parent involvement, or a "culture of poverty" (Valencia, 1997). Counter-storytelling thus becomes a vehicle for self-empowerment, as students use concepts, readings, and other literacy practices as mediating artifacts for arriving at a critical, reflexive understanding of the problems encountered in their communities (Parker and Stovall, 2004). *I believe counter-storytelling is a rich tradition and powerful strategy for challenging the dominant stories or myths about historically dominated groups.*

## Healing

Healing is the social space interwoven throughout the experience of coming to name one's pain (hooks, 1989). Wrought by the violence of colonialism, decolonizing pedagogies seek to generate spaces of healing and community, where students can come together in spaces that are seldom experienced in public schools. In their analysis of schooling, students not only strive to think critically about colonialism and how it is experienced personally in relation to schooling, they speak against this violence and oppression. This speaking against or *naming* generates spaces of self-worth, cultural validation, and a vision of community that involves a love for their peers, families, and broader community.

The development of a political and social consciousness emerges out of this sense of community. Precisely because of colonialism, *Raza* students experience personal violence, marginalization, and dehumanization every day and everywhere. The development of political clarity among urban *Raza* youth requires that critical educators work toward the constitution of healing spaces. *I believe healing is perhaps the most important goal of a decolonizing pedagogy—education is more than cognitive development, it is about the recovery and healing of the mind, body, and spirit.*

## Experiential, Dialogical Approach to the Curriculum

> The starting point for organizing the program content of education or political action must be the present, existential, concrete situation, reflecting the aspiration of the people.
>
> *Freire, 1970, p. 95*

*I believe in an experiential, dialogical approach to the design and analysis of social issues across formal and non-formal learning spaces.* Linear and thematic representations of curricula cannot do justice to the complex, dynamic, and experiential nature of educational encounters. My approach to education is informed by cultural-historical theories of learning (Cole, 1996; Vygotsky, 1978) that ask us to reconceptualize pedagogy as both art (creative activity) and politics. Further, an experiential, dialogical approach places dialogue and experience at the center of the curriculum (see Gay, 2010). The object of learning is not so much driven by the mastery of knowledge; rather, the transformation of knowledge, how students and teachers internalize, process, and reinvent what is learned is prioritized. Nevertheless, by placing experience at the center of learning, I am not suggesting that learning, and education more broadly, is "student-centered." The praxis of learning includes students and teachers (who are also caught in the process of conscientization and transformation), but is more than these: the development of a critical social and political consciousness whose praxis is self and social transformation.

From an experiential, dialogical approach to curriculum development, the curriculum can be characterized as constantly moving from the abstract to the concrete and back again, as students struggle to critically understand their individual lived experiences in relation to others, and in relation to systems of oppression. This successive movement from the abstract to the concrete and back again is a general pedagogical strategy that generates and activates a series of interesting contradictions.

## Cultural-Historical Approaches to Pedagogical Mediation

The concept of mediation has its origins in Karl Marx's historical-materialism, and was further articulated by Lev Vygotsky in his cultural-historical approach to the formation of consciousness. Mediation describes the historical process that emerges with the separation between human beings and their world. As historical subjects, Marx had argued, we act upon our world, and in so doing both shape our environment and are thus transformed by it. *I believe that our world and the people that inhabit the world are in a process of historical transformation, and that our struggle as colonized people entails the transformation of the world that oppresses us.*

From a historical-materialist perspective, human consciousness develops with the production of culture, i.e. tools and artifacts, and is carried on by its successive transformation, as it is transmitted across individuals and communities. Paulo Freire's (1985) idea of "cultural action" is useful in understanding the historical character of education as a process whereby teachers and students are engaged in the co-construction of knowledge. A fundamental premise of the concept of mediation is the idea that we are conscious historical subjects, shaping and being shaped by what we do: "Consciousness is generated through the social practice that we participate in" (Freire and Macedo, 1987, p. 47).

## The Role of the Educator

Education—as opposed to socialization—is a dynamic, historical process arched towards life and human development. Diaz and Flores's (2001) metaphoric description of the educator as a "socio-historical mediator" is congruent with cultural-historical approaches to learning that define the teacher as someone who works deliberately in the construction of learning contexts. This view is often at odds with commonly held notions among progressive educators who, translating Paulo Freire's work, believe that their role is simply to "facilitate" learning through "dialogue."[3] Facilitation is seen as a political response to the banking model of education, in which teachers impose their knowledge upon students. From a cultural-historical approach to learning, facilitation is one form of mediation, the effectiveness of which should be assessed based on concrete learning situations. *I believe decolonizing educators are never passive, nor are they mere facilitators, but are actively shaping and remaking the contexts that make learning possible.*

## Learning as Socio-Historical Praxis

Cultural-historical theory proposes a radical view of learning as a material social practice that is rooted in a dialectical view of humans and their social environment. This view of learning challenges dominant perspectives that assume both (a) that learning is an individual act, and (b) that learning is a purely mental or cognitive process. From a cultural-historical perspective, learning is not individual, but a collective, social practice.

This cultural-historical approach to learning should not be confused with the pragmatist's "learning by doing" perspective. Although people learn through experience, these consciousness-raising oriented experiences are guided by specific goals, and, one would hope, are intentionally built from the accumulated knowledge of the past. Thus, we are able to learn through the experiences of others, through storytelling, and by observation. These practices, in turn, are not "natural" but are culturally specific, goal-oriented, and make sense within the broader context in which they take form. *I believe that learning is a collective, human activity that is culturally specific.*

## Cultural Resources in the Mediation of a Critical Social Consciousness

Cultural-historical approaches see the potential in all cultural knowledge and experience as a resource in the generation of new forms of knowledge. *I believe that the kinds of teaching strategies that are useful in any given learning context will depend on the goals, where the learning takes place, and who is a part of the learning, etc.* Often, progressive educators gravitate to inclusive theories of learning as a way of acknowledging "diversity" and the different ways in which learning happens. However, we must take caution in reducing the richness of mediational means to the popularized "multiple intelligences" or "learning styles," as these stereotype particular groups of students or they delimit the different array of possibilities in which teachers can move creatively in a given learning context. From a cultural-historical perspective, instead of thinking of learning styles we are apt to think of cultural resources; instead of the individual learner, the community of practice.

*Finally, I cannot overemphasize cultural mediation in the process of the formation of consciousness.* The series of interchanges that are both designed and unplanned are as important as the learning content. Progressive educators have rightly oriented the discussion of education to *what* we teach, but questions of process, i.e. pedagogical mediation, need to be raised along with questions of curricular content. Simply "exposing" students to *The Autobiography of Malcolm X*, assigning Eduardo Galeano's *The Open Veins of Latin America*, listening to Tupac's Shakur's lyrics, or viewing *Che: The Movie* is insufficient in generating a rich learning experience that mediates political education and clarity in our students. More important is what we do with these mediating artifacts, how we structure activities through lesson-structures, down to the kinds of talk we use to guide the interaction within those activities, and how these are interwoven with the goal of developing a critical social and political consciousness.

## Contradictions: The Genesis of Development and Learning

> Utilizing certain basic contradictions, we must pose this existential, concrete, present situation to the people as a problem which challenges them and requires a response—not just at the intellectual level, but at the level of action.
>
> *Freire, 1970, pp. 95–96*

One of the underlying principles of historical materialism is that historical transformations emerge in and through "contradictions." The resolution of contradictions or "unity of opposites," in the Marxist sense, generates new historical forms. Contradictions are found in any given activity. Within formal learning contexts, contradictions emerge between the teacher and student, between teachers' and students' cultural worlds, between the individual goals of students and the collective object, etc. Contradictions, in this sense, need not be considered negatively. *On the contrary, I believe contradictions are resources that we should strive to resolve and sometimes generate.* Distancing is a useful spatial metaphor for understanding the generation and resolution of contradictions.

There is yet a third dimension to contradictions—sometimes referred to as 'contrareities' because they are not strict contradictions in the traditional sense—that emerges when the historical conditions that have led to the formation of primary/secondary contradictions are brought to the surface. Literacy, for instance, and academic writing in particular, is a tool that is forged throughout the year as students work their way towards its mastery/appropriation. Given the political economy of literacy and academic writing in the United States, who produces it, and who gets to have access to it, for historically dominated groups such as Black and Chicano/Mexicano communities, (il)literacy has been used as a tool for colonial domination. What happens when students learn to master academic writing yet at the same time become conscious of the oppressive histories of literacy? That is, what happens when students learn to master academic forms of writing while at the same time writing instruction involves a critical appraisal of colonialism and literacy as a form of dis/empowerment?

## Conclusion: Why Re-Humanization?

I want to argue for dialogue and collective reflection as tools and processes that assist in the deliberate generation of contradictions. These generative contradictions, from a decolonizing pedagogical framework, should strive for healing, which inevitably leads to the re-humanization of colonized peoples. Contradictions are always present in any given practice. In attempting to create learning contexts that lead to student learning, mastery of knowledge, and self-transformation, it is important to move towards a collective reflection, through dialogue, on the practice itself. In a previous learning situation working with migrant students, this was achieved by bringing together the mediation of Paulo Freire's *Pedagogy of the Oppressed*, in particular his chapter on Banking Education, with a general reflection on the program itself, opening a dialogue with the question posed during the third week of the program: "Are we banking?" At this point, Freire's text shifted from the object of learning to a tool for reflection on the program. The significance of this kind of strategic reflection is the attempt to transform consciousness and social practice itself; in this case, the ways in which we were engaging around texts and teaching. Thus, learning can be viewed more broadly as an individual's appropriation of cultural tools or her change in participation within a given practice. Learning also goes hand in hand with the development of historically new cultural practices. What progressive educators and grassroots cadre have yet to resolve is how this dynamic view of learning is reinvented within the context of collective, political struggle, like the kind we are seeing in Indigenous and Socialist movements throughout Latin America. *I believe that, while a decolonizing pedagogical praxis is attuned to the tensions of generating an education by the colonized, how this generative experience is taken up in political movements for oppressed groups is in constant dialectical tension.*

## Notes

1   I use the term "migrate" rather than "immigrate" because for Chicanos the Southwest is viewed as an occupied territory; it is stolen Mexican land appropriated by the United States in 1848 with the forced Treaty of Guadalupe Hidalgo.
2   By *"Raza"* I mean a sociopolitical identity that encompasses the indigenous-mestizo, working class peoples of Latin America. *"Raza"* is typically used as a signifier for "the people" but my use of the term is akin to Gramsci's (1926) use of "the subaltern."
3   See Paulo Freire's (1993) discussion on "directivity" in the learning process in *Pedagogy of the City*. Also, see Peter Mayo's (1999) *Gramsci, Freire and Adult Education*, pp. 67ff. for a thorough discussion on the role of "authority" and interpretation of Freirean education as facilitator and midwife.

## References

Acuña, R. (1988). *Occupied America: A History of Chicanos*. New York, NY: Harper & Row.

Cole, M. (1996). *Cultural Psychology: A Once and Future Discipline*. New York, NY: Cambridge University Press.

Delgado, R., and Stefancic, J. (2001). *Critical Race Theory: An Introduction*. New York, NY: New York University Press.

Diaz, E., and Flores, B. (2001). "Teacher as Sociocultural, Sociohistorical Mediator." In M. L. Reyes and J. J. Halcon, eds., *The Best for Our Children: Critical Perspectives on Literacy for Latino Students* (pp. 29–47). New York, NY: Teachers College Press.

Freire, P. (1970). *Pedagogy of the Oppressed*. New York, NY: Continuum.

Freire, P. (1985). *The Politics of Education: Culture, Power, and Liberation*. Westport, CT: Bergin & Garvey.

Freire, P. (1993). *Pedagogy of the City*. New York, NY: Continuum.

Freire, P., and Macedo, D. (1987). *Literacy: Reading the Word and the World*. Westport, CT: Bergin & Garvey.

Gay, G. (2010). *Culturally Responsive Teaching: Theory, Research, and Practice*. New York, NY: Teachers College.

Gramsci, A. (1926). "Some Aspects of the Southern Question." Retrieved February 12, 2009. http://www2.cddc.vt.edu/marxists/archive/gramsci/works/1926/10/southern_question.htm

Grande, S. (2004). *Red Pedagogy: Native American Political and Social Thought*. Lanham, MD: Rowman & Littlefield.

Harding, S. (2009). "Standpoint Theories: Productively Controversial." 24(4) *Hypatia*, pp. 192–200.

hooks, b. (1989). *Talking Back: Thinking Feminist, Thinking Black.* Cambridge, MA: South End Press.

Iseke-Barnes, J.M. (2008). "Pedagogies for Decolonizing." 31(1) *Canadian Journal of Native Education*, pp. 123–148.

Mayo, P. (1999). *Gramsci, Freire, and Adult Education: Possibilities for Transformative Action.* New York, NY: Zed Books.

Nakata, M., Nataka V., Keech, S., and Bolt, R. (2012). "Decolonial Goals and Pedagogies for Indigenous Studies." 1(1) *Decolonization, Education & Society*, pp. 120–140.

Parker, L., and Stovall, D.O. (2004). "Actions Following Words: Critical Race Theory Connects to Critical Pedagogy." 36(2) *Educational Philosophy and Theory*, pp. 167–182.

Shor, I. (1992). *Empowering Education: Critical Teaching for Social Change.* Chicago, IL: University of Chicago Press.

Smith, L.T. (1999). *Decolonizing Methodologies: Research and Indigenous Peoples.* New York, NY: Palgrave.

Spring, J. (2012). *Deculturalization and the Struggle for Equality: A Brief History of the Education of Dominated Cultures in the United States.* Columbus, OH: McGraw-Hill.

Tejeda, C., Espinoza, M., and Gutierrez, K. (2003). "Toward a Decolonizing Pedagogy: Social Justice Reconsidered." In Peter P. Trifonas, ed., *Pedagogies of Difference: Rethinking Education for Social Change* (pp. 10–40). New York, NY: Routledge.

Valencia, R. (ed.). (1997). *The Evolution of Deficit Thinking: Educational Thought and Practice.* Abingdon, UK: Routledge Falmer.

Vygotsky, L.S. (1978). *Mind in Society: The Development of Higher Psychological Processes.* Cambridge, MA: Harvard University Press.

Yosso, T. (2006). *Critical Race Counterstories along the Chicana/Chicano Educational Pipeline.* New York, NY: Routledge.

Zavala, M. (2013). "What Do We Mean by Decolonizing Research Strategies? Lessons from Decolonizing, Indigenous Research Projects in New Zealand and Latin America." 2(1) *Decolonization: Indigeneity, Education & Society*, pp. 55–71.

Zavala, M. (2014). "Organizing Against the Neo-liberal Privatization of Education in South Los Angeles: Reflections on the Transformative Potential of Grassroots Research." 29(2) *Journal of Curriculum Theorizing*.

# 17

# POSITIONALITY, RECOGNITION, AND DIALOGUE IN DEMOCRATIC EDUCATION

*Steven P. Camicia*

ASSOCIATE PROFESSOR, SOCIAL STUDIES EDUCATION, UTAH STATE UNIVERSITY

From a very young age, I knew that there were some fundamental disparities between what I had been taught about what my gender and sexual identities *should be* and what they *are*. I saw my body as a site of contention where education and society attempted to eradicate one identity deemed to be deficient in order to inscribe another that was deemed "normal." I do not conflate gender and sexuality, but in both cases it was apparent that my formal and informal education reflected society's heteronormative desire to either pathologize or eradicate my identities. My body type is large, which intensified demands for my performance of masculinities in activities such as competitive sports and violence, all of which have always repulsed me. My first boyfriend and I were eight at the time of my first sexual relation. None of these identities were represented in the curriculum of my formal and informal educations.

A couple of years ago, I attended a panel discussion during banned book week. One of the topics was book bans in public libraries and schools. One of the panelists proposed that librarians in school libraries should protect the rights of parents by removing books from the shelves that parents find offensive, including books on same-sex families or relationships. I asked the panelist the following question, and then commented as follows:

> What about the right of children to see themselves recognized in the books on library shelves and curriculum? As a child and adolescent, I was denied the experience of seeing myself as a gay male in romantic relationships. My heterosexual classmates were able to see themselves in heterosexual relationships, and their relationships were often prevalent in their families and media. My parents are not LGB, which made it even more necessary for me to see positive examples of same-sex relationships in the school curriculum.

Neither that panel member nor any of the others responded to my question, although I could see that most panelists were sympathetic.

Two of the top ten most challenged books in 2012 portray same-sex relationships (American Library Association, 2013). In addition to an absence in libraries, the silencing of lesbian, gay, bisexual, transgender, and queer (LGBTQ) individuals in the social studies curriculum has been (and continues to be) widespread (Mayo, 2007; Schmidt, 2010; Thornton, 2010).

As a public school student, my identities had a great impact on whether and how I would contribute to classroom discussions, although rare, on issues of gender and sexuality. My current work involves increasing LGBTQ recognition and perspectives in curriculum (Camicia, 2012; forthcoming; in press). Such an increase in perspectives in curriculum provides a safe and inclusive environment for LGBTQ students, as well as an increase in the understanding of LGBTQ issues in both LGBTQ and non-LGBTQ students.

In contrast to my marginalized identities, my identities as a White, male, middle-class citizen of the United States have been privileged. I was not aware of this privilege throughout my public schooling years because my privilege kept me from seeing that women, people of color, and people from other countries were not represented in almost every school subject.

It wasn't until I studied at the university level that I was able to see this inequity. During my first Introduction to Education course at the University of Nevada, Reno, we watched Lee Mun Wah's documentary, *The Color of Fear* (Lee, 1994). After the film, our professor skillfully led a class discussion where our all-White student class confronted our shared ignorance related to White privilege. The film set the tone for all of my education classes because I began to look for ways that my privilege and education kept me from seeing non-dominant perspectives and social inequalities. I realized that the lack of recognition and/or misrecognition of women and people of color bolsters messages of sexism and racism in the curriculum. I also realized that while some of the White men represented in my education have been dead for a long time, and mainly lived in Europe, some lived closer to contemporary times and mainly in the United States. This latter group emphasized American exceptionalism, nationalism, and xenophobia in the curriculum by placing the United States as the "norm" by which the world would be judged. As a student, these aspects of my privileged identities had a great impact on whether, and how, I would contribute to classroom discussions, although rare, on racism, sexism, and nationalism.

## My Pedagogical Creed

My pedagogical creed has developed from a desire for democratic education in which multiple perspectives and social justice flourish.

## *Positionality*

I believe that students and teachers do not enter classrooms with the same power of voice because the social inequalities that exist in society follow students and teachers into classrooms. These inequalities function in the form of perceived identities such as race, gender, class, sexuality, and ability. Inequality of voice due to social hierarchies of identity undermines education and democratic communities because dominant voices and perspectives perpetuate social inequality.

Identities are defined by relational factors rather than essential qualities (Maher and Tetreault, 1993). The sum of these identities are inscribed on each individual's body and called a person's positionality.

Teachers and students all have unique positionalities that contribute to their privilege or marginalization. This is central to learning and teaching about social issues because knowledge is situated, contextual, dynamic, and reflective of power relations (Foucault, 1990; Haraway, 1991; Hartsock, 1997).

I believe that students and teachers are embedded in relational networks both inside and outside of classrooms. My experiences in different communities have shown me that teaching and learning about social issues is different in different communities. As students and teachers move through various communities, the networks of power relations change along with positionalities (Camicia and Bayon, 2012; Franklin and Camicia, 2011).

When teachers educate every student in every community the same, they perpetuate hierarchies of oppression by perpetuating knowledge of dominant identities.

I believe that inequitable power relationships in society are reflected in school curriculum (Camicia, 2008, 2010; Camicia and Franklin, 2011). Because the curriculum represents an official knowledge (Apple, 2000), the positionalities of dominant groups are overly recognized in the curriculum and the positionalities of marginalized groups are not. An examination of positionality strengthens democratic education by decentering dominant positionalities and deconstructing the belief that knowledge is "objective" or "neutral."

I believe that democratic education centers on learning and teaching about social issues in a way that recognizes multiple perspectives and hierarchies of oppression. Harding (1993) writes, "An effective pursuit of democracy requires that those who bear the consequences of decisions have a proportionate share in making them" (p. 3). The effectiveness of education for democracy requires that students and teachers recognize that social issues are viewed differently depending upon a person's positionality.

I agree with feminist epistemologists that emphasize that knowledge about social issues is most valid when viewed from the positionality of those most marginalized by a social issue (Code, 1991; Harding, 1992; Hekman, 1997). This realization is central to authentic democratic education. If it is not central, education is democratic in name only.

I believe that the authenticity of democratic education increases when the diverse positionalities in classrooms and communities are recognized in the curriculum (Camicia, 2009, 2010). This requires that dominant positionalities be decentered in curriculum and classroom dialogue (Boler, 2004).

## *Recognition*

I believe that students and teachers enter classrooms with positionalities that are recognized, misrecognized, or not recognized. I cannot dialogue authentically about social issues with my students unless I recognize how our positionalities are related and situated within hierarchies of oppression.

I believe that recognition has many meanings, including providing praise or a legal right, but the meaning that I use here involves seeing someone as they see themselves. It means to see something that is already there but was initially unseen. This way of seeing or recognizing is aimed at appreciating the complexity and fluidity of identity and positionality.

I use queer theory as a lens for understanding identity as it relates to education (Pinar, 1998). One of the most prominent themes in queer theory extends Foucault's observation that knowledge and power are related in ways that maintain power relations through "norms" (Foucault, 1972, 1981, 1990).

I believe that normalization is a tool for maintaining power relations because it is a process that imbues socially constructed categories with an air of objectivity (Foucault, 2003). For example, categories related to race, gender, ability, and sexuality are social constructions developed by scientists. Democratic education can function to deconstruct these social constructions in order to increase social justice.

I believe that rather than understanding socially constructed categories as constructions, communities take them to be objective realities. Power relations and inequalities are constructed and maintained by defining "norms" related to these categories. For example, the category of gay has been constructed in relationship to the "norm" of the category of heterosexuality.

I believe that "norms" are sites where privilege is perpetuated and hierarchies of oppression are maintained. Britzman (2012) writes, "Where queer theory meets pedagogy is in how it conceptualizes normalcy as negation" (p. 295). As long as students and teachers work within dominant constructions of "normalcy" in their learning about social issues, they are limited to outcomes that are defined by those with dominant interests and positionalities.

I believe recognition exists within a system of ethics. Based upon the work of Levinas (1981), Butler (2006) describes an ethics of recognition where we "create a sense of the public in which oppositional voices are not feared, degraded, or dismissed, but valued for the instigation to a sensate democracy" (p. 151).

I believe that the process of recognition is possible through recognizing the diversity of positionalities and the intersections of identities on bodies (Collins, 2000; Crenshaw, 1991).

I believe the process of recognition in education is contingent and paradoxical. Butler writes, "For representation to convey the human, then, representation must not only fail, but it must show its failure" (p.144). I believe authentic democratic education is a way to show these failures and deconstruct hierarchies of oppression.

Recognition has enormous implications when people speak because the voices of those closer to the "norm" are given more attention and power (Bakhtin, 1981). When my students and I question "norms," we seek ways to decenter dominant voices and privilege marginalized voices.

I believe that dialogue about positionality, "norms," power relations, and recognition can function within teaching and learning to increase the diversity of perspectives and positionalities represented in the curriculum.

An ethics of recognition in learning and teaching creates possibilities for opening a third space (Bhabha, 2009; Fine and Weiss, 2003; Soja, 2009). It is a space where dialogue, learning, and teaching about social issues can occur with an eye toward creating socially just education and communities.

## Deliberation of Social Issues

I believe that students and teachers enter classrooms that are embedded in contexts of local and global controversial issues. Deliberation of these issues provides the material for understanding how differences in positionality express themselves in different worldviews. While we share the same experiences, we experience them differently depending upon our positionalities and our locations in networks of power relations.

I believe that even if controversial issues are not discussed, they exist in the experiences of teachers and students, whether they experience them firsthand, secondhand, or through various media.

Students and teachers experience issues such as transgender rights, inequitable learning outcomes, human migration, or poverty whether the curriculum recognizes these social issues or not.

I believe that rather than silence these social issues and perspectives, public schools are in a unique position to teach democracy through deliberation (Hess, 2009; Parker, 2003). During deliberation, students and teachers discuss different perspectives on controversial issues in order to deepen their understandings of issues and plan a course of action. The aim is education that increases knowledge, civic awareness, and civic action through their synthesis.

I believe that controversial issues emanate from differences in perspective. When dominant positionalities are the only ones recognized in deliberation, "democratic education" is counterproductive because it excludes marginalized positionalities and perspectives.

I believe democratic education is soft when on the surface there appears to be multiple perspectives voiced during deliberation but, in reality, only dominant positionalities and perspectives are expressed (Camicia, 2009).

Democratic education is democratic in name only if students are provided with *and* taught *and* encouraged to pursue multiple perspectives in the curriculum.

I believe that classroom deliberation of an issue such as immigration policy provides an opportunity for students to recognize a wide range of positionalities. Identities such as race, gender, ability, sexuality, class, and geopolitical belonging are central to this deliberation. If they are not, then deliberation is largely composed of dominant "norms" and positionalities.

I believe that classroom deliberation of social issues such as immigration policy, related to systems of inequality such as racism, sexism, ableism, heteronormativity, cisgenderism (prejudice against people whose gender identity does not align with that assigned at birth), classism, and nationalism can encourage deeper understanding of these social issues and civic action.

Democratic education is strengthened when it includes authentic deliberation that recognizes multiple positionalities and perspectives. The deliberation of controversial issues such as immigration policy does not occur within a vacuum. It occurs within the historical and contemporary contexts of social inequalities and oppressions. Student and teacher deliberation of social issues that recognizes these inequities aims to increase knowledge of significant social issues, civic attitudes, civic action, and social justice.

## *Dialogue*

I believe that students and teachers enter classrooms with more or less dialectical relationships that can be used to deconstruct hierarchies of oppression.

I believe that authentic democratic education is built upon dialectical relationships where the boundaries between student and teacher dissolve. Freire (1998) writes, "When we live our lives with the authenticity demanded by the practice of teaching that is also learning and learning that is also teaching, we are participating in a total experience that is simultaneously directive, political, ideological, Gnostic, pedagogical, aesthetic, and ethical" (pp. 31–32). This can only occur if learning is dialogical between students and teachers.

I believe that learning takes place when teachers learn from students as students learn from teachers.

I believe that authentic democratic education requires students and teachers to dialogue within an ethics of recognition. This involves a classroom atmosphere where the complexity, contextually, and locality of identities are expressed.

I believe that dialogue and recognition are necessary to decenter dominant identities and deconstruct them of their "normalizing" functions in the curriculum, functions that maintain hierarchies and boundaries of oppression.

Dialogue and recognition encourage students and teachers to, as hooks (1994) writes, "collectively imagine ways to move beyond boundaries, to transgress" (p. 207). As a teacher, a transparent and reflexive examination of my privilege offers an invitation to students to enter a dialogue that crosses boundaries and silenced positionalities.

Democratic education centers upon the discussion and deliberation of social issues. When a diversity of identities and positionalities are recognized in the learning of social issues, teachers and students are able to transgress the boundaries that construct and maintain social inequalities.

## Conclusion

After living in San Francisco, Hong Kong, Reno, the Philippines, and Seattle, my transition to a rural, university town in northern Utah has intensified my reflection on teaching, learning, and social education. The differences of ideas, politics, and cultures between these communities have helped form my pedagogical creed because I understand teaching and learning to be contextual. Authentic democratic education is a process of recognition and dialogue aimed at increasing social justice within different contexts. Authenticity increases when students and teachers form dialogical relationships that recognize the diversity of positionalities within classrooms and communities. Recognition is aimed at increasing social justice by uncovering power inequities related to social issues.

My understanding of recognition and lack of recognition stems from my positionality as a White, gay, male, middle-class citizen of the United States. All of these identities were privileged in my education and society with the exception of my identity as a gay male. My awareness of my positionality has ebbed and flowed through my experiences with different communities. This is especially true with formal and informal learning environments.

My pedagogical creed has developed from understanding that dominant education and cultures do not recognize people and perspectives from marginalized identities. In other cases, they tend to misrecognize people and perspectives from marginalized identities. A democratic education aimed at equity must focus on increasing the recognition of marginalized perspectives and deconstructing oppressive structures such as racism, ableism, heteronormativity, sexism, cisgenderism, and nationalism. Essentially, and ultimately, then, my work is intended to increase perspectives in learning and teaching about unrepresented perspectives in THE curriculum by increasing global, multicultural, postcolonial, and queer perspectives (Camicia, 2009, 2012; Camicia and Bayon, 2012; Camicia and Saavedra, 2009; Camicia and Zhu, 2011, 2012).

## References

American Library Association. (2013). Frequently Challenged Books of the 21st century. Retrieved from http://www.ala.org/bbooks/frequentlychallengedbooks/top10

Apple, M.W. (2000). *Official Knowledge: Democratic Education in a Conservative Age* (2nd edn.). New York, NY: Routledge.

Bakhtin, M.M. (1981). *The Dialogic Imagination: Four Essays by M.M. Bakhtin* (C. Emerson and M. Holquist, trans.). Austin, TX: University of Texas Press.

Bhabha, H.K. (2009). "In the Cave of Making: Thoughts on Third Space." In K. Ikas and G. Wagner, eds., *Communicating in the Third Space.* New York, NY: Routledge.

Boler, M. (2004). "All Speech Is Not Free: The Ethics of 'Affirmative action Pedagogy.'" *Democratic Dialogue in Education: Troubling Speech, Disturbing Silence,* pp3–13.

Britzman, D.P. (2012). "Queer Pedagogy and its Strange Techniques." In E.R. Meiners and Q. Therese, eds., *Sexualities in Education: A Reader* (pp. 292–308). New York, NY: Peter Lang Publishing, Inc.

Butler, J. (2006). *Precarious Life: The Powers of Mourning and Violence.* New York, NY: Verso.

Camicia, S.P. (2008). "Deciding What Is a Controversial Issue: A Case Study of Social Studies Curriculum Controversy." 36(4) *Theory and Research in Social Education,* pp. 290–307.

Camicia, S.P. (2009). "Identifying Soft Democratic Education: Uncovering the Range of Civic and Cultural Choices in Instructional Materials." (May/June) *The Social Studies,* pp. 136–142.

Camicia, S.P. (2010). "Deliberation of Controversial Public School Curriculum: Developing Processes and Outcomes that Increase Legitimacy and Social Justice." 6(2) *Journal of Public Deliberation,* pp. 1–20.

Camicia, S.P. (2012). "An Ethics of Recognition in Global and Teacher Education: Looking through Queer and Postcolonial Lenses." 4(1) *International Journal of Development Education and Global Learning,* pp. 25–35.

Camicia, S.P. (forthcoming). *LGBTQ Curriculum and Heteronormativity in the Classroom: Democratic Education as Social Change.* New York, NY: Routledge.

Camicia, S.P. (in press). "Navigating/Embodying Controversy in Classrooms in the United States and Philippines: Using Autoethnography to Understand the Complexities of Democracy in Different Contexts." In T. Misco and J. De Groof, eds., *Cross-cultural Case Studies of Teaching Controversial Issues: Pathways and Challenges to Democratic Citizenship Education.* Oisterwijk, Netherlands: Legal Wolf Publishers, in cooperation with UNESCO/Paris.

Camicia, S.P., and Bayon, A. (2012). "Curriculum Development Collaboration between Colonizer and Colonized: Contradictions and Possibilities for Democratic Education." In T.C. Mason and R.J. Helfenbein, eds., *Ethics and International Curriculum Work: The Challenges of Culture and Context* (pp. 73–92). Charlotte, NC: Information Age.

Camicia, S.P., & Franklin, B. (2011). "What Type of Global Community and Citizenship? Tangled Discourses of Neoliberalism and Critical Democracy in Curriculum and its Reform." 9(3–4) *Globalisation, Societies, and Education,* pp. 311–322.

Camicia, S.P., and Saavedra, C. (2009). "A New Childhood Social Studies Curriculum for a New Generation of Citizenship." 17 *The International Journal of Children's Rights,* pp. 501–517.

Camicia, S.P., & Zhu, J. (2011). "Citizenship Education under Discourses of Nationalism, Globalization, and Cosmopolitanism: Illustrations from China and the United States." 6(4) *Frontiers of Education in China,* pp. 602–619.

Camicia, S.P., & Zhu, J. (2012). "Synthesizing Multicultural, Global, and Civic Perspectives in the Elementary School Curriculum and Educational Research." 17 *The Qualitative Report,* pp. 1–19.

Code, L. (1991). *What Can She Know? Feminist Theory and the Construction of Knowledge.* Ithaca, NY: Cornell University Press.

Collins, P.H. (2000). *Black Feminist Thought: Knowledge, Consciousness, and the Politics of Empowerment.* New York, NY: Routledge.

Crenshaw, K. (1991). "Mapping the Margins: Intersectionality, Identity Politics, and Violence against Women of Color." 43(6) *Stanford Law Review,* pp. 1241–1299.

Fine, M., and Weiss, L. (2003). *Silenced Voices and Extraordinary Conversation: Re-imagining Schools.* New York, NY: Teachers College, Columbia University.

Foucault, M. (1972). *Power/Knowledge: Selected Interviews and Other Writings 1972–1977* (C. Gordon, L. Marshall, J. Mepham, and K. Soper, trans.). New York, NY: Pantheon Books.

Foucault, M. (1981). "The Order of Discourse." In R. Young, ed., *Untying the Text: A Post-Structuralist Reader* (pp. 48–79). Boston, MA: Routledge & Kegan Paul.

Foucault, M. (1990). *The History of Sexuality: Volume I: An Introduction* (R. Hurley, trans.). New York, NY: Vintage Books.

Foucault, M. (2003). *Abnormal: Lectures at the Collège de France, 1974–1975* (G. Burchell, trans.). New York, NY: Picador.

Franklin, B., and Camicia, S.P. (2011). "Critical Civic Literacy and the Building of Community for a Globalized World." In J.L. Devitis, ed., *Critical Civic Literacy: A Reader* (pp. 131–140). New York, NY: Peter Lang Publisher.

Freire, P. (1998). *Pedagogy of Freedom: Ethics, Democracy, and Civic Courage* (P. Clarke, trans.). Lanham, MD: Rowman & Littlefield Publishers.

Haraway, D. (1991). "A Cyborg Manifesto: Science, Technology, and Socialist-Feminism in the Late Twentieth Century." In D. Haraway, *Simians, Cyborgs and Women: The Reinvention of Nature* (pp. 149–181). New York, NY: Routledge.

Harding, S. (1992). "After the Neutrality Ideal: Science, Politics, and 'Strong Objectivity.'" 59(3) *Social Research,* pp. 567–587.

Harding, S. (ed.). (1993). *The "Racial" Economy of Science: Toward a Democratic Future.* Bloomington, IN: Indiana University Press.

Hartsock, N.C.M. (1997). "Comment on Hekman's 'Truth and Method: Feminist Standpoint Theory Revisited': Truth or Justice?" 22(2) *Signs,* pp. 367–374.

Hekman, S. (1997). "Truth and Method: Feminist Standpoint Theory Revisited." 22(2) *Signs,* pp. 341–365.

Hess, D.E. (2009). *Controversy in the Classroom: The Democratic Power of Discussion.* New York, NY: Routledge.

hooks, b. (1994). *Teaching to transgress: Education as the practice of freedom.* New York, NY: Routledge.

Lee, M.W. (Writer). (1994). *The Color of Fear.* In StirFry Seminars and Consulting (Producer). United States.

Levinas, E. (1981). *Otherwise Than Being or Beyond Essence* (A. Lingis, trans.). Boston, MA: Martinus Nijhoff Publishers.

Maher, F.A., and Tetreault, M.K. (1993). "Frames of Positionality: Constructing Meaningful Dialogues about Gender and Race." 66(3) *Anthropological Quarterly,* pp. 118–126.

Mayo, J.B. (2007). "Negotiating Sexual Orientation and Classroom Practice(s) at School." 35(3) *Theory and Research in Social Education,* pp. 447–464.

Parker, W.C. (2003). *Teaching Democracy: Unity and Diversity in Public Life.* New York, NY: Teacher's College Press.

Pinar, W.F. (ed.). (1998). *Queer Theory in Education.* Mahwah, NJ: Lawrence Erlbaum Associates, Publishers.

Schmidt, S.J. (2010). "Queering Social Studies: The Role of Social Studies in Normalizing Citizens and Sexuality in the Common Good." 38(3) *Theory and Research in Social Education*, pp. 314–335.

Soja, E.W. (2009). "Toward a New Consciousness of Space and Spatiality." In K. Ikas and G. Wagner, eds., *Communicating in the Third Space*. New York, NY: Routledge.

Thornton, S.J. (2010). "Silence on Gays and Lesbians in Social Studies Curriculum." In W.C. Parker, ed., *Social Studies Today: Research and Practice*. New York, NY: Routledge.

**PART IV**

# Continuing to Move from the Classroom into the World

# 18

# SEARCHING FOR UNDERSTANDING, FINDING THE PEACEMAKERS

*Elizabeth Yeager Washington*

PROFESSOR, SOCIAL STUDIES EDUCATION, UNIVERSITY OF FLORIDA

## Beginnings: Social Issues in My Country

I am a White woman who grew up in Alabama during the 1960s, and I have lived in three other Southern states since I left Alabama in 1983. I have come to believe that at some point in their lives, Whites who grew up in the Deep South must face reality about the places they call home. I have seen White Southerners deal with this reality in many different ways. Some take a path that leads them through confrontation, hostility, and alienation—both from themselves and from people they have known all their lives—but they end up in a place of understanding and responsibility. I have seen others take this same path, understanding the reality but growing bitter and defensive, with an even deeper sense of White privilege—yet I know from personal experience that there may still be reason to hope for a change of heart among these people. I have seen still others take a path that begins with a deep hunger to question why things are the way they are and a sense that what they see around them is wrong, and their anguish grows the more they learn—but they, eventually, live their lives in a way that is true to what they have learned, and they seek out the peacemakers with whom they can talk and solve problems.

I have seen others who share my heritage take no path at all, living in a make-believe world where "things were fine around here until . . .," and racism is over when they say it is. As a Buddhist, I know I must acknowledge that no one really exists the way they seem to me, but as a White Southerner I just feel angry and ashamed of them.

I lived in Tuscaloosa, which had become a peaceful city since the days of George Wallace, I went to integrated schools, and I had casual friendships with African American classmates. Yet, I also grew up with a sense that something was wrong in Alabama. It was not until 1977, in high school, that I found a close friend who shared my unease and wanted to talk about it. I never had a teacher who discussed the history of the South in an open, honest way. But ever since that friendship formed (and it continues to be a touchstone for me), I have been able to look back and understand other ways that racism could be expressed in families, schools, communities, and government.

While in high school, I had two powerful experiences—one spiritual, one ugly—that shaped how I thought about issues of race and racism. First, the spiritual. As a sophomore, I became friends with an African American classmate who, for reasons I never quite understood, thought I would be a good speaker at her church during its Youth Week. My topic was "young people as the future church." I scarcely remember what I said because I was so nervous about public speaking, but I do remember experiencing for the first time the joy and expressiveness of an African American worship service, and I thought of this many years later when I attended worship services at Glide Memorial Church in the Tenderloin district of San Francisco. Most of all, I remember the warm welcome, the embraces, and the blessings I received from everyone in the congregation. However, it was hard for me to hold on to the warmth of the experience when I thought of the cold shoulder my friend probably would have received at my White church.

The ugly experience occurred on graduation night in 1979. I piled into a car with several of my closest friends (all White), and we headed to McDonald's. In the parking lot, we met a car full of African American friends who had also graduated that night. All of us were in high spirits. We greeted each other loudly and with excitement, jumped around high-fiving each other, and generally acted full of ourselves. Within minutes, the McDonald's manager, an older White man, barged out of the restaurant and ordered us off the property. He asked no questions, did not want to hear any explanations about how we knew each other—he just wanted us to leave because he did not "want any racial trouble" on his property. All of us quickly complied, and I remember just riding around in the car with my friends in stunned silence for a while. Finally, one of my friends spoke up: "That was our fault." We all knew what he meant. Even though we believed the manager was a racist who had made a terrible assumption, we also felt that somehow we had gotten our African American friends into trouble. Our presence had created a dynamic that led to a bad ending.

Nonetheless, back then I did live mostly in a sheltered world.

When I left Alabama for The University of Texas at Austin in 1983, I began to meet people from all over the United States. They quickly jerked me out of my shelter by assuming that, because I was from Alabama, I must be a racist. At an academic social gathering, someone made fun of my accent and said, "I certainly hope you're not proud of being from such a goddamn racist place."

Almost everyone wants to believe he or she is not a racist. When I was confronted so publicly at that miserable party, this man was not telling me anything

I did not already know about my home state. But I soon realized that he was not just talking about geography and history. Had I ever really looked inside my own heart and questioned my beliefs? I thought I had, but I wasn't even close. It would take many years and many soul-searching experiences for me to put the pieces together.

## Beginnings: Social Issues in Another Country

At sixteen, I was selected as an exchange student to attend high school in the city of Cochabamba, Bolivia. I had already developed an interest in history, geography, and world events, but nothing had prepared me for the culture shock of living in one of the world's poorest countries. In school and in my host family, I was again sheltered from some of the harshness of what was around me, but I still had daily encounters with beggars living on the streets, the sick and the crippled, orphans, and others who had no social safety net on which to depend for some of the necessities of life. I found myself giving away all of my *bolivianos* until Bolivian friends discouraged me by assuring me that it would make no difference. They were probably right.

Perhaps the most profound realization I had was that poverty, racism, and oppression are matters of degree, rather than kind. They began to seem rooted in the same place of hatred, misunderstanding, willful ignorance, and lack of compassion. The street people I saw were all indigenous Bolivians, treated in much the same way as Native Americans and African Americans in the United States. When I returned to the United States after two months in Cochabamba, I felt disoriented. But the experience had taken hold, and I decided to major in Latin American Studies and minor in Spanish at the University of Alabama. Later, I earned a Master of Arts in Teaching, specializing in Latin American history, while I was teaching in Atlanta.

## The Journey

It is difficult to pinpoint with any degree of certainty when I began to think of myself as a social justice-oriented person, but I believe that I had no opportunity to flourish in this identity until I became a professor of social studies education at the University of Florida. There I found that I could bring together my intense consumption of news about social issues (both domestic and international) with my teaching of social studies methods courses, civics methods courses, and global studies methods courses (the latter two being courses that I was able to create and make a permanent part of the Social Studies M.Ed. program that I coordinate). I also became involved in my own social activism in matters of local and national civil rights and civil liberties issues, as well as global human rights issues such as human trafficking. My involvement was an organic process that felt inevitable.

A variety of people have guided me along this path. It is hard to separate the personal from the professional, so I will not try to do so, but to simply identify their specific, profound influence.

- John Dewey, who argued that schools should be a democracy in microcosm where pupils learn particular processes, values, and attitudes to live effectively as citizens. Democracy, to Dewey, largely meant a form of active community life—a way of being and living with others. Moreover, he emphasized that democracy entails certain habits of the mind that must be cultivated throughout citizens' lives as they participate in various institutions and groups in which they have a voice in setting goals, sharing knowledge, communicating, and taking direct action.

- Walter Parker, who has continued to raise important questions about what it means to educate children for the demands of an increasingly diverse society that is trying to realize the democratic ideal. He argues that our view of citizenship in the U.S. must not be based upon national homogeneity; it must be pluralistic and allow for a wide range of cultural and ethnic identities. He also asserts that the school's primary moral obligation is to give children an education that will equip them to take advantage of their citizenship.

- Benjamin Barber and Jesse Goodman, who taught me about "critical democracy," which implies a moral commitment to place the public good over individual power and privilege. It implies an effort by citizens to address meanings of deliberation, civic responsibility, social equity, group conflict and cooperation, community, individual rights, institutional organization, public interest, and the distribution of power. Goodman views critical democracy as part of a broader notion of care, justice, common concern for the social good, and a restructuring of economic, social, and political power. Democracy, he states, is incompatible with racism, sexism, and poverty and must enfranchise more people for democratic participation. He emphasizes participatory action grounded in a commitment to eliminating prejudice and oppression.

- Reggie Holder, my high school friend who was troubled by what he saw in Tuscaloosa and wanted to talk about it with me. He now works at a United Methodist Church in downtown Birmingham where he ministers to the homeless and has been welcomed into the African American community to address social justice issues.

- Gonzalo Barrientos, a Texas state legislator. He was the first person I had ever witnessed exercising his First Amendment rights during a speech, all the while being viciously heckled by a group of White University of Texas students. He maintained his poise while speaking out about a racist incident against Mexican Americans in Austin.

- Cynthia Tyson, whom I met at the National Council for the Social Studies Conference, and who opened my eyes to critical race theory. I also admire the gentle, loving way she approaches teaching African American children about their precious heritage and identity.

- Elizabeth Bondy and Dorene Ross, two White UF colleagues who are committed to social justice and to education in high-poverty schools with large populations of students of color. They have been role models of gentle but persistent questioning of the status quo and of intellectual integrity.
- Vaclav Havel, Aung San Suu Kyi, and Nelson Mandela, who have endured unimaginable horror while remaining steadfast in their commitment to social justice and democratic values.
- The Navajo people of Chinle, Arizona, who welcomed me into their community, told me their stories, and allowed me to ask them questions.
- My husband, Ray Washington, an attorney who has dedicated most of his practice to representing those who have been denied their due process rights and who has forged strong connections with the African American community in Gainesville. Like me, he is a news and current events junkie who will happily sit and talk endlessly with me about the Constitution and social justice outrages. Unlike me, he is calm and analytical and always gives me a deeper understanding of complex issues.
- My sons, Benjamin, David, and John. Last year, Benjamin, at age 13, was brave enough to make a Citizen Comment at a City Commission meeting long before I got up the nerve to do so. My sons David and John are both interns for the American Civil Liberties Union in Los Angeles, and, through them, I have learned how to be a better Bill of Rights watchdog.

## My Pedagogical Creed

As in Margaret Crocco's chapter (Chapter 4), I have tried to outline belief statements that resemble the approach Dewey took. Also like Crocco, my pedagogical creed mostly comprises "convictions for which I have no evidentiary warrant other than the values I bring to my teaching":

- First and foremost, I believe I must be willing to be "troubled" by social justice issues, and then to be brave enough to talk about them in class. As a White Southern woman, I have sometimes felt constrained by my cultural upbringing, which emphasized polite agreement and fear of causing offense. To others, this "bravery" is second nature, and I have tried to learn from them.
- Most of my students are from the South. It is counterproductive to make my students feel defensive. From a practical standpoint, I find that putting people on the defensive usually creates nothing but ill will. I also believe it is wrong to make assumptions about my students because of where they are from. They continually surprise me.
- I believe that I should let my students know who I am from the beginning—what might be called "full disclosure." I believe that I should tell them

where I grew up and when, and that this now influences almost everything I do in my teaching. It is who I am, and they deserve to know it: but they also deserve to know that we will discuss social issues openly, respectfully, and safely, taking multiple perspectives into account.

• I believe that social issues are an essential part of the school curriculum and that they can and must be incorporated into every social studies course. It is not hard to find social issues worthy of study in history, government, geography, economics, and so on. I believe the issues are sitting right there in front of us. People's quest for social justice has driven much of history. One cannot study the geography of, for example, Sub-Saharan Africa without understanding the social issues that arise from poverty, the remains of colonialism, and the exploitation of the continent's resources. One is not really learning economics unless one is studying how economic inequality is created and sustained, and, of course, the study of civics and government would have no value without an examination of social issues stemming from violations of civil liberties and "hot button" topics that revolve around issues of racial inequality.

• I believe that in my social studies methods courses, my students should have the opportunity to explore and apply a variety of approaches to teaching the social science disciplines, but all of these approaches must be reflected upon, revised in changing circumstances, and—most importantly—based on the integrity of the discipline itself. I believe that, since they are unlikely to find a job teaching a stand-alone course on social issues in Florida, they must be creative and persistent in looking for opportunities to infuse social issues into every course they teach. Throughout the three semesters they are with me, my students and I explore the possibilities. Furthermore, the content and pedagogy they choose must be enveloped within an ethic of care for their students, as expressed by Nel Noddings and others.

• I believe that in my civics methods courses, my students should focus on both *engaged* and *enlightened* citizenship, as Patricia Avery and others have suggested. Civics content must be connected with civics skills and dispositions, and the children they teach should be viewed as "citizens in training."

• I believe that in my global studies methods courses, my students should address three essential questions: How do we find out what we need to know about global issues? How do we live together justly? How do we live together safely? As we explore media conglomerates, citizen journalism, human rights issues ranging from sex trafficking to children orphaned because of AIDS, and national security challenges, I believe in letting my students gravitate toward a topic that is compelling to them. I often find that the issue they choose is reflected in their work throughout the course, and that, by the end of the semester, they have achieved some depth of knowledge and personal meaning about, for example, the Rwandan genocide, Guantanamo Bay detainees, or child soldiers. Issues of race and ethnicity are embedded in many of the topics they choose, and they learn about the many ways that racism drives violence, war, and the exploitation of human life.

- While I believe in guiding my students through the complexities of race in the United States and other countries, ultimately I know that my students came to me with an entire lifetime of beliefs and assumptions, and I will not be able to "undo" anything I believe is misguided or "wrong" in three semesters. I do believe in remaining hopeful that students will think about, reflect on, and question some of their beliefs—whatever they may be—and come to a better understanding of how their beliefs and assumptions will affect the children they teach.

- I believe that my students must think deeply about how they will teach social issues that are likely to be controversial, depending on the community in which they live and other unpredictable factors. We frankly discuss their concerns and fears—everything from losing control of the classroom to losing their jobs. By the end of the program, they develop a philosophy statement that reflects their goals for teaching controversial issues and their position on disclosing their own views with their future students.

- Finally, I believe—and teach—that democracy, as Dewey said, is a not just a form of government but a way of living and being with other people. The way we talk to each other and solve problems in this country must be based on that shared understanding.

## Conclusion

Am I still atoning for the sins of George Wallace and his ilk? Maybe. Am I still seeking peace within myself every time I see something on the news that reminds me of the past and makes me ashamed of what is happening now? Probably. Most of all, I believe I am trying to do what the wise people in my life have taught me—to never stop my search for understanding, and to always seek out the peacemakers. Living my life as both a student and teacher of social issues is my roadmap.

# 19

# DELVING INTO THE WORLD WITHIN AND BEYOND THE CLASSROOM DOOR: LESSONS ABOUT INEQUALITY AND OPPORTUNITY

*Chara Haeussler Bohan*

ASSOCIATE PROFESSOR, SOCIAL STUDIES EDUCATION, GEORGIA STATE UNIVERSITY

I was handed my 8th grade diploma from my father, who was the board of education president in our small New Jersey town, Florham Park. The town was so tiny it did not have its own high school. My father had served on the local school board during my time in grade school and continued in this role for several more years while my younger siblings attended the schools, as well. A decade earlier, my mother proudly served as the same town's first librarian. Our family summer vacations were spent driving along the East coast in our Chrysler station wagon visiting museums, battlefields, and other historic sites. Through these experiences, I learned, at a very young age, about the importance of social issues, education, civic involvement, and history. My father's German immigrant family had come to New York in the 1890's and enjoyed modest financial success. My father attributed their achievement to the opportunities afforded by the high quality of public education in America. He gave back to his country by serving in several local public official roles, including three terms on the local board of education.

With such childhood experiences, it came as little surprise to my family that I became a teacher. Studying about social issues and education was certainly in my DNA. Now, as I reflect on my professional work during the past quarter century and articulate my pedagogical creed, I believe I was destined to devote my career to teaching and learning about social issues.

I began my teaching career in New York City in the fall of 1989. While working on an MAT degree at Teachers College, Columbia University, I engaged in pre-service teaching at Brooklyn Technical High School, one of the crown jewels of the New York City public education system. The following year, I started my first full-time teaching position at an elite private school, Horace Mann, that was established by Nicholas Murray Butler in 1887 as the laboratory school of Teachers College (TC). At these two New York City schools I taught a range of social studies and history courses, and when my spouse's job was transferred to Austin, Texas, I continued as a social studies teacher at William B. Travis High School, a Title I school with a predominantly low income Hispanic population. Thus, I had a diverse range of teaching experiences—in different geographical areas, with different student populations, and a range of courses, including but not limited to: Global Issues, U.S. History, European History, World History, U.S. Government, and World Geography. Tellingly, in each and every one of these high schools and courses, I taught about social issues.

Developing the "itch" to learn more (teachers are overgrown students), I began doctoral studies in 1995 at the University of Texas at Austin (UT) in Curriculum and Instruction under the mentorship of Dr. O.L. Davis, Jr. who had been recommended to me by my T.C. advisor, Mike Whelan.

Dr. Davis was an outstanding mentor, and he taught me how to research, write, and guide students. He introduced me to academic publishing, scholars, and conferences. I began my foray into higher education instruction in January 1996 when I was given the opportunity to supervise social studies student teachers. Working with social studies interns and teachers at a variety of schools broadened my education horizons even further.

After completing my doctoral degree, I taught undergraduate education students at Baylor University and, later, graduate students in social studies education at Georgia State University. All these experiences, from childhood forward, have strongly shaped my pedagogical beliefs. The practice of teaching, researching, and writing in the field of social education has also informed my educational outlook. In the following narrative, using Dewey's creed as a guide, I discuss my own pedagogical creed as it relates to teaching and learning about social issues. Social concerns have been the focus of my entire professional career. Dewey's creed is organized into five sections; 1) what education is, 2) what school is, 3) the subject matter of education, 4) the nature of method, and 5) the school and social progress. These categories serve to organize my own discussion about teaching and learning social issues.

## Article I: What Education Is

I believe education is the acquisition of life-long learning. Although many theories of learning have been espoused over the years—such as functionalism, behaviorism, developmentalism, information processing, and constructivism (Schunk, 1996)—they all share commonalities. At a basic level, all learning theories connote a change in behavior or performance that has resulted from experience (Driscoll, 1994). In the context of teaching and learning about social issues, I believe that the social nature of education cannot be overemphasized. Teaching and learning about social issues involves understanding the world and the humans who live in it. Education is a result of humans learning from one another. Experiences also shape learning, especially with regard to social education. Consider the experience of visiting, or perhaps living in, a foreign country, compared to simply reading about the country. The two kinds of learning are vastly different. Educational aims are most often meant to be beneficial, but they can produce unintended harmful results, too. Robert Oppenheimer's experience with the creation of the atomic bomb serves as a keen reminder of the destructive power of knowledge.

Learning takes a variety of forms. Learning involves cognition centered in the brain. Howard Gardner's (1983) theory of multiple intelligences first offered in his book *Frames of Mind* informs my understanding of education as a process of learning. Although Gardner's theory has undergone revision and has received criticism for its subjective nature and lack of empirical evidence, the theory helps to remind teachers about the wide range of human intelligence and the variety of student interests/natural strengths.

Gardner's list of multiple intelligences include logical-mathematical, spatial, linguistic, bodily-kinesthetic, musical, interpersonal, intrapersonal, naturalistic, and existential. As an educator, with respect to teaching and learning social issues I tend to emphasize linguistic and interpersonal learning over other kinds of learning. While the world of words and human connections is paramount, when I focus on teaching about social issues in my classroom I do my utmost to try to nurture students' strengths in other areas, be they logical-mathematical, spatial, linguistic, bodily-kinesthetic, musical, interpersonal, intrapersonal, naturalistic, or existential.

Dewey posited that learning begins at birth (Milson, Bohan, Glanzer, and Null, 2010, p. 362). Humans typically build upon the knowledge of previous generations and learn synchronously or asynchronously from one another. In the context of learning about social issues, human connections are of utmost import. Learning does not always progress forward, and can, of course, regress or be lost. One such example was the vanished ability to read Egyptian hieroglyphs until the 1799 discovery of the Rosetta Stone. Learning about social issues can derive from a variety of sources and experiences, such as apprenticeship, literature, technology, repetition, movement, and observation, and involve use of the five senses: sight, sound, touch, taste, and smell. Dewey believed that the child's interests should serve as a starting point for education. I concur, but would add that the child ought to be introduced to new ideas, concepts, skills, activities, environments, and cultures, as well, in order to facilitate an educative process. In regard to teaching and learning about social issues, education centers on humans.

## Article II: What School Is

I believe that in the traditional sense, school is the location where students and teachers gather to learn. School is a structure that the community designates for education. Teachers College professor Lawrence Cremin (1970), however, frequently encouraged his students to think of education in a broader sense, beyond the institution of schooling. He reminded his pupils that learning can take place anywhere, in any form. Cremin wanted his students to expand their understanding of education beyond the schoolhouse door, and to think of learning that occurs in a wider range of institutions such as "families, churches, libraries, museums, publishers, benevolent societies, youth groups, agricultural fairs, radio networks, military organizations, and research institutions" (Cremin, 1970, p. xi). The recent development of online learning has helped revolutionize traditional notions of school, but, at its core, school facilitates learning between humans; hence the inherently social nature of education, even if technology serves as the primary, or, only, link between people.

Although education is experienced in an extensive range of institutions, I have devoted my career to the teaching and engaging my students in learning about social issues in the traditional setting of formal schooling. Within the school setting, I encourage student learning about social issues through a variety of activities, including, but not limited to, research papers, in-class presentations, book reviews, and imagining and creating dinner party conversations among historical figures, leading politicians, educators, or other prominent figures. We have also attended viewings of *Waiting for Superman*, and arranged for my students to view Ken Burns' Civil War series and listen to Franklin Delano Roosevelt's fireside chats. In informal settings, I arrange for and/or encourage students to visit Presidential libraries, archives, local history and art museums, and historical monuments. More specifically, for example, I have taken students to the Jimmy Carter and Lyndon Baines Johnson Presidential libraries, where we viewed historical artifacts and discussed the lives and careers of these particular presidents. I brought history students to Ellis Island to discuss U.S. immigration. In each particular situation, the social issue varied and was related to the context of what we were studying at the time.

In each setting, formal and informal, I work to foster a sense of community learners. In discussing the origins of European residential colleges in his recent work *College: What it Was, Is, and Should Be*, Andrew Delbanco (2012, p. 38) notes that the meaning of the Latin term *collegium* is society or community. This, of course, complements what Cremin said about school and beyond being educative in a host of different and significant ways.

## Article III: The Subject Matter of Education

I believe that the teaching and learning of social issues is the foundation of American democracy. In 1816, Thomas Jefferson advised, "If you expect a nation to be ignorant and free and in a state of civilization, you expect what never was and never will be" (Thomas Jefferson's letter to Charles Yancey, 6 January 1816; Graham, 2005, p. 3). Democracy depends on an educated populace. Understanding the nation's history and government, as well as those of other countries, is vital to human relations and advancement.

In "What Knowledge Is of Most Worth?" Herbert Spencer (1919, reprint of 1884 article) asserted that the latter question had to be answered before school curricula could be developed. I agree. Schools reflect the answer to Spencer's question in a variety of ways, including the allotment of time devoted to particular content. Students spend more time learning subject matter that the community prioritizes, and this is particularly true in those school districts obsessed with standardized test scores. In contemporary formal school settings, testing of linguistic and logical-mathematical skills often reflects the value placed on subject matter. A common saying in schools is, "If it is not tested, it is not taught."

For my specific work in teaching and learning about social issues, the world, the country, the region, the state, and the local community is my classroom and the subject matter with which I am concerned. The time frame can be past, present, or future. People, places, and events comprise the learning narratives.

The ten thematic strands of the National Council for the Social Studies (2010) function as a comprehensive guide to important social studies subject matter education. These ten themes include: culture; time, continuity, and change; people, places, and environments; individual development and identity; individuals, groups, and institutions; power, authority, and governance; production, distribution, and consumption; science, technology, and society; global connections; and civic ideals and practices. These ten broad themes are comprehensive with respect to teaching and learning social issues. I often refer back to them when developing formal lessons for teaching about social issues.

## Article IV: The Nature of Method

I believe in the old saying that "variety is the spice of life," and that the principle of variety is particularly important when considering the nature of methods when teaching and learning social issues. I also believe that learning is keener when it is active; thus individuals learn best when they have to teach ideas to other people. Dewey emphasized the importance of learning as an active process. He noted that

> the active side precedes the passive in the development of the child nature; that expression comes before conscious impression; that muscular development precedes sensory; that movements come before conscious sensations; I believe that consciousness is essentially motor or impulse; that conscious states tend to project themselves in action.
>
> *Quoted in Milson, et al., 2010, p. 368*

In my courses, I model my belief in the importance of variety and implement several activities to foster active learning. Over the years these have included, but were not limited to, simulations, role-playing, group work, lectures, discussions, student presentations, student-created television ads or newspapers, interpretation of primary source documents, field trips, debates, mapping the school building or larger geographical area, and research projects.

## Article V: The School and Social Progress

I believe that schools are a means of social betterment, but they do not provide equal opportunities to all children, especially not to impoverished students from racial and ethnic minorities. Who can forget Kozol's (1991) description of horrid conditions in East Saint Louis schools? Similarly, who does not wish for genuine futures for the brilliant students in Kohl's (1967) Harlem classroom who appear condemned to a life of poverty, neglect, and violence? Yet, I long to believe in the American dream. In the context of teaching and learning about social issues, I lead classroom discussions about reasons for immigration to the U.S., and examine its impact on schooling. I have conducted studies on citizenship examinations with several colleagues (Doppen, et al., 2011), as well as research on foreign-born social studies education professors who wrestle with the decision whether or not to pursue American citizenship (Bohan, et al., 2008). I have written about adopting a daughter from China and how such a potentially sensitive issue can be handled in the classroom (Bohan, 2003). As the great-granddaughter of German immigrants who came to America for a better life, education in public schools was instrumental in providing the opportunity for familial intellectual and financial achievement.

Yet, the path my ancestors followed was not one of continuous progression; it included a few bumps in the road. Shame came to the family when my grandmother's older sister was held back in first grade because she spoke German and not English. During World War Two my father recalls getting in trouble in elementary school for punching a child who called him a Nazi. His ire was aroused particularly because his father had served in the U.S. Army during World War One and he did not want to be associated with the enemy. But my father survived this elementary school incident as well as the difficulty at age 12 of having a bed-ridden father who suffered from an incapacitating stroke. Long before my father could vote, he filled out tax forms, made family economic decisions, and effectively served as the head of household. He went on to become high school valedictorian, and a first generation college student at MIT. He credits his success to the public schools in New York, which established standards through the Regents examination (as far back as the Civil War).

As a teacher and teacher educator, I believe that the school is an important vehicle of social progress. Nevertheless, opportunities are not the same for all students, nor are they equal among schools. Having taught in two high schools, one with predominantly affluent students and one with largely poor students, the disparity in educational opportunities in America was strikingly evident to me each and every day. A keen awareness of differences developed because my teaching experience in an elite New York City private school (Rupert Murdoch's son James was on the track team that I coached) immediately preceded working in a Title I predominantly Hispanic public school, where my infant son spent his first months of life in the on-campus childcare facility designated for the children of those students who were teenage mothers. These teaching experiences led me to develop a college course on poverty and education in order to help future teachers understand the vast socio-economic differences in students who populate American schools. In class we read books by Jonathan Kozol (*Savage Inequalities* [1991] and *Shame of the Nation*), Herbert Kohl (*36 Children* [1967]), and Martin Haberman (*Star Teachers of Children in Poverty* [1995]). These authors profoundly influenced my thinking about whether the schools serve as vehicles of social progress.

Even in difficult economic times, I believe in the power of education. I believe that the school can serve as a means of social progress, but this goal is not always achieved. In the context of teaching and learning social issues, I believe teachers and students need to carefully examine the nature and purpose of education, the role of schooling, the knowledge and subject matter of most worth, the nature of teaching methods used to convey learning of subject matter, and the means by which schools serve and do not serve to enable social progress. In the context of teaching and learning about social issues, real concerns can generate ideas for active learning that lead to social betterment.

As Nigel Hamilton (2008) explains:

> Biography was the record of real lives; but if its great benefit to society was its ability to provide insights into human nature that could be useful to the reader in his own life, then there was no intrinsic reason biographers should chronicle only the lives of the famous.

*p. 11*

The methods of learning about social issues can and should vary, but the goals ought to be clear. We should teach and learn about social issues in order to work to understand our lives and ourselves. Over my office door, I have a sign hanging to remind me of my grander purpose: "live your life in a way your children will know you stood for something wonderful." I would change "your children" to "all people." I hope that my first quarter century in education and the quarter century to come will serve as a model for the importance of education for all humans. I work to teach about social issues as a way to honor my past teachers and to provide an example to future teachers.

## References

Bohan, C.H. (2003). "One Child's Happy Face: Teaching and Learning about Adoption from China." 15(3) *Social Studies and the Young Learner*, pp. 9–14.

Bohan, C.H., Doppen, F., Feinberg, J., and O'Mahony, C. (2008). Citizens of Today and Tomorrow: An Exploration of Social Studies Preservice Teachers' Knowledge and their Professor's Experiences with Citizenship Education. 10(1–2) *Curriculum and Teaching Dialogue*, pp. 117–134.

Cremin, L.A. (1970). *American Education: The Colonial Experience, 1607–1783*. New York, NY: Harper & Row.

Delbanco, A. (2012). *College: What it Was, Is, and Should Be*. Princeton, NJ: Princeton University Press.

Doppen, F., Feinberg, J., O'Mahony, C., Lucas, A., Bohan, C., Lipscomb, G., and Ogawa, M. (2011). Social Studies Preservice Teachers' Citizenship Knowledge and Perceptions of the U.S. Naturalization Test. 33(1) *Action in Teacher Education*, pp. 81–93.

Driscoll, M.P. (1994). *Psychology of Learning for Instruction*. Boston, MA: Allyn & Bacon.

Gardner, H. (1983). *Frames of Mind: The Theory of Multiple Intelligences*. New York, NY: Basic Books.

Graham, P.A. (2005). *Schooling America: How the Public Schools Meet the Nation's Changing Needs*. New York, NY: Oxford University Press.

Haberman, M. (1995). *Star Teachers of Children in Poverty*. West Lafayette, IN: Kappa Delta Pi.

Hamilton, N. (2008). *How to do Biography: A Primer*. Cambridge, MA: Harvard University Press.

Jefferson, T.J. (1816). Letter to Charles Yancey. January 6. Accessed online at *Thomas Jefferson Encyclopedia*. http://wiki.monticello.org/mediawiki/index.php/Quotations_on_Education.

Kohl, H. (1967). *36 Children*. New York, NY: Signet.

Kozol, J. (1991). *Savage Inequalities: Children in America's Schools*. New York, NY: Crown.

Milson, A., Bohan, C.H., Glanzer, P., and Null, J.W. (eds.). (2010). *American Educational Thought: Essays from 1640–1940*. Charlotte, NC: Information Age Publishers.

National Council for the Social Studies. (2010). *National Curriculum Standards for the Social Studies: A Framework for Teaching, Learning and Assessment*. Washington, D.C.: National Council for the Social Studies.

Schunk, D.H. (1996). *Learning Theories: An Educational Perspective* (2nd edn.). Englewood Cliffs, NJ: Prentice Hall.

Spencer, H. (1919). "What Knowledge Is of Most Worth?" *Essays on Education and Kindred Subjects: Everyman's Library*. New York, NY: E.P. Dutton & Co.

# 20

# QUESTIONING AND BLURRING BOUNDARIES IN A CONTEXT OF CHANGE

## Science, Technology, Engineering, and Mathematics (STEM) Education

*Barbara Solomon Spector*

PROFESSOR, SCIENCE EDUCATION, UNIVERSITY OF SOUTH FLORIDA

### Genesis of My Pedagogical Creed

Asked why I did something in a certain way while teaching high school biology early in my career, my usual answer was, "It just seemed reasonable, or logical." I discovered the subconscious context for what I thought was reasonable when I began to engage in metacognition. I recognized everything in my pedagogical creed emerged from my Judaic cultural heritage and experiences growing up in a Jewish community in Brooklyn: the charity boxes in my grandmother's kitchen taught me I had responsibility to contribute to solving societal problems. My grandfather's study of the Torah every day of his adult life taught me the power of social interaction and life's experiences as perceptual screens for making meaning. He read a daily portion with neighborhood men in the synagogue and participated in vigorous discussion (arguing) as they continuously reinterpreted the Torah and the sages' commentaries to use the moral lessons for current day living. Valuing multiple interpretations made by sages, past and present (reminiscent of a theoretical base in science), made me tolerant of ambiguity and accepting of the notion there is no one right answer or right way to resolve a human dilemma. Climbing on my great uncle's lap as a young child during Hanukkah parties, I was told I would be given a silver dollar if I asked a good question. My family rewarded me in many ways for asking insight-generating questions. My own study of Torah, encouraged by my parents, led to my penchant for analyzing everything. Whether in personal situations or with regard to issues in society, it seems natural for me to conduct systematic inquiry, gathering and analyzing evidence and using logic to support my ideas (reminiscent of the nature of science).

When it was time to go college, I had to decide whether to follow a path in art, dance, or science. I had experience with and was intrigued by all three. I chose science to enable me to become a physician, to serve society by healing people's bodies. Unfortunately, even though I graduated cum laude, several medical school recruiters told me I was not a good investment, because I was newly married, would have children, and never practice. (Fortunately, that attitude no longer dominates medicine.) My fall back was to enhance people's minds by becoming a high school biology teacher. For eighteen years, I taught general, Regents, and Advanced Biology in Syracuse, New York. The latter was my favorite, because my students and I were free to choose what should be in the course. I used this course as my way of staying current in the science needed to understand social issues (e.g., right to die law, extraordinary life-prolonging technologies, fluoridation of water, controversial psychiatry issues, aging, etc.). Scientists, engineers, and other professionals (e.g., a law school dean) from the community came to class to help us learn many ideas I knew little or nothing about. We also traveled out of the school building to the local medical school, laboratories, and eventually to Woods Hole, Massachusetts, the land of the Nobel Laureates, to engage firsthand with the cream of the scientific world. This course was a wonderful adventure that eventually led to me being offered a fellowship to attend graduate school leading to a doctoral degree. Although my Ph.D. was in science education, I also took courses on qualitative research, organizational development, and techniques to facilitate change. This knowledge served me well when I became the Program Director for Education in the National Sea Grant College Program Office in Washington, D.C., in 1979. A congressional mandate to infuse marine education in K-12 schools required me to use my new research and change agent skills and combine them with my experiences in art, music, and dance from my youth. Addressing real world social issues involving the ocean required the perspective of every discipline; therefore, marine education could be infused in every discipline taught in K-12 schools. I worked with stakeholders from marine businesses, government agencies, and education institutions across the United States to develop this vehicle for a transdisciplinary approach to education.

As I developed a national perspective, I learned I had been pioneering a shift from the dominant reductionist paradigm to a holistic paradigm in science education throughout my career. The latter is currently referred to as the Science/Technology/Society Interaction (STS) reform movement or STEM (science, technology, engineering, and mathematics) reform. Things I started doing early in my teaching career "just because they seemed reasonable," such as teacher as mediator, student-centered inquiry, cooperative learning, Socratic questioning, project-based learning, integration of community resources, and more, now have distinctive labels as part of the literature facilitating the paradigm shift from traditional transmission science teaching to the desired state for teaching described in the *National Science Education Standards* (NSES) (1996), *A Framework for K-12*

*Science Education: Practices, Crosscutting Concepts, and Core Ideas* (2011), and *The Next Generation Science Standards* (2013).

I became a science teacher educator at the university level in 1981. Among the forces that have driven me over the years are: (a) an insatiable curiosity about why things are as they are, (b) a low threshold for boredom, (c) needing an outlet for my creativity, (d) needing to continually learn something new, and (e) needing to share and do something with what I learn, compare it with what others know, and integrate it all. My self-declared mission was, and still is, enabling out-of-the-box science teachers to change science education into an effective instrument for resolving social issues and making life better for our species while preserving this precious planet.

## What Should Education Be For?

Education about social issues should be to facilitate learning, defined as the integration of thinking, feeling, and acting that empowers learners to make meaning of their experiences in the world around them (Novak, 1977). (Meaningful learning does not occur when an authority "transmits" information and a learner "catches" it.) Learning requires a person to construct his/her own meaning through self-reflection and subsequent modifications of one's mental models comprising his/her cognitive framework. Systematically reflecting on one's own thinking usually reveals questions for further exploration or inconsistencies with previously held mental models (preconceptions/incomplete conceptions/misconceptions). These inconsistencies and/or need for extensions stimulate questions for further investigation and, subsequently, learning. Learning is thus iterative. There is an opportunity for more connections to be made in the brain each time a learner experiences an idea. More connections result in a deeper, more complex understanding of an idea.

The catalyst for this iteration is self-reflection, a deliberate voluntary process of slowing down the thinking process to become more aware of how one forms mental models (Sengay et al., 1994). Mental models are images in our long-term memory of how the world works in the short term, perceptions we build up as part of everyday reasoning. The cognitive framework in each person's mind is composed of many mental models accumulated during an individual's lifetime, and is therefore idiosyncratic.

Learning about social issues should enable a person to function effectively in today's world where the only constant is change. Effective functioning should enable one to reach his/her genetic potential (self-actualize), to build relationships, to pursue one's genetically-based curiosity (which is inherently insatiable), and foster creativity.

Education about social issues should help a person learn how to learn and be an autonomous life-long learner (in contrast to a dependent learner), who uses innate and learned processes, skills, and tools to be self-efficacious and successfully interact socially. A socially interactive person enacts many roles in a lifetime, such as wage earner, family member, civic participant, leisure actor, health guardian, spiritual actor, consumer, and more. Education should enable a person to exercise judgments that result in decision-making and actions to generate a life of personal fulfillment, contentment, and joy. Such decisions and actions should improve the quality of one's life while effectively enacting multiple roles in a democratic society, and assist in smooth passage through inevitable stages of a human's life.

Education about social issues should contribute to affirmation of self and perpetuate a "can do" attitude leading to creation of a peaceful, sustainable, win-win world, in contrast to a win-lose world. Education should foster the following perspectives: It is not what happens, but how you react to what happens that matters. Turning the proverbial lemons into lemonade is automatic. Engaging with diverse ideas, people, places, and things enriches life and opens new opportunities for fulfillment. New ventures are joyous opportunities. Being aware of what is going on in society and contributing to making it better is an individual's responsibility and is personally fulfilling. Each day is lived to its fullest as an adventure in harmony with planet earth and all its inhabitants.

## What should the School Be for?

Schools should be community institutions designed to: (a) provide opportunity to identify, access, and guide use of resources as tools for learning about social issues; (b) provide for social interaction and building relationships among peers and across generations to promote learning; (c) provide mentoring, critique, and guidance for reflection on inquiries (metacognition); (d) extend one's range of experience and interest beyond initial perception of environmental boundaries; and (e) provide mechanisms to answer the questions, "What is going on here?" and "What can I do about it ?"

Resources include human expertise and print material, physical and digital objects, and events. Human expertise within schools should be available to provide guidance to expedite learning about social issues. Resources should provide exposure to diverse ideas, attitudes, people, events and objects, both natural and human-made throughout the history of the world. These resources should enable learners to build on the shoulders of giants who have come before them.

Furthermore, school should be a place for adventures of mind and heart by providing a physically and emotionally safe environment for one to ask questions, explore via inquiry, and in which to test new ideas. Schools should provide learning opportunities accommodating the iterative nature of learning, such as time for reflection and metacognition, sharing, gathering feedback from multiple perspectives (peers and experts), self-assessment and evaluation, and revision. Rewards for those who think out-of the box should be plentiful.

The label "school" can be applied to various community institutions, including formal and informal education institutions. Formal education institutions include pre-K-through-16 schools and potentially religious institutions. Informal education institutions include the following: museums, aquaria, zoos, research laboratories, botanic gardens, nature centers, science centers, civic organizations, government agencies, after-school programs, digital media, gaming, and science journalism. All these institutions share the goal of developing a scientifically and technologically literate citizenry capable of solving societal problems. These institutions should have porous borders expediting the flow of ideas from and into the near and far community, extending from the home to a space station. Lines, therefore, should be blurred among formal and informal education institutions, as well as other civic organizations. Society is best served when "schools" provide articulated learning opportunities establishing continuity between and among various institutions in a community.

## Subject Matter of Education

Real world social issues should serve as cameos to connect all the disciplines. The similarities, differences, convergences, and connections existing among the humanities, arts, sciences, mathematics, and engineering should be accented (in contrast to solely focusing on the basic concepts of each discipline in its own silo). The varied subject matter categorized by disciplines in libraries should be woven together for study in a transdisciplinary tapestry, reflecting the way this information exists in the natural and human made worlds. Crosscutting concepts such as cause-and-effect, patterns, systems, scale, energy, structure and function, stability and change (NRC, 2011) illustrates connections that are threads for weaving a tapestry. The interfaces among disciplines provide potent stimulation for the expression of creativity in solving social problems.

Additionally, subject matter should contribute to individuals adding to, deleting, or rearranging their idiosyncratic cognitive frameworks that serve as perceptual screens for incoming stimuli. Subject matter should be generated with input from stakeholders throughout the community and serve the needs of the individual and the community. Real world situations and issues, of obvious consequence to the learner, should be the context used for developing learning opportunities. Social issues stimulate a "need to know", which is critical to learners developing an interest in, and ownership of, knowledge.

Systematic inquiry processes explicated by science and engineering (technology) disciplines should be both the subject of study and the processes used to learn. Such subject matter fosters use of reason and evidence to support decisions and actions to resolve social issues in our scientifically and technologically driven democratic society. Thus, processes of planning an investigation, explicating a question or problem, observing an event/object, designing a test, identifying, collecting, organizing, and interpreting data to form explanations or design solutions, and communicating conclusions should dominate learning opportunities. These processes integrate stimuli from the environment, supporting the way the human brain functions when addressing all disciplines.

Learning opportunities should vary. Subject matter should provide choice of topics to learn, the level of entry into a topic, the order of study, and time devoted to a topic. Learning cycles, such as the 5Es (engage, explore, explain, elaborate, evaluate) (Bybee et al., 2006), should be both a subject of study and a process used to learn. Questioning strategies and the role of questions in active learning, engaging in argument from evidence, developing and using models, and communicating are vital subject matter, as are theories of how people learn and how theories are translated into practice.

## Nature of Method

Experiential learning, learners having choice, metacognition, and instructors serving as facilitators modeling inquiry behaviors in a community of practice (of co-learners) (Wenger et al., 2002) are keys to effective method. Additional features of method follow:

- Virtual and/or physical resource collections combined with access to stakeholders and their environments provide opportunity for learner immersion in a wide variety of relevant interactions with social issues from which to induce patterns.
- Establishing a community of practice, in which both the instructor and students share responsibility for teaching and learning individually and collaboratively, empowers learners to take charge of their own meaning-making. It enables them to make choices consistent with their own idiosyncratic cognitive frameworks (prior knowledge), learning styles, interests, and capacity to make decisions regarding their own learning.
- Instructional configurations should encompass face-to-face small and large group interactions combined with online capabilities for reflection, discussion, and sharing products.
- Open-ended developmental instructional tasks (assignments) are stimuli for learning opportunities (in contrast to being tests of whether a person has learned what the authority transmitted).
- Embedding assessments in such tasks and learning products, including reflective journals, fosters autonomous learning.
- Through journals, learners chronicle changes and growth in their thinking, feeling, and acting in electronic fora shared with their learning community. This gives practice in making explicit the way one is changing mental models when connecting current experiences to prior knowledge.
- Conducting ongoing inquiry into what is being learned and how it is being learned is engaging in metacognition. Gathering and analyzing data about one's own learning processes and sharing those in the community of practice (i) helps make sense of course experiences, (ii) provides data for self-assessment that helps a person determine what else one needs and wants to

learn, and (iii) provides insight to varied ways future audiences are likely to learn.

- Responding to each other's journals by asking clarifying questions, critiquing what was written, evaluating the evidence and reasoning presented, and making comments creates multidirectional dialogue. This dialogue provides an opportunity for learners to articulate and compare patterns and interpretations emerging for each of them personally, engage in argument supported by evidence, and collectively construct meaning; and

- Learners should be invited to (i) communicate about real situations in which they are, or have been, involved in relation to an intended outcome, and (ii) share articles, media and events encountered out of class with the potential to enrich discussions and deepen understandings. This is one way to establish relevance for an individual and enable an individual's particular area of interest to become part of the learning milieu.[1]

## School and Social Progress

Schools facilitating the development of a meaningful understanding of the interaction among science, technology, and society is critical to social progress. Individuals who understand STS are aware of their responsibility to affect social progress, and recognize opportunities to have a positive impact. Advances in both science and technology have the potential to change the way humans think about their lives and their environment and what they can do to address those social issues they confront. Advances in both science and technology affect each other, and advances impact our scientific and technologically driven society. Society, via public policy and funding for research and development, impacts what science discoveries will emerge and what technologies will be developed, thus creating a cycle. Intervening at any point in the cycle can stimulate, or inhibit, social progress.

The development of electronic communication technologies, such as the Internet, has resulted in immediate world-wide communication. Because of these technologies, today's schools have more opportunity to influence social progress than ever before. A school student can produce a YouTube video about a social issue that goes viral and influences the thoughts and actions of millions of viewers in a very short time. Thus, youngsters can become the watchful eye of the environment and take advocacy positions influencing their peers and adults worldwide by using the tools of their everyday life, long before they reach voting age. It is, therefore, incumbent on schools to ensure that learners have the knowledge, skills, and inclination to ask productive questions, research information, distinguish information useful to resolve a social issue from among the mass of available information, vet it, and use it in a reasoned way for decision-making, so as to construct solutions advancing social progress.

# Note

1  These features of method can be combined by structuring a course (or unit) as an open-ended inquiry into a focus question, (e.g., "What is STS and how does it relate to science teaching?"), and inviting learners to plan their own inquiries to construct responses to the focus question, unrestricted by sequence and time. Learners should be invited to conduct a self-designed investigation in an instructor-designed physical and/or virtual resource center and in learner-selected community sites (e.g., public media sources, business and industry, informal education agencies, and schools). Learners generate questions, explore resources, gather data, make interpretations, share their interpretations through electronic fora, receive feedback from their community of practice, explore more resources, reinterpret their data, and share their ideas again. The process repeats continuously as learners make more connections to deepen the understandings they construct and generate their personal grounded theory about a social issue.

# References

Achieve. (2013). *The Next Generation Science Standards.* http://www.nextgenscience. org/next-generation-science-standards

Bybee, R.W., Taylor, J.A., Gardner, A., Van Scotter, P., Carlson Powell, J., Westbrook, A., and, Landes, N. (2006). *The BSCS 5E Instructional Model: Origins, Effectiveness, and Applications.* Colorado Springs, CO: BSCS.

National Research Council. (1996). *National Science Education Standards.* Washington, D.C.: National Academy Press.

National Research Council. (2011). *A Framework for K-12 Science Education: Practices, Cross-cutting Concepts, and Core Ideas.* Washington, D.C.: National Academy Press.

Novak, J.D. (1977). *Theory of Education.* Ithaca, NY: Cornell University Press.

Senge, P., Kleiner, A., Roberts, C., Ross, R.B., and Smith, B.J. (1994). *The Fifth Discipline Fieldbook.* New York, NY: Doubleday.

Wenger, E.C., McDermott, R., and Snyder, W.C. (2002). *Communities of Practice: A Guide to Managing Knowledge.* Cambridge, MA: Harvard Business School Press.

# 21

# DEVELOPING GLOBAL CONSCIOUSNESS

*Merry M. Merryfield*

PROFESSOR EMERITA, SOCIAL STUDIES AND GLOBAL EDUCATION,
THE OHIO STATE UNIVERSITY

My interest in social issues is rooted in my childhood. I grew up in Knoxville, Tennessee in the 1950s and 1960s, a time of transition from overt racism and segregation to the integration of restaurants, schools, and, eventually, neighborhoods. One of the transformative moments in my childhood was an experience at the Tennessee Theatre in downtown Knoxville. As I and my pre-teen friends approached to purchase tickets, we saw Black students protesting segregation by lying on the payment and singing freedom songs, as they were not allowed inside the theatre. A white usher came out to lead me and my white friends over the Black bodies into the movie. It was a profound moment as I realized the privilege I had because my skin was white. Although I had grown up in an all-white neighborhood with "colored" maids (the language of the 1950s and early 1960s in my community), and was used to seeing "white" and "colored" water fountains at department stores, it was the experience at the theatre that made me begin to examine and question the inequities and prejudices that permeated my community, church, and school.

By the time I entered college I was well versed in white privilege, xenophobia, cultural capital, discrimination against "The Other," and the corollaries of a worldview that devalued and, to some degree, feared anyone who was different. Eventually, I would draw on this tacit knowledge in my work on issues of equity and diversity and infuse those concerns into the field of global education. I also came to realize that no matter how parochial or racist one's background, one's upbringing does not prevent one from learning to teach for social justice and global mindedness.

In an effort to understand the racism of my world, I majored in history and took all the courses offered in "Black Studies" at Georgia State University. By the late 1960s, I was well into African American literature—*The Autobiography of Malcolm X*, *Black Rage*, *Invisible Man*, *The Fire Next Time*, the histories of John

Hope Franklin, the seminal works of W.E.B. DuBois, and more. I also became close friends with an African American principal, and socialized in Atlanta's vibrant Black community. I learned to try to see events and issues through the eyes and experiences of others, a lesson in perspective consciousness that has infused my work since that time.

During my first year of teaching in South Atlanta, I began to study issues of what was then called "the Developing World." As a teacher of world cultures I often invited people from other world regions into my classes. After one such day during my first year of teaching, a Nigerian guest told me that my students were not interested in the real Nigeria, that they just wanted to focus on the exotic, the superficial, the extreme: the Africa of the movies. It was then that I began to rethink the curriculum and textbooks not only about Africa, but the world. Is the content superficial? Is it reinforcing stereotypes? Have I been teaching American superiority? Over time, I had learned to rely on African American scholars and friends to understand African American experiences and perspectives, so why had I depended on white American scholarship to teach about Africa? I focused on Africa in my Master's program at Georgia State and changed school districts to teach courses such as "Protest and Reform" and "African Studies" in Fulton County.

Feeling a need to understand global racism and poverty, I became a Peace Corps volunteer teaching geography and African literature in Sierra Leone in 1977. Within days of being in the country I realized that just about everything I had learned about Africa or development was either outdated or useless in living and teaching in Sierra Leone, and thus my education about African began anew. My fellow teachers taught me about the politics of ethnicity. Both they and my principal, a Mende who had been imprisoned on a trumped up charge because he was elected as a member of the SLPP opposition party, explained why the ballot boxes never showed up in our town when the country supposedly voted 100% for a one-party state. My students taught me about manning the barricades when the secret police tried to overrun their community the year before. They wanted me to understand why they were 19 and 20 years old and still in secondary school. Friends explained about female circumcision and secret societies. Men at the mosque next door to my flat taught me about the call to prayers and the tenets of Islam. I read works by Camara Laye, Ngugi waThiongo, and Edward Said to try to understand post-colonial societies and the irony of teaching Shakespeare's *Macbeth* in a town with no running water or electricity.

Through the years, I have had many other profound learning experiences while living in Kenya, Malawi, Nigeria, Botswana, the Philippines, Indonesia, China and, of course, the United States. I believe in the power of cross-cultural experiences because such events have created insights in my thinking into issues of ethnic and religious conflict, justice, development, poverty, power, and the inheritance of colonialism that I would never have glimpsed without working in other countries. The elements of global education that I expand upon below are grounded in my life's work, both personal and academic.

## What Are Social Issues?

I believe that social issues are those touchstones of humanity that divide people and societies.[1] They may deal with rights or treatment of different groups within a society, the role of government or other institutions (religious, academic, legal, etc.) in people's lives, or they may grow out of responses to new phenomena that affect people (e.g., HIV/AIDS, the Columbine shootings, a new wave of immigration). I see social issues as often arising from changing mores and customs.

In my work, I often articulate social issues as questions to be examined: Should undocumented workers be allowed to become citizens? Can people be fired for their religious beliefs? Why does a neighborhood want to keep out people of a certain ethnicity, race, or national origin? How should people be protected from toxic wastes? What works in helping people to overcome poverty?

I have found that as values and norms change over time, social issues evolve. For example, hotly debated issues related to women's rights in the United States continue even today yet, they are quite different in substance from those that characterized American perspectives a hundred years ago.

## Why should Schools Teach Social Issues?

I believe that social issues need to be taught as they are central to understanding any society and critical in understanding the world today. If students only learn about social issues from their out of school environments, they will likely only hear one side of the issue and never appreciate how other knowledge and other points of view can illuminate the issue and provide insights into ways to resolve it. I believe schools, if they choose, can play a critical role in student understanding of social issues. Teachers can assess their students' own knowledge, attitudes, and experiences and then work to overcome possible biases and broaden their students' foundational knowledge through historical, multicultural, and global perspectives on the social issues that characterize their world. If schools want to teach students how to work at resolving social issues and managing conflict they need to provide opportunities for them to work with people of diverse cultures and walks of life in examining and evaluating social issues locally, nationally, and globally. I know that the ability to learn from and collaborate with people of diverse backgrounds is a lifelong skill that is essential in today's interconnected world, if we are to reduce conflict. Below are some specific beliefs I have developed about teaching and learning social issues.

## Teaching Perspective Consciousness and Multiple Perspectives

I believe that students need to develop skills perspective consciousness if they are to understand social issues from conflicting points of view. Perspective consciousness is the ability to recognize how people different from one-self construct events and issues through their own histories, cultural lenses, knowledge bases, and experiences (Hanvey, 1975). I have learned about perspective consciousness through 30 years of work in classrooms where students study different cultures, issues, and events from diverse people's points of view.

Teachers need to use—and, in fact, many do—primary sources, films, online videos, first-hand experiences, and literature written by people in cultures under study so that students come to understand the complexity of social issues in people's lives over time and space. With online technologies, teachers may develop online discussions with teachers and students in other countries or work collaboratively through projects such as iEARN and e-Pals (Merryfield, 2007).

## Teaching Global Interconnectedness

I believe that people must come to understand their own personal connections to the larger world and to social issues that characterize the human story. These connections—through a common language, religion, customs, interests, purchases and products, or a shared problem or event—help students see how they influence, and are influenced, economically, politically, technologically, and culturally by the actions and beliefs of people around the planet.

I believe students need to see the world as a system. Issues-oriented instruction situates current and historical events and issues (such as movement of people, use of violence, or labor issues) within a world context. In this way, students come to understand global political systems, global economic systems, and global environmental systems.

From human rights to the role of governments in people's lives, I believe many social issues cannot be understood without a knowledge of many countries and the global commons. Educators need to integrate global content into their instruction of topics such as loss of manufacturing jobs, biodiversity, and new immigrants in the community, so that their students see local issues through global perspectives and recognize that global issues are often significant within their own community, state, or region (Kasai and Merryfield, 2004).

## Analyzing Power and Resistance

If students are to understand the social issues of our time, I believe they must come to understand power in many contexts. Teachers need to facilitate student learning about how governments, non-governmental organizations, multinational corporations, individuals, and other groups have acquired and used economic, cultural, technological, political, and military power locally and globally. Students also need to learn how groups of people, nations, organizations, and individuals have resisted or challenged or changed the power exerted by others.

## Building Cross-Cultural Competence

I believe students must develop skills in communicating and interacting with people different to themselves in order to understand social issues at home and abroad. Through cross-cultural experiential learning, students learn skills and cultural knowledge that help them understand issues in a variety of contexts, and collaborate with people to address them.

Part of building intercultural competence is work on reducing chauvinism and prejudice. Through such efforts, students learn to recognize and reduce their own parochialism, resist stereotyping, and develop the ability to empathize. Teachers need to work at opening students' minds so that they can see their local community and nation from a global perspective. In their teaching of history, teachers should strive to help students see connections between prejudice and inequities across time and space.

Ideally, intercultural competence is developed, in part, for students to be able to participate in local and global communities through service learning projects or other collaboration. Participation may be part of a required assignment or a voluntary extra-curricular activity. It may be local, such as work with neighborhood groups concerned with racism or poverty, or more global, such as online work with Amnesty International, the noted international human rights organization.

New electronic technologies have revolutionized the teaching of social issues in the last decade. The Internet not only provides teachers and students with instant access to documents, media, and other print and visual resources across the planet, it allows interaction with people and organizations in every world region. Making use of online newspapers in other regions will provide students with primary source material on a daily basis. Organizing video-conferencing relationships with schools, organizations, or experts allows students opportunities to talk with people in other countries about the social issues under study (Merryfield, 2003).

## Conclusion

Students cannot understand life on the planet, past and present, without studying social issues, as they are integral to human interaction. In a globally connected world the study of social issues allows students to connect events and issues across time and space and encourages inquiry, participation, and problem solving. Such study also requires the development of skills—critical literacy and intercultural competence—needed by citizens in a globally connected world.

## Note

1   See http://catdir.loc.gov/catdir/toc/ecip0516/2005018778.html for social issues listed by the Library of Congress.

# References

Hanvey, Robert. (1975). *An Attainable Global Perspective.* New York, NY: Center for War/Peace Studies.

Kasai, Masataka and Merryfield, Merry. (2004). "How are Teachers Responding to Globalization?" 68(5) *Social Education*, pp. 354–359.

Merryfield, Merry. (2007). "The Web and Teachers' Decision-Making in Global Education." 35(2) *Theory and Research in Social Education*, pp. 256–275.

Merryfield, Merry. (2003). "Like a Veil: Cross-Cultural Experiential Learning Online," 3(2) *Contemporary Issues in Technology and Teacher Education.* Accessed February 6, 2010, at http://www.citejournal.org/vol3/iss2/socialstudies/article1.cfm.

# 22

# BIG HISTORY AS CORE CURRICULUM

*Cynthia Brown*

PROFESSOR EMERITA, HISTORY, DOMINICAN UNIVERSITY OF CALIFORNIA

John Dewey wrote "My Pedagogic Creed" in 1897, when he was 38 years old, at the start of his ten years at the University of Chicago (1894–1904). I am writing this in 2013, at the age of 75, after a lifetime of work in teacher education and big history.

Dewey's ideas were passed to me early, by my mother, Louise Bast Stokes, who trained as a biology teacher at the University of Wisconsin in a lab school modeled on Dewey's lab school in Chicago. Through her, his ideas became second nature to me, including his humanism. (He signed the Humanist Manifesto in 1933, but later called himself a "Reconstructionist": one who reconstructs the definition of God to refer to human values instead of a supernatural deity.) (Epstein, 2010)

In the public schools of my small town, Madisonville, in western Kentucky, I experienced confirmation of Dewey's ideas. The academic content proved undemanding, with time to learn by doing extra-curricular activities during school hours, and by reading mother's Harvard Classics rather spending hours on homework. Despite the absence of African American students, segregated in their own schools, I became familiar with the lives of classmates from many social and economic levels. My interest in understanding everybody increased as my opportunities for travel opened up.

At Duke University, I chose to major in history because it seemed the only discipline that encompassed all the others, and because only history could begin to explain how segregation in the South came to be—a pressing question for me. I helped organize the first sit-in in Durham, North Carolina, and wrote my senior thesis on the Peabody Education Fund, which gave aid to African American schools in the South.

After receiving my Master of Arts in Teaching, I taught two years of high school in Baltimore, at Eastern High School. It was the early days of racial integration. About a third of my students were African American. They were not hesitant about adding social issues to my world history course. They taught me the song, "We Shall Overcome." I added a unit on the U.S.S.R., since the textbook had none, and students became so interested that they requested that the principal start classes in Russian language.

After finishing my Ph.D. at Johns Hopkins University, I spent two years as the wife of a Peace Corps doctor assigned to northeast Brazil (1965–1967). I discovered the work of Paulo Freire (1970), recently exiled after a military coup took over the country in 1964. Freire put social issues at the center of teaching adult literacy; the importance of his ideas provoked my first writing, "Literacy in Thirty Hours" (Brown, 1975; Kirylo, 2011). Freire's ideas reinforced my preference for dialogue and discussion in the classroom, rather than lecture mode, and helped me be more aware of oppression wherever it existed.

For three years I worked with Herb Kohl in Berkeley to develop an alternative elementary teacher training program to credential teachers of color for the public schools (Kohl, 1998). Following my work with Herb, I learned about the importance of free speech by writing about Alexander Meiklejohn, philosopher and college president (Brown, 1981), and more about the importance of social issues in the curriculum by constructing the oral biography, *Ready from Within*, of Septima Clark, civil rights teacher (Brown, 1986). Clark was saying what I thought but couldn't yet say myself; she became the major catalyst in my development as a writer and teacher, since, of course, I needed a woman as my role model. *Ready from Within* is still used in adult literacy classes because it confirms the power of adult learners.

From 1981 to 1995, I directed the secondary credential program at Dominican University of California (then Dominican College), then taught in it full time until 2001. Racism, sexism, and homophobia continued to be dominant social issues. I also taught a unit in a high school class to model teaching current social issues (genocide) as a way to connect with the past, which resulted in my book, *Connecting with the Past* (1994). During these years I began to see other social issues as well—the disjointed, disconnected nature of the prevailing school curriculum and the emerging environmental problems that few seemed to be noticing at the time.

In 1991, I read an article in the *Journal of World History* by David Christian, a history professor in Sydney, Australia (Christian, 1991). Entitled "The Case for Big History," this article changed the focus of my life. Big History seemed the best response to the pressing new issues—how to integrate many disciplines into a coherent curriculum and how to understand our environmental challenges.

As soon as possible, I began teaching Big History, and from 2002 to 2007 I wrote my own account of it (Brown, 2007). Later, with David Christian and Craig Benjamin, I wrote the first college textbook in this new synthesis of science and the humanities, *Big History: Between Nothing and Everything* (2014). In 2010, the faculty at Dominican University of California implemented its decision to require Big History for all incoming freshmen (www.dominican.edu/academics/bighistory). During 2012, I wrote essays for the development of a high school curriculum in Big History, funded by Bill Gates. This curriculum became available online in August 2013 for all teachers and administrators to use (www.bighistoryproject.com).

Can we achieve any real democracy, or will it always be a cover for the plutocracy hiding behind it? Can sufficient technological fixes, conservation, and savings from waste slow down or reverse climate change? Will people understand the current stakes well enough to change their lives and demand government action? It is hard to see how any current curriculum can avoid dealing with these critical social issues.

## Human Nature

I believe that humans are a unique kind of animal, special because, in the continuum from loners (sharks) to the most social animals (ants, termites, and bees), we sit right in the center, both separate individuals and socially enmeshed creatures. We are paradoxical in our deepest nature—both defensive and competitive, while at the same time altruistic and cooperative (Wilson, 1979).

We humans are also unique because our ability to communicate symbolically and precisely enables us to accumulate our learning over the generations. Certain other species (chimps and dolphins, for example) can teach one generation of their young rudimentary skills, but no others can build upon its knowledge generation after generation, as we have done. Our amazing accumulation of knowledge over almost 200,000 years—our collective learning, in the term of big historians—has brought us to the present moment in which the human capacity is so great that we are unintentionally changing the biosphere of our planet. At the same time that our knowledge is immense, it also remains vastly incomplete and seems likely always to remain so (Christian, 2004).

## The Historic Moment

I believe that the human species has now entered a historical moment in which the continuation of our civilization, or possibly even of our species, is in doubt because of our self-inflicted transformation of our planetary biosphere. A majority of scientists and historians agree with this analysis. The extreme challenge of the next decades puts all aspects of human social life in a new light, including education (Spier, 2010; McKibben, 2011).

When we look at the human species globally, we see how similar all humans are and how similar the patterns of our cultural development are everywhere. We see a period of hunting and gathering that began about 200,000 years ago; by 13,000 years ago it had been extended worldwide. Hunting and gathering constituted more than 95% of human existence on the planet through extreme periods of climate change (Christian, Brown, and Benjamin, 2014).

Beginning about 10,000, we see the start of agriculture and the domestication of certain plants and animals as humans found it necessary to settle down into village life. As surplus food accumulated, populations increased and life in cities and states developed into what we call agrarian civilizations. Only two hundred years ago, with the addition of fossil fuel (coal) to our systems of energy flow, we began to develop industrial capitalism. With the additional use of oil in the 20th century, we increased both our population and our use of Earth's resources at a startling rate, until now we face large-scale climate changes, death of oceans and fisheries, and massive extinctions of animals and plants (Christian, Brown, and Benjamin, 2014).

At the beginning of the 21st century, our empirical knowledge and technological skill have reached astonishing levels, giving us the ability to communicate globally at speeds unimaginable only a few years ago. Computers and cell phones are rapidly changing all aspects of human life, including, of course, education.

The national context that educators in the U.S. face has changed profoundly since that of Dewey's adulthood (1884–1930), when the U.S. led the world in industrial output by a large margin. Now the U.S. is an industrial power in a world of industrials powers, with fierce competition from the large nations that were slower to industrialize. Our national government, which rallied to help capitalism survive the Great Depression and to fight World War II, has gradually been reduced in scale as a result of reducing the income tax rate since Ronald Reagan's election to the presidency in 1981. The percentage of voters in national elections has been less than 60% of those qualified since 1968. Campaigns for office are so costly that candidates are deeply beholden to their wealthy donors. Certainly, the survival of democracy seems at stake. Those who wish to reduce U.S. government were behind the passage of the 2007 No Child Left Behind Act, ostensibly to hold schools accountable. Yet it set standards so narrowly that schools could not possibly meet them, with the result (probably intended) that the legislation has served as a way to label public schools as failures (Miner, 2013).

## The First Five Years

I believe that human infants begin learning at birth. They absorb from their interactions with others the social values and issues of the day, while at the same time they acquire the basic knowledge and vocabulary that will serve as a framework for lifetime learning. Around the world wealthy and middle class educated families can provide the circumstances their children need from birth to five years. Yet poor and uneducated families cannot. To break the cycle of poverty, governments need to provide some kind of pre-school programs like Head Start for children from families under a certain income level, followed by excellent elementary and secondary schools.

Young children worldwide need to learn attitudes that Maria Montessori envisioned 70 years ago. They need to learn that they are children of the universe, that they are a human family stretching around the planet, and that they are inter-dependent members of a highly complex biosphere rather than dominators of it. These basic facts and attitudes cannot wait until later; they must form the bedrock neural passages in our children's brains (Duffy and Duffy, 2002).

## The Role of Public Schools in a Multicultural Democracy

I believe that public schools exist to make democracy possible. Government by the people cannot succeed unless it operates with an educated electorate—edu-cated in the empirical knowledge available, and imbued with the values necessary for large-scale cooperation.

Across the globe, some 57 million children in 2013 had no access to public education, most of them in sub-Sahara Africa and Pakistan. Countries that lack access to public education are called failed states. Does the lack of education cause the failure of states? Or does the weakness of government structures cause the lack of education? Together they form a self-reinforcing negative loop.

Education is an individual right, the only way to develop one's skills and tal-ents for living in a knowledge-rich world. At the same time, education is also a social responsibility—the only way for an individual to assume the responsible role required in a democracy for the governance of one's community and nation.

Public schools teach not only knowledge but also shared civic values that bind people together and make complex social life possible. These values include respect for each person, equality before the law, separation of church and state, transparency in government, freedom of speech and religion, and consideration of multiple cultural and class perspectives. Freedom of speech merits special atten-tion, including the freedom to criticize religion, since free speech is the bedrock principle of a free society (Rushdie, 2012).

Because students cannot experience this range of values if they are schooled in homogeneous cultural/religious settings, I believe that all students should attend public school, with specific, family-chosen religious and cultural education taking place in after-school programs and on weekends. Students need to experience, early on, the cultural and class diversity of their society, or they come to adult-hood unprepared for it.

Young people do not wait until adolescence or adulthood to learn social values and attitudes. They absorb them before adolescence from their experiences and interactions at home and at school. Social issues cannot be avoided in the elemen-tary grades; they are imparted, silently or by articulation, by the structure of the school, the values of its staff, and the make-up of the student body.

## Curriculum

I believe that every child in the world has the right to learn the modern scientific origin story, often called "Big History." This is the coherent story from the Big

Bang to the present that scholars have been able to construct only in the last 35 years (Cloud, 1978; Spier, 1996; Christian, 2004; Chaisson, 2006).

Big History combines the latest knowledge based on empirical evidence in the sciences and the humanities to provide a map, or overview, of human collective learning. It explains how humans got to the present moment. It is indispensable to students for understanding their current world. It transforms the curriculum by giving each discipline its place in a meaningful story.

Social studies curriculum in the West since World War II has evolved rapidly from Western civilization to world history and now to Big History. Big History is the global story for the present global civilization; it encompasses everything that humans know.

Yet just as we have reached a globally interconnected and communicating civilization, we can see that our whole structure of civilization, based on burning fossil fuels, is threatened by rapid global climate change. To face this challenge, we must mobilize our efforts on the scale of mobilization during World War II, requiring the participation of every citizen in the world. This is the issue that will take priority in our schools in the immediate future, and this is due to the sense that we may only have a decade or so to prevent climate change catastrophic to humans. Informed students are insisting on being part of the effort to change our old systems and find new ones that will permit civilization to continue in sustainable ways; teachers from around the world must also exert their leadership.

## Teaching as a Career

I believe that public school teaching serves as a fulfilling career for those who devote themselves to it. Through teaching, one can be of service to interlocking levels of life—one's community, state, nation, and world. At the same time, one can enjoy the thrill of keeping up with new knowledge and sharing it immediately with students who can use it. One can also garner the satisfaction of engaging the pressing social issues of one's time, leading students in considering all perspectives and in seeking common solutions.

Public school teaching in the U.S., and probably anywhere in the world, is not for the faint-hearted. It requires extreme stamina and self-respect, since some forces seem constantly bent on disrespecting teachers and dismantling public education. At the end of the day, public school teaching is a noble and heroic calling, serving the purposes of a self-governing society.

## References

Brown, C.S. (1975). *Literacy in Thirty Hours: Paulo Freire's Process in Northeast Brazil*. London, U.K.: Writers and Readers Publishing Cooperative.

Brown, C.S. (1981) *Alexander Meiklejohn: Teacher of Freedom*. Berkeley, CA: Meiklejohn Civil Liberties Institute.

Brown, C.S. (1986). *Ready From Within: Septima Clark and the Civil Rights Movement.* Navarro, CA: Wild Trees Press. (Re-issued by Africa World Press, 1990.)

Brown, C.S. (1994). *Connecting with the Past: History Workshop in Middle and High School.* Portsmouth, NH: Heinemann.

Brown, C.S. (2007). *Big History: From the Big Bang to the Present.* (Second edition, 2012). New York, NY: New Press.

Chaisson, E. (2006). *Epic of Evolution: Seven Ages of the Cosmos.* New York, NY: Columbia University Press.

Christian, D. (1991). "The Case for Big History." 2(2) *Journal of World History,* pp. 223–238.

Christian, D. (2004). *Maps of Time: An Introduction to Big History.* (Second edition, 2011). Berkeley, CA: University of California Press.

Christian, D., Brown, C. S., and Benjamin, C. (2014). *Big History: Between Nothing and Everything.* New York, NY: McGraw-Hill.

Cloud, P. (1978). *Cosmos, Earth and Man: A Short History of the Universe.* New Haven, CT: Yale University Press.

Duffy, M., and Duffy, D'N. (2002). *Children of the Universe: Cosmic Education in the Montessori Elementary Classroom.* Santa Rosa, CA: Parent Child Press.

Epstein, G. (2010). *Good Without God: What a Billion Non-Religious People Do Believe.* New York, NY: Harper.

Freire, P. (1970). *Pedagogy of the Oppressed.* (30th anniversary edition, 2000). New York, NY: Continuum.

Kirylo, J.D. (2011). *Paulo Freire: The Man from Recife.* New York, NY: Peter Lang.

Kohl, H. (1998). *The Discipline of Hope: Learning from a Lifetime of Teaching.* New York: Simon and Schuster.

McKibben, B. (2011). *The Global Warming Reader.* New York, NY: OR Books.

Miner, B.J. (2013). *Lessons from the Heartland: A Turbulent Half-Century of Public Education in an Iconic American City.* New York, NY: New Press.

Rushdie, S. (2012). *Joseph Anton: A Memoir.* New York, NY: Random House.

Spierv, F. (1996). *The Structure of Big History: From the Big Bang Until Today.* Amsterdam, The Netherlands: Amsterdam University Press.

Spier, F. (2010). *Big History and the Future of Humanity.* Malden, MA: Wiley-Blackwell.

Wilson, E.O. (1979). *On Human Nature.* Cambridge, MA: Harvard University Press.

www.dominican.edu/academic/bighistory

www.bighistoryproject.com

# 23

# THE CENTRALITY OF STUDENTS AND THEIR APPRECIATION AND UNDERSTANDING OF SOCIAL ISSUES

*Robert E. Yager*

PROFESSOR, SCIENCE EDUCATION, THE UNIVERSITY OF IOWA

My interest in teaching and learning began with my start in a small rural school which had been "consolidated" after closing all one-room schools in Viola Township, Audubon County, Iowa, in 1923. My mother was the first of her generation to graduate from college and become a teacher. In some sense, her encouragement and teaching ideas were the beginnings of my personal Creed—though they were opposite to my current philosophy for teaching seven decades later. My experience as a K-12 student only involved remembering what teachers and textbooks said—and how my own efforts compared with the performances of other students. I graduated from high school as Valedictorian when I had just turned seventeen years old.

My plan was to attend the University of Northern Iowa, from which my mother had graduated to be a teacher. I chose English (and drama) as a major. Eventually, I changed majors because of my greater successes with science courses. (I did not succeed in college drama with but two lines in a major stage production!) I continued the B.A. college program with a science major, finishing in three years (including two summer sessions). I also completed strong minors in English and government, both of which moved me closer to concerns with social issues.

My student teaching at the University of Northern Iowa Laboratory School was the first experience that shaped my "to be" Pedagogical Creed. The Laboratory School building was just across the street from the science research center, where study and research continued with teachers using the typical rote methods most popular in university science departments.

Both the Lab School and science faculty differed drastically concerning effective methods for teaching. The focus in the Lab School was getting the students to engage and analyze. My experiences there were my first to deal with the use of social issues in the extant curriculum and the first to provide a means for authentic learning.

After graduation with a Bachelor's degree in science (at age 20), I got a position teaching science and English in a small rural school (Chapin Consolidated School) in north central Iowa. It was similar to the K-12 school in which I began my education in Viola Township. It was a place for me to try the ideas which were opposite to those I personally experienced as a student; that is, instead of emphasizing note taking, rote lectures, and memorization I engaged my students in experimenting with plants and animals in the classroom and around school. Many experiments related to weeds, food needs, bird migration, nutrition, habitats, and seasonal changes.

Following my first year of teaching, I decided to undertake graduate studies in Botany at the University of Iowa. I wanted to learn more about science, plus more about how to engage my students in interesting learning activities. I chose plant physiology because it best fit what I "liked" and how it could be used with students. Unfortunately, my experience in the three graduate classes in Botany during my first summer at the University of Iowa reintroduced me to all the traditional ways of teaching, which included outlines to be copied in order to prepare for class exams. Any hope to learn more about engaging students in hands-on science was a lost cause, as the course largely called for remembering what was in the textbooks and lectures in order to repeat the information in exams.

Ultimately, my success resulted in my being offered a research assistantship and encouragement to remain enrolled in graduate school. I, however, chose to return to Chapin and a second year of teaching. This second year was significant for the development of my own Pedagogical Creed as I focused even more on student interests and student engagement with scientific issues.

As my second year of teaching at Chapin began, the Korean War was becoming a major national concern. Fearful of being drafted, I decided to return to the master's program at the University of Iowa which I had started the previous summer. Subsequently, I also joined the National Guard hoping to avoid the Army draft. But that is not how it worked out. While I ended up finishing the Master's degree I also ended up heading to basic training in the U.S. Army.

After basic training I was lucky enough to be sent to Germany, where I was placed in an Army school enrolling soldiers whose skills were extremely limited in mathematics and reading. Most, in fact, had skills below that of a typical fourth grader. They were to be released from the Army unless they gained more skills in both areas. That provided another great learning experience for me in regard to developing my skills as a teacher and understanding how to work with students with limited abilities.

Ultimately, I returned to the University of Iowa where I married my wife, a teacher in home economics and diversity. I decided I wanted to earn a Ph.D. in plant physiology.

After my first year of study for my Ph.D., I was chosen to head (temporarily) the University of Iowa Laboratory School science program. Four faculty members (each of whom had headed the university science education program for five years) had not been promoted with tenure due to their lack of significant research and publications. I was to serve as the head of the science department for a single year while they located a named "full professor" to formulate and direct a new program at the University of Iowa. I viewed this as a great possibility for sharing ideas and learning more about teaching.

The new chairperson, a Dr. Porter, who was hired a year later, insisted on several "conditions" before accepting the offer of becoming a full professor at the University of Iowa. One of the conditions was bringing in an assistant professor to head the Laboratory School, who would also work with students who were to be future secondary school teachers.

Interestingly, Dr. Porter's ideas concerning successful teaching and learning were the same as my own. First, he insisted that our teaching "team" be enhanced! Furthermore, he wanted to focus on application courses in the sciences which illustrated learning, *not rote memorization*. Moreover, he wanted me to teach and be the *permanent* head of the science department at the Lab School. All of this, of course, significantly impacted my curricular and instructional efforts, leading to a Pedagogical Creed centered on problems, students, and personal and group projects.

My primary goal of teaching through the years focused on preparing students to "understand and respond to individual interests, strengths, experiences, and needs" (Khan, 2006). It is important to remember that both science and learning always start with questions. Central to the Yager Creed is that student questions are vital to motivate and accomplish learning. For me, the questions must relate to four key features to accomplish the goals. This means that student learning best occurs when the questions are: 1) Personal, 2) Current, 3) Local, and 4) Collaborative.

Lev Vygotsky (1934, 1978, 1987) was considered an early prophet of constructivist ideas. Vygotsky wrote extensively about "real learning" and how it is to be accomplished. His work has been an important focus for developing my Pedagogical Creed. Specific aspects of Vygotsky's work that I have found particularly influential are as follows:

- Language itself becomes a very powerful tool of intellectual adaptation.
- Encouraging and accepting student autonomy, initiation, and leadership.
- Allowing student thinking to drive lessons instead of depending on content and instructional strategies that are based on textbooks or state edicts.
- Asking students to elaborate on responses from others.
- Allowing wait-time after asking questions.
- Encouraging students to interact with each other and with others also identified as "the" teacher.
- Asking thoughtful, open-ended questions while encouraging students to do the same.
- Asking students to articulate their theories about concepts before accepting, using, and repeating teacher (or textbook) explanations of concepts.

- Looking for alternative concepts from students, and encouraging them to address any misconceptions and/or differences.

The greatest impact in the development of my Pedagogical Creed was the Science/Technology/Society (STS) efforts of the 1970s and 1980s. I first came across the term/concept in a book entitled *The Manmade World* by J.G. Truxal and E.J. Piel (1971), both of whom were engineers. The focus on STS was dramatically enhanced by Rustum Roy (1984), who was also an engineer and who helped to establish an international organization on STS. Roy contacted me about helping to create an "educational" component to STS in order to fit educational reform efforts.

Many argued against STS, especially the last "S," as they asserted that "society" should not be construed as being part of science. I was actually interested in having the first "S" be Society, thus serving as the starting point: Society, Technology, and Science. Some of the most vociferous critics asserted that that STS meant to Stop Teaching Science. Tellingly, in the end the STS efforts resulted in an emphasis on just what the term "effective teaching" meant in the real world of teaching and learning.[1]

Another effort in which I was involved was with the National Center for Learning and Teaching Nanoscale Science and Engineering (NCLT) at Northwestern University. Robert Chang, also engineer, was the Principal Investigator of the project, which ran from 2005 to 2010. The focus was on Nanotechnology as an "enlargement and corrective" focus for the whole of science.

Another one of my recent experiences comes from the impressive staff of the Iowa Children's Museum (see Weld, 2004). They argue that children's play has come under attack and seems too often to detract from learning. But, play can give children a head start on academic successes. Lines have been drawn between playing and learning, with more children spending too much time in didactic settings, such as those in traditional schools with the teacher in control! Should play simply be purposeless?—Fun?—A freeing experience? Evidence indicates that the openness of play—where the process is more important than the product—can provide a terrific framework for real learning. It is important to note also that play is important in the everyday lives of children! Play brings joy, fun, and exploration of new ideas. Play is also important for life-long learning, and creates a foundation for reading, mathematics, science, and art, bringing these skills together with a motivation to learn, as opposed to solely experiencing the teacher and textbook directions.

Teaching for over 60 years at the University of Iowa has allowed me to grow each year in terms of changing from the traditional teaching model I experienced as a boy and as an undergraduate and graduate student to a more personal, experimental, hands-on/minds-on approach, and social issues driven approach.

## Yager's Pedagogical Creed

The first and foremost aspect of the Yager Creed is a focus on student-centered learning. I maintain that students should be asked to consider the following questions (National Research Council, 1996):

- Is it a personal problem or issue?
- How did it become such a problem or issue?
- What are some alternative approaches to its solution?
- What are the potential effects of applying alternatives for individuals and/or society generally?

Essentially, then, all learning must be personal, starting with a personal problem or issue; it must be something that inspires an ever-increasing number of questions. It puts the student in charge.

Tied to this, I believe it is essential to start the learning process in science with positing questions, and this is critical to get the students involved in "doing" real science.[2] This is, I believe, basic to personal learning. Furthermore, "questions" promote "constructivist" learning and provide ways to assess teaching success.

I have developed five examples of questioning which I believe are the featured questions that should frame classroom actions for promoting learning:

1. Asking questions that describe: "What did you do?" and "What happened?"
2. Asking students for advice: "What evidence do you have for that idea?" and "What thinking/observations led you to suggest that?"
3. Seeking explanations: "How would you explain that?" and "What may have caused it to happen?"
4. Asking questions that relate to responses from others: (e.g., students, parents, other students, industrial leaders): "What did other people suggest?" and "How do these compare with your ideas?"
5. Asking questions that predict: "What will you do next?" and "What will happen if you . . .?"

Such questions illustrate my Teaching Creed concerning appropriate teacher interactions with students; these result in the following ways to accomplish learning:

- Class activities that are student-centered and which are planned and carried out by students;
- Classes are individualized and personalized, recognizing student diversity;
- Classrooms are directed by student questions and experiences;
- Students and teachers are using a variety of resources, both written and personal;
- Cooperative work is encouraged for addressing problems and issues;

- Students are considered active contributors to instruction and to the curriculum;
- Teachers build on student experiences which illustrate that students learn best from their own experiences and ideas as well as those from other students;
- Teachers plan and carry out their teaching around student problems and current issues—preferably those planned by students; and
- Teachers encourage their students to question and respond with possible answers for which substantiating evidence is expected and needed.

I maintain that successful learning should:

- Identify problems with local interest and impact;
- Use local resources (human and material) to locate information that can be used in problem resolution;
- Promote active involvement of students as they seek information that can be applied to solve real-life problems;
- Be extended beyond class periods, the classroom, the school;
- Use process skills which can help resolve students' own problems;
- Include the experiences of citizenship roles and attempt to resolve issues they have identified;
- Focus on the potential of personal and civic actions after weighing all possible consequences of alternative options;
- Defend decisions and actions using rational arguments based on evidence;
- Display curiosity about and appreciation for the natural as well as the human-made world;
- Apply skepticism, logical reasoning, and creativity to investigate the objects and events in the observable universe;
- Use new evidence and realize the tentativeness of current explanations;
- Consider the political, economic, moral, and ethical aspects of school programs as they relate to personal and global issues.

All of the following examples are fundamental to the Yager Creed for establishing and improving student learning:

I believe all educational programs should focus on real-world problems, and that the latter should be student-generated.

I believe that the learning activities must be age appropriate and learner-centered.

I believe it is essential to support and develop a classroom community in which cooperation, shared responsibilities, and respect are integral components.

I believe instruction should affect the daily living of students, which result in responsible personal decision-making.

I believe students should be engaged in learning activities in which investigation, analysis, and the application of concepts and processes are integral components.

I believe it is essential to provide ample opportunity for discussion and debates among students.

I believe continuous assessment of student assessing student understanding is critical.

I believe it is critical to engage students in ongoing assessments of their own work as well as that of others (Khan, 2006).

I believe that opportunities for students to extend beyond the classroom and into their local communities is essential.

I believe that the empowerment of students as future citizens who believe they have the power to make changes and take responsibility for doing so is critical.

I believe that, in order to empower students to become citizens who believe they can make changes in a responsible manner, education must focus on current issues and ways of bringing about the resolution of such issues. This means identifying local, regional, national, and international problems with students, planning for individual and group activities which address them, and moving to actions designed to resolve the issues.

I believe that learner-centered curricula provide more opportunities for graduates to become creative, autonomous learners, which are the sort of people most needed for the 21st century workforce. The typical curriculum as manifested in the modern era continues to be the instructional paradigm in which teachers are in control of what is done in classrooms, and then used to report what is seen as an indication of learning. A learner-centered curriculum is not just a theoretical construct but one with real and varying options. Practical ways of supporting learner-centered curricula, through assessment practices, use of technology, and consideration of physical space are all features for realizing the needed reforms.

Basic to my Educational Creed is never to stop learning!! Learning must continue as a major factor about which I share as my philosophy and experiences. There is still more to learn! It is the heart and soul of science!!

In closing, I wish to note that following 60 years in education I retired from the Head of the Science Education Center at the University of Iowa in 2008, after authoring hundreds of articles/publications and supervising over 130 Ph.D. dissertations. I am pleased to note that all share my interest and use of social issues as a means of improving education generally.

Finally, I recommend more teaching along the lines advocated by Salmon Khan in his *The One World School House*. I have found his ideas to be shockingly similar to my own development, and that they indicate the power and success of using social issues to improve real student learning (Khan, 2006).

## Notes

1  Currently the new national reform effort in science in the United States—the Next Generation Science Standards (NGSS)—moves away from STS, in that its focus is now Science, Technology, Engineering, and Mathematics (STEM).
2  I believe that institutions should work together to create more engaging situations that bring real-world research experiences to students. For scientists, confronting the unknown is a way of life. The idea of risk that an experiment might not yield expected results or that a line of reasoning might be wrong are not considered negatives. On the contrary, they are inherent to the process of discovery; more learning usually results from mistakes than those from anticipated results. Transformative breakthroughs often come from the boldest thinking which challenges conventional wisdom.

## References

Khan, S. (2006). *The One World School House: Education Reimaged*. Accessed at: www. khanacademy.org. Also available as an ebook.

National Research Council. (1996). *National Science Education Standards*. Washington, D.C.: National Academy Press.

Roy, R. (1984). *S-S/T/S Project: Teaching Science via Science, Technology and Society Material in the Pre-college Years*. University Park, PA: Pennsylvania State University.

Truxal, J.G., and Piel, E.J. (1971). *The Man-made World*. Brooklyn, NY: McGraw-Hill Book Company.

Vygotsky, L.S. (1934/1986). *Thought and Language*. Cambridge, MA: MIT Press.

Vygotsky, L.S. (1978). *Mind in Society: The Development of Higher Psychological Processes*. Cambridge MA: Harvard University Press.

Vygotsky, L.S. (1987). *Thinking and Speech*. New York, NY: Plenum Press.

Weld, J. (2004). *The Game of Science Education*. Boston, MA: Allyn and Bacon.

# APPENDIX

## My Pedagogic Creed

*John Dewey*

(JANUARY 6, 1897) LIV(3) *SCHOOL JOURNAL*, PP. 77–80

### Article One: What Education Is

I believe that all education proceeds by the participation of the individual in the social consciousness of the race. This process begins unconsciously almost at birth, and is continually shaping the individual's powers, saturating his consciousness, forming his habits, training his ideas, and arousing his feelings and emotions. Through this unconscious education the individual gradually comes to share in the intellectual and moral resources which humanity has succeeded in getting together. He becomes an inheritor of the funded capital of civilization. The most formal and technical education in the world cannot safely depart from this general process. It can only organize it; or differentiate it in some particular direction.

I believe that the only true education comes through the stimulation of the child's powers by the demands of the social situations in which he finds himself. Through these demands he is stimulated to act as a member of a unity, to emerge from his original narrowness of action and feeling and to conceive of himself from the standpoint of the welfare of the group to which he belongs. Through the responses which others make to his own activities he comes to know what these mean in social terms. The value which they have is reflected back into them. For instance, through the response which is made to the child's instinctive babblings the child comes to know what those babblings mean; they are transformed into articulate language and thus the child is introduced into the consolidated wealth of ideas and emotions which are now summed up in language.

I believe that this educational process has two sides—one psychological and one sociological; and that neither can be subordinated to the other or neglected without evil results following. Of these two sides, the psychological is the basis.

The child's own instincts and powers furnish the material and give the starting point for all education. Save as the efforts of the educator connect with some activity which the child is carrying on of his own initiative independent of the educator, education becomes reduced to a pressure from without. It may, indeed, give certain external results but cannot truly be called educative. Without insight into the psychological structure and activities of the individual, the educative process will, therefore, be haphazard and arbitrary. If it chances to coincide with the child's activity it will get a leverage; if it does not, it will result in friction, or disintegration, or arrest of the child nature.

I believe that knowledge of social conditions, of the present state of civilization, is necessary in order properly to interpret the child's powers. The child has his own instincts and tendencies, but we do not know what these mean until we can translate them into their social equivalents. We must be able to carry them back into a social past and see them as the inheritance of previous race activities. We must also be able to project them into the future to see what their outcome and end will be. In the illustration just used, it is the ability to see in the child's babblings the promise and potency of a future social intercourse and conversation which enables one to deal in the proper way with that instinct.

I believe that the psychological and social sides are organically related and that education cannot be regarded as a compromise between the two, or a superimposition of one upon the other. We are told that the psychological definition of education is barren and formal—that it gives us only the idea of a development of all the mental powers without giving us any idea of the use to which these powers are put. On the other hand, it is urged that the social definition of education, as getting adjusted to civilization, makes of it a forced and external process, and results in subordinating the freedom of the individual to a preconceived social and political status.

I believe each of these objections is true when urged against one side isolated from the other. In order to know what a power really is we must know what its end, use, or function is; and this we cannot know save as we conceive of the individual as active in social relationships. But, on the other hand, the only possible adjustment which we can give to the child under existing conditions, is that which arises through putting him in complete possession of all his powers. With the advent of democracy and modern industrial conditions, it is impossible to foretell definitely just what civilization will be twenty years from now. Hence it is impossible to prepare the child for any precise set of conditions. To prepare him for the future life means to give him command of himself; it means so to train him that he will have the full and ready use of all his capacities; that his eye and ear and hand may be tools ready to command, that his judgment may be capable of grasping the conditions under which it has to work, and the executive forces be trained to act economically and efficiently. It is impossible to reach this sort of adjustment save as constant regard is had to the individual's own powers, tastes, and interests—say, that is, as education is continually converted into psychological terms. In sum, I believe that the individual who is to be educated is a social individual and that society is an organic union of individuals. If we eliminate the social factor from the child we are left only with an abstraction; if we eliminate the individual factor from society, we are left only with an inert and lifeless mass. Education, therefore, must begin with a psychological insight into the child's capacities, interests, and habits. It must be controlled at every point by reference to these same considerations. These powers, interests, and habits must be continually interpreted—we must know what they mean. They must be translated into terms of their social equivalents—into terms of what they are capable of in the way of social service.

## Article Two: What the school Is

I believe that the school is primarily a social institution. Education being a social process, the school is simply that form of community life in which all those agencies are concentrated that will be most effective in bringing the child to share in the inherited resources of the race, and to use his own powers for social ends.

I believe that education, therefore, is a process of living and not a preparation for future living.

I believe that the school must represent present life—life as real and vital to the child as that which he carries on in the home, in the neighborhood, or on the play-ground.

I believe that education which does not occur through forms of life, forms that are worth living for their own sake, is always a poor substitute for the genuine reality and tends to cramp and to deaden.

I believe that the school, as an institution, should simplify existing social life; should reduce it, as it were, to an embryonic form. Existing life is so complex that the child cannot be brought into contact with it without either confusion or distraction; he is either overwhelmed by multiplicity of activities which are going on, so that he loses his own power of orderly reaction, or he is so stimulated by these various activities that his powers are prematurely called into play and he becomes either unduly specialized or else disintegrated.

I believe that, as such simplified social life, the school life should grow gradually out of the home life; that it should take up and continue the activities with which the child is already familiar in the home.

I believe that it should exhibit these activities to the child, and reproduce them in such ways that the child will gradually learn the meaning of them, and be capable of playing his own part in relation to them.

I believe that this is a psychological necessity, because it is the only way of securing continuity in the child's growth, the only way of giving a background of past experience to the new ideas given in school.

I believe it is also a social necessity because the home is the form of social life in which the child has been nurtured and in connection with which he has had his moral training. It is the business of the school to deepen and extend his sense of the values bound up in his home life.

I believe that much of present education fails because it neglects this fundamental principle of the school as a form of community life. It conceives the school as a place where certain information is to be given, where certain lessons are to be learned, or where certain habits are to be formed. The value of these is conceived as lying largely in the remote future; the child must do these things for the sake of something else he is to do; they are mere preparation. As a result they do not become a part of the life experience of the child and so are not truly educative.

I believe that moral education centres about this conception of the school as a mode of social life, that the best and deepest moral training is precisely that which one gets through having to enter into proper relations with others in a unity of work and thought. The present educational systems, so far as they destroy or neglect this unity, render it difficult or impossible to get any genuine, regular moral training.

I believe that the child should be stimulated and controlled in his work through the life of the community.

I believe that under existing conditions far too much of the stimulus and control proceeds from the teacher, because of neglect of the idea of the school as a form of social life.

I believe that the teacher's place and work in the school is to be interpreted from this same basis. The teacher is not in the school to impose certain ideas or to form certain habits in the child, but is there as a member of the community to select the influences which shall affect the child and to assist him in properly responding to these influences.

I believe that the discipline of the school should proceed from the life of the school as a whole and not directly from the teacher.

I believe that the teacher's business is simply to determine on the basis of larger experience and riper wisdom, how the discipline of life shall come to the child.

I believe that all questions of the grading of the child and his promotion should be determined by reference to the same standard. Examinations are of use only so far as they test the child's fitness for social life and reveal the place in which he can be of most service and where he can receive the most help.

## Article Three: The Subject-Matter of Education

I believe that the social life of the child is the basis of concentration, or correlation, in all his training or growth. The social life gives the unconscious unity and the background of all his efforts and of all his attainments.

I believe that the subject-matter of the school curriculum should mark a gradual differentiation out of the primitive unconscious unity of social life.

I believe that we violate the child's nature and render difficult the best ethical results, by introducing the child too abruptly to a number of special studies, of reading, writing, geography, etc., out of relation to this social life.

I believe, therefore, that the true centre of correlation of the school subjects is not science, nor literature, nor history, nor geography, but the child's own social activities.

I believe that education cannot be unified in the study of science, or so-called nature study, because apart from human activity, nature itself is not a unity; nature in itself is a number of diverse objects in space and time, and to attempt to make it the centre of work by itself, is to introduce a principle of radiation rather than one of concentration.

I believe that literature is the reflex expression and interpretation of social experience; that hence it must follow upon and not precede such experience. It, therefore, cannot be made the basis, although it may be made the summary of unification.

I believe once more that history is of educative value in so far as it presents phases of social life and growth. It must be controlled by reference to social life. When taken simply as history it is thrown into the distant past and becomes dead and inert. Taken as the record of man's social life and progress it becomes full of meaning. I believe, however, that it cannot be so taken excepting as the child is also introduced directly into social life.

I believe accordingly that the primary basis of education is in the child's powers at work along the same general constructive lines as those which have brought civilization into being.

I believe that the only way to make the child conscious of his social heritage is to enable him to perform those fundamental types of activity which makes civilization what it is.

I believe, therefore, in the so-called expressive or constructive activities as the centre of correlation.

I believe that this gives the standard for the place of cooking, sewing, manual training, etc., in the school.

I believe that they are not special studies which are to be introduced over and above a lot of others in the way of relaxation or relief, or as additional accomplishments. I believe rather that they represent, as types, fundamental forms of social activity; and that it is possible and desirable that the child's introduction into the more formal subjects of the curriculum be through the medium of these activities.

I believe that the study of science is educational in so far as it brings out the materials and processes which make social life what it is.

I believe that one of the greatest difficulties in the present teaching of science is that the material is presented in purely objective form, or is treated as a new peculiar kind of experience which the child can add to that which he has already had. In reality, science is of value because it gives the ability to interpret and control the experience already had. It should be introduced, not as so much new subject-matter, but as showing the factors already involved in previous experience and as furnishing tools by which that experience can be more easily and effectively regulated.

I believe that at present we lose much of the value of literature and language studies because of our elimination of the social element. Language is almost always treated in the books of pedagogy simply as the expression of thought. It is true that language is a logical instrument, but it is fundamentally and primarily a social instrument. Language is the device for communication; it is the tool through which one individual comes to share the ideas and feelings of others. When treated simply as a way of getting individual information, or as a means of showing off what one has learned, it loses its social motive and end.

I believe that there is, therefore, no succession of studies in the ideal school curriculum. If education is life, all life has, from the outset, a scientific aspect; an aspect of art and culture and an aspect of communication. It cannot, therefore, be true that the proper studies for one grade are mere reading and writing, and that at a later grade, reading, or literature, or science, may be introduced. The progress is not in the succession of studies but in the development of new attitudes towards, and new interests in, experience.

I believe finally, that education must be conceived as a continuing reconstruction of experience; that the process and the goal of education are one and the same thing.

I believe that to set up any end outside of education, as furnishing its goal and standard, is to deprive the educational process of much of its meaning and tends to make us rely upon false and external stimuli in dealing with the child.

## Article Four: The Nature of Method

I believe that the question of method is ultimately reducible to the question of the order of development of the child's powers and interests. The law for presenting and treating material is the law implicit within the child's own nature. Because this is so I believe the following statements are of supreme importance as determining the spirit in which education is carried on:

1. I believe that the active side precedes the passive in the development of the child nature; that expression comes before conscious impression; that the muscular development precedes the sensory; that movements come before conscious sensations; I believe that consciousness is essentially motor or impulsive; that conscious states tend to project themselves in action.

I believe that the neglect of this principle is the cause of a large part of the waste of time and strength in school work. The child is thrown into a passive, receptive or absorbing attitude. The conditions are such that he is not permitted to follow the law of his nature; the result is friction and waste.

I believe that ideas (intellectual and rational processes) also result from action and devolve for the sake of the better control of action. What we term reason is primarily the law of orderly or effective action. To attempt to develop the reasoning powers, the powers of judgment, without reference to the selection and arrangement of means in action, is the fundamental fallacy in our present methods of dealing with this matter. As a result we present the child with arbitrary symbols. Symbols are a necessity in mental development, but they have their place as tools for economizing effort; presented by themselves they are a mass of meaningless and arbitrary ideas imposed from without.

2. I believe that the image is the great instrument of instruction. What a child gets out of any subject presented to him is simply the images which he himself forms with regard to it.

I believe that if nine-tenths of the energy at present directed towards making the child learn certain things, were spent in seeing to it that the child was forming proper images, the work of instruction would be indefinitely facilitated.

I believe that much of the time and attention now given to the preparation and presentation of lessons might be more wisely and profitably expended in training the child's power of imagery and in seeing to it that he was continually forming definite, vivid, and growing images of the various subjects with which he comes in contact in his experience.

3. I believe that interests are the signs and symptoms of growing power. I believe that they represent dawning capacities. Accordingly the constant and careful observation of interests is of the utmost importance for the educator.

I believe that these interests are to be observed as showing the state of development which the child has reached.

I believe that they prophesy the stage upon which he is about to enter.

I believe that only through the continual and sympathetic observation of childhood's interests can the adult enter into the child's life and see what it is ready for, and upon what material it could work most readily and fruitfully.

I believe that these interests are neither to be humored nor repressed. To repress interest is to substitute the adult for the child, and so to weaken intellectual curiosity and alertness, to suppress initiative, and to deaden interest. To humor the interests is to substitute the transient for the permanent. The interest is always the sign of some power below; the important thing is to discover this power. To humor the interest is to fail to penetrate below the surface and its sure result is to substitute caprice and whim for genuine interest.

4. I believe that the emotions are the reflex of actions.

I believe that to endeavor to stimulate or arouse the emotions apart from their corresponding activities, is to introduce an unhealthy and morbid state of mind.

I believe that if we can only secure right habits of action and thought, with reference to the good, the true, and the beautiful, the emotions will for the most part take care of themselves.

I believe that next to deadness and dullness, formalism and routine, our education is threatened with no greater evil than sentimentalism.

I believe that this sentimentalism is the necessary result of the attempt to divorce feeling from action.

## Article Five: The School and Social Progress

I believe that education is the fundamental method of social progress and reform.

I believe that all reforms which rest simply upon the enactment of law, or the threatening of certain penalties, or upon changes in mechanical or outward arrangements, are transitory and futile.

I believe that education is a regulation of the process of coming to share in the social consciousness; and that the adjustment of individual activity on the basis of this social consciousness is the only sure method of social reconstruction.

I believe that this conception has due regard for both the individualistic and socialistic ideals. It is duly individual because it recognizes the formation of a certain character as the only genuine basis of right living. It is socialistic because it recognizes that this right character is not to be formed by merely individual precept, example, or exhortation, but rather by the influence of a certain form of institutional or community life upon the individual, and that the social organism through the school, as its organ, may determine ethical results.

I believe that in the ideal school we have the reconciliation of the individualistic and the institutional ideals.

I believe that the community's duty to education is, therefore, its paramount moral duty. By law and punishment, by social agitation and discussion, society can regulate and form itself in a more or less haphazard and chance way. But through education society can formulate its own purposes, can organize its own means and resources, and thus shape itself with definiteness and economy in the direction in which it wishes to move.

I believe that when society once recognizes the possibilities in this direction, and the obligations which these possibilities impose, it is impossible to conceive of the resources of time, attention, and money which will be put at the disposal of the educator.

I believe it is the business of every one interested in education to insist upon the school as the primary and most effective instrument of social progress and reform in order that society may be awakened to realize what the school stands for, and aroused to the necessity of endowing the educator with sufficient equipment properly to perform his task.

I believe that education thus conceived marks the most perfect and intimate union of science and art conceivable in human experience.

I believe that the art of thus giving shape to human powers and adapting them to social service, is the supreme art; one calling into its service the best of artists; that no insight, sympathy, tact, executive power is too great for such service.

I believe that with the growth of psychological science, giving added insight into individual structure and laws of growth; and with growth of social science, adding to our knowledge of the right organization of individuals, all scientific resources can be utilized for the purposes of education.

I believe that when science and art thus join hands the most commanding motive for human action will be reached; the most genuine springs of human conduct aroused and the best service that human nature is capable of guaranteed.

I believe, finally, that the teacher is engaged, not simply in the training of individuals, but in the formation of the proper social life.

I believe that every teacher should realize the dignity of his calling; that he is a social servant set apart for the maintenance of proper social order and the securing of the right social growth.

I believe that in this way the teacher always is the prophet of the true God and the usherer in of the true kingdom of God.

# CONTRIBUTORS

**Chara Haeussler Bohan** is an Associate Professor in the College of Education at Georgia State University. She earned her doctoral degree in curriculum and instruction with a concentration in education history and social studies education at The University of Texas at Austin where she studied with O.L. Davis. In 2011, she won the Outstanding Faculty Research Award from Georgia State University College of Education.

**Cynthia Brown** (Ph.D. Johns Hopkins, 1964) taught history and education at Dominican University of California from 1981 to 2001. From 2001 to 2010 she taught Big History part-time. Currently, she is resident historian in Dominican's Freshman Year Experience Big History Program. She also serves on the board of the International Big History Association.

**Steven P. Camicia** earned his Ph.D. in curriculum and instruction from the University of Washington, where he was mentored by Walter Parker and James Banks. In 2010, Camicia was awarded the School of Teacher Education and Leadership Researcher/Scholar of the Year Award at Utah State University. Currently, he is an Associate Professor of Social Studies Education at Utah State University

**Margaret Smith Crocco** is Chair of the Department of Teacher Education at Michigan State University. She earned a master's and doctoral degree in American Civilization at the University of Pennsylvania. Previously, she served as Professor and Dean of the College of Education at the University of Iowa, and Professor and Chair of the Department of Arts and Humanities at Teachers College, Columbia University.

**O.L. Davis, Jr**. is Catherine Mae Parker Centennial Professor of Curriculum and Instruction, Emeritus, at The University of Texas at Austin. He holds a Ph.D. (1958) from George Peabody College for Teachers. He is the author/co-author/editor of more than 30 books and almost 200 reports of research and essays. He retired from The University of Texas at Austin in February 2007.

**Ronald W. Evans** is currently a Professor in the School of Teacher Education at San Diego State University. He attended Stanford from 1983 to 1986 and was awarded a Doctorate (Ed.D.) in 1987. Professor Richard Gross was his advisor, and David Tyack and Decker Walker were members of his dissertation committee. Many of Evans' publications have been award-winning.

**William R. Fernekes** earned an Ed.D. in social studies education and curriculum from Rutgers Graduate School of Education in 1985 under the tutelage of Jack L. Nelson. In 2011, Fernekes received the Mel Miller Award from the National Social Studies Supervisors Association as the outstanding social studies supervisor in the United States.

**Geneva Gay** is Professor of Education at the University of Washington, Seattle, where she teaches multicultural education and general curriculum theory. She is nationally and internationally known for her scholarship in multicultural education, particularly as it relates to curriculum design, staff development, classroom instruction, and intersections of culture, race, ethnicity, teaching, and learning.

**Diana E. Hess** is currently on leave from her position as a Professor of Curriculum and Instruction at the University of Wisconsin, Madison. She earned a Ph.D. from the University of Washington in Seattle, where her major professor was Professor Walter Parker. Currently, Hess is the Senior Vice President of the Spencer Foundation, a foundation devoted to supporting high-quality investigation of education.

**Charlene Johnson-Carter** is an Associate Professor in the Department of Curriculum and Instruction at the University of Arkansas, Fayetteville. She earned her Ph.D. in Educational Leadership at Emory University (1992). She is a member of the American Educational Research Association's Special Interest Group, Research Focus on Black Education.

**Merry M. Merryfield** is Professor Emerita of Social Studies and Global Education at The Ohio State University. She earned an Ed.D. in Social Studies Education, African Studies, and Educational Inquiry, at Indiana University (1986). In 2009, Merryfield received both the Global Scholar Award and the James M. Becker Award for Global Understanding from the National Council for the Social Studies.

**Jack L. Nelson** is Professor II (Distinguished) Emeritus at Rutgers University, where he was on the faculty of the Graduate School of Education for 30 years. He received his doctorate at the University of Southern California, and served on the faculties of California State University, Los Angeles, and SUNY, Buffalo. His publications include 17 books. In 2013, he was the recipient of the National Council for the Social Studies Lifetime Achievement Award.

**Mark A. Previte** is Associate Professor of Secondary Education (Social Studies) at the University of Pittsburgh, Johnstown. He earned his doctorate at Pennsylvania State University. Before entering academia, Previte was a secondary social studies teacher and department chair for 28 years at Northern Cambria High School in Pennsylvania.

**E. Wayne Ross** is Professor in the Department of Curriculum and Pedagogy and Co-Director of the Institute for Critical Education Studies at The University of British Columbia. Ross received his Ph.D. in Curriculum and Instructional Development at The Ohio State University. Ross has published more than 20 books on curriculum studies, social studies education, teacher education, and critical pedagogy.

**William B. Russell III** is Associate Professor of Social Science Education at the University of Central Florida. Russell earned his Ph.D. at Florida State University. He has been the recipient of numerous awards, including the Scholarship of Teaching and Learning Award. Dr. Russell serves as the director for The International Society for the Social Studies, and is the Editor-in-Chief of *The Journal of Social Studies Research*.

**Barbara Solomon Spector**, a Fellow of the American Association for the Advancement of Science, is Professor of Science Education at the University of South Florida (USF) and Director of the Informal Science Institutions Environmental Education Graduate Certificate Program. She earned her Ph.D. at Syracuse University.

**Carlos Alberto Torres** is Distinguished Professor of Social Sciences and Comparative Education at the University of California, Los Angeles (UCLA), Director of the UCLA Paulo Freire Institute, and Associate Dean for Global Programs. He is also the Founding Director of the Paulo Freire Institute in São Paulo, Brazil, Buenos Aires, Argentina, and at UCLA. He is a political sociologist of education who got his Ph.D. in International Development Education at Stanford University.

**Samuel Totten** earned a doctorate in Curriculum and Teaching from Teachers College, Columbia University. He studied under Maxine Greene at Teachers

College. He taught at the University of Arkansas, Fayetteville from 1987 to 2012. In 2011, he was the recipient of Teachers College, Columbia University's Distinguished Alumini Award.

**Elizabeth Yeager Washington** is Professor of Social Studies Education at the University of Florida in Gainesville. She is also a Senior Fellow of the Florida Joint Center for Citizenship, and a Knight Fellow at the Bob Graham Center for Public Service. She earned her Ph.D. in Curriculum and Instruction from The University of Texas at Austin under Professor O. L. Davis, Jr.

**William G. Wraga** received an Ed.D. in Social and Philosophical Foundations of Education with a specialization in Curriculum Theory and Development from Rutgers University in 1991. Currently he is Professor of Education in the College of Education at the University of Georgia, Athens. In 2007 Wraga received the Russell H. Yeany, Jr. Research Award from the College of Education, University of Georgia.

**Robert E. Yager** has been on the faculty at the University of Iowa for 50 years as a Professor of Science Education. He received his M.S. and Ph.D. in plant physiology from the University of Iowa. Currently he heads the NSTA Exemplary Science Programs. His publications total over 600.

**Miguel Zavala** is Assistant Professor in the Department of Secondary Education at California State University, Fullerton, where in 2012 he was the recipient of the Junior Faculty Research Award. He received his Ph.D. from UCLA in 2010 and studied under the guidance of well-known critical scholars, such as Sandra Harding, Peter McLaren, and Carlos Torres.

**Jack Zevin** is Professor of Secondary Education at Queens College of the City University of New York. He received his Ph.D. at the University of Michigan (1969). He was a doctoral student of Byron G. Massialas. In 1997, he was the recipient of the Presidential Teaching Award at Queens College; he has also been a National Endowment for the Humanities Fellow.

# INDEX

28386224R00151

Made in the USA
Lexington, KY
14 January 2019